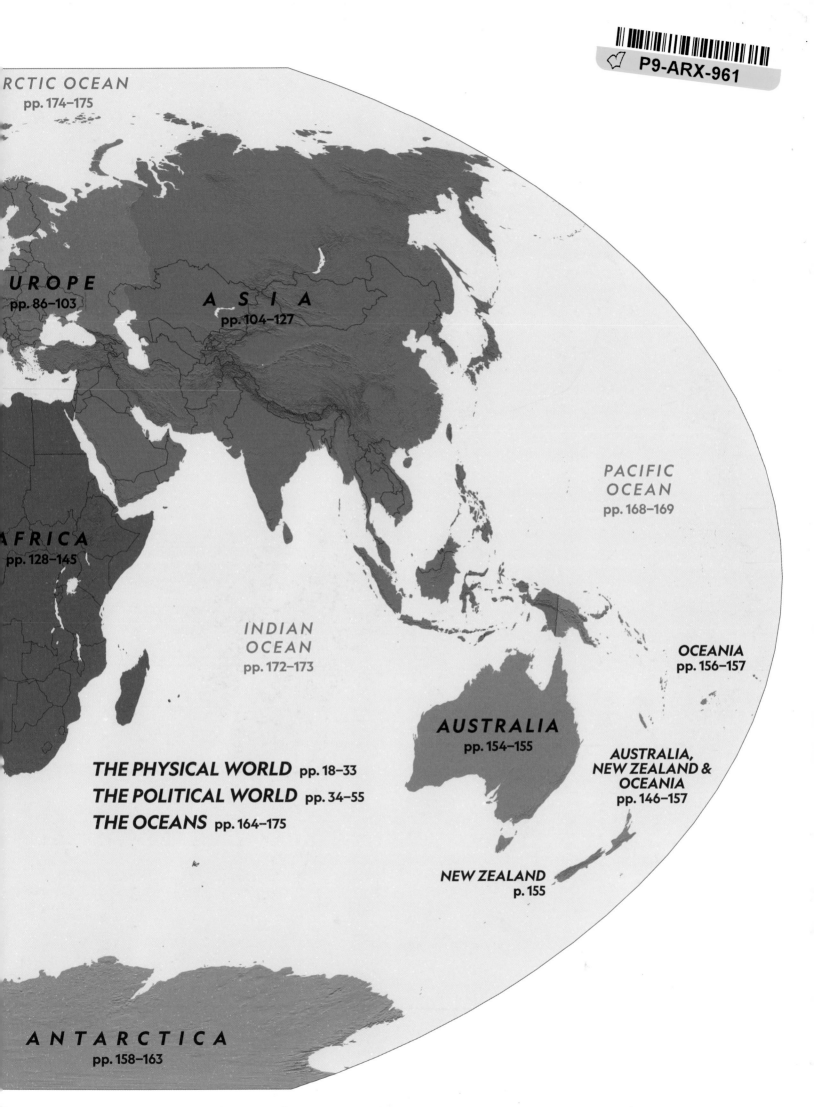

YOU ARE HERE

NATIONAL GEOGRAPHIC
KiDS

WORLD ATLAS

SIXTH EDITION

NATIONAL GEOGRAPHIC
WASHINGTON, D.C.

TABLE OF CONTENTS

North America: Mexican boy, page 60

South America: Llama, page 77

Europe: Colosseum, pages 92–93

Title page (left to right): tarsier, Philippines; Lower Yellowstone Falls, Wyoming, U.S.A; young boy, Brazil; Montreal skyline, Quebec, Canada; lion, African savanna; Guggenheim Museum, Bilbao, Spain; young girl, Gambia, Africa; fall foliage, U.S.A.

Antarctica: Penguins, page 160

Australia, New Zealand & Oceania: Maori man, page 150

Africa: Mother and child, page 133

Asia: Panda, page 108

How to Use This Atlas

This atlas is a window for exploring the world. To learn about maps, use the first section, Understanding Maps. Basic facts about Earth as a planet are presented in the section called Planet Earth. Maps in the Physical World section focus on different aspects of nature and the environment. The Political World section contains world maps about how humans live on the planet. In the pages that follow, the maps, photographs, and essays are arranged by continent and region. You can find details about specific countries in the Flags & Facts section beginning on page 176.

"YOU ARE HERE"

Locator globes help you see where one area is in relation to others. On regional pages (as shown here), the area covered by the main map is yellow on the globe, and its continent is green. On pages with continent maps, the locator globe shows the whole continent in yellow. The surrounding land is gray.

STATS & FACTS

At the left-hand edge of each continent opener and regional page is a bar that includes basic information about the subject. This feature is a great first stop if you're writing a report.

CHARTS & GRAPHS

Each region includes a chart or graph that shows information visually.

WHERE ARE THE PICTURES?

If you want to know where a picture in a regional section of this atlas was taken, look for the map in the photo essay. Find the label that describes the picture you're curious about, and follow the line to its location.

Maps use symbols to represent political and physical features. At right is the key to the symbols used in this atlas. If you are wondering what you're looking at on a map, check here.

82 NORTHEASTERN SOUTH AMERICA

THE CONTINENT:
SOUTH AMERICA

Northeastern South America

GOAL! Fans of soccer cheer on the women from Brazil and Jamaica in the 2019 FIFA Women's World Cup in Grenoble, France.

THE BASICS

STATS
Largest country
Brazil
3,287,611 sq mi (8,514,877 sq km)
Smallest country
Suriname
63,251 sq mi (163,820 sq km)
Most populous country
Brazil 208,847,000
Least populous country
Suriname 598,000
Predominant languages
Portuguese, English, Dutch, Hindi
Predominant religions
Christianity, Hinduism, Islam
Highest GDP per capita
Brazil $15,600
Lowest GDP per capita
Guyana $8,200
Highest life expectancy
Brazil 74 years
Lowest life expectancy
Guyana 68 years

GEO WHIZ

Guyana's roughly 300 species of catfish are hunted for the international aquarium trade.

Brazil's Pantanal is the world's largest freshwater wetland.

Paramaribo, Suriname's capital, is a mix of Dutch, Hindu, Chinese, East Indian, and Javanese cultures. Dutch is the only official language.

Brazil dominates the region as well as the continent in size and population. It is the world's fifth largest country in area, and it is home to about half of South America's 430 million people. São Paulo and Rio de Janeiro are among the world's largest cities, and the country's vast agricultural lands make it a top global exporter of coffee, soybeans, beef, orange juice, and sugar. The Amazon rainforest, once a dense wilderness of unmatched biodiversity, is now threatened by farmers, loggers, and miners. Lands colonized by the British, Dutch, and French make up sparsely settled Guyana and Suriname as well as French Guiana, a French overseas department. Formerly known as the Guianas, these lands are populated by people of African, South Asian, and European heritage.

VAST WATERSHED

The United States and South America are shown at the same scale.

Amazon Basin

SOUTH AMERICA

The Amazon River basin includes 2.4 million square miles (6.1 million sq km). It would cover much of the contiguous, or lower 48, U.S. states.

NATIONAL RHYTHM. Samba, often called Brazil's national music, combines the music traditions of the country's populations—Amerindian, Portuguese, and African. Here, a samba band practices on Rio de Janeiro's Ipanema Beach.

92 ABOUT THE CONTINENT

THE CONTINENT:
EUROPE

more about
Europe

ABOUT THE CONTINENT **93**

EUROPE

WHERE THE PICTURES ARE

GETTING STARTED

INDEX AND GRID

Look through the index for the place-name you want. Next to it is a page number in bold, a letter, and another number. Go to the page. Draw imaginary lines from the letter along the side of the map and the number along the top. Your place will be close to where the lines meet.

COLOR BARS

Every section of this atlas has its own color. Look for the color on the Table of Contents pages and across the top of every page in the atlas. Within that color bar, you'll see the name of the section and the title for each topic or map. These color bars are a handy way to find the section you want.

NORTHEASTERN SOUTH AMERICA | 83

THE CONTINENT:
SOUTH AMERICA

◖ THE SIX-BANDED ARMADILLO, found throughout the dry grassland areas of the region, lives on plants and insects. Unlike others of its species, it remains active during the day.

Map Key
- ⊛ Country capital
- • City or town
- ····· Boundary
- ····· Claimed boundary

◖ BAUXITE TO ALUMINUM. By exploiting rich deposits of bauxite, the ore from which aluminum is made, and inexpensive hydropower, Suriname produces aluminum ingots, such as these headed for global markets.

North America

South America

Europe

Asia

Africa

Australia, New Zealand & Oceania

Antarctica

BAR SCALE

To find out how far on Earth's surface it is from one place on a map to another, use the scale. A bar scale appears on every map. It shows how distance on paper relates to distance in the real world.

MAP KEY

• • • City or town	★ Pole	⊢⊣⊢ Waterfall	⬭ Dry salt lake
⊛ Country capital	791 ft + 241 m Mountain peak with elevation above sea level	⌁ Dam	⬭ Glacier
◉ Dependency, state, provincial or territorial capital	-282 ft • -86 m Low point with elevation below sea level	⊢⊣⊢ Canal	⬭ Swamp
⊗ Capital of Northern Ireland, Scotland, or Wales		⋀⋀⋀ Ice shelf	⬭ Sand
◎ Other capital	······ Defined boundary	⌒ Reef	⬭ Tundra
◆ Small country	··· ··· Disputed or undefined boundary	⬭ Lake	⬭ Lava
∴ Ruin	······ Claimed boundary	⬭ Intermittent lake	⬭ Below sea level
▪ Point of interest	⌇ River		

Exploring Your World

Earth is a big place. Even from space you can't see it all at one time. But with a map you can see the whole world—or just a part of it. Thanks to the internet, you can experience Earth from space, pick a place you want to explore, and zoom closer and closer until you are "standing" right there! These screenshots (right) take you from London to space at the click of a mouse. You can even find a satellite view of your neighborhood (box below).

Compare the computer-enhanced satellite images with the maps on the opposite page. You will see how the same places can be shown in very different ways.

FIND YOUR HOUSE

This image shows the offices of National Geographic in Washington, D.C. To see where you live, go to showmystreet.com, one of several websites that allow you to view satellite imagery of the world.

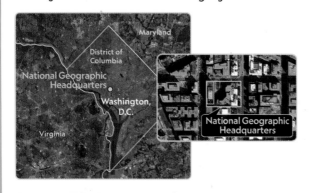

COMPUTER ENHANCED VIEWS OF ...

CITY

London

REGION

UNITED KINGDOM

London.

COUNTRY

London.

E U R O P E

CONTINENT

London

THE WORLD

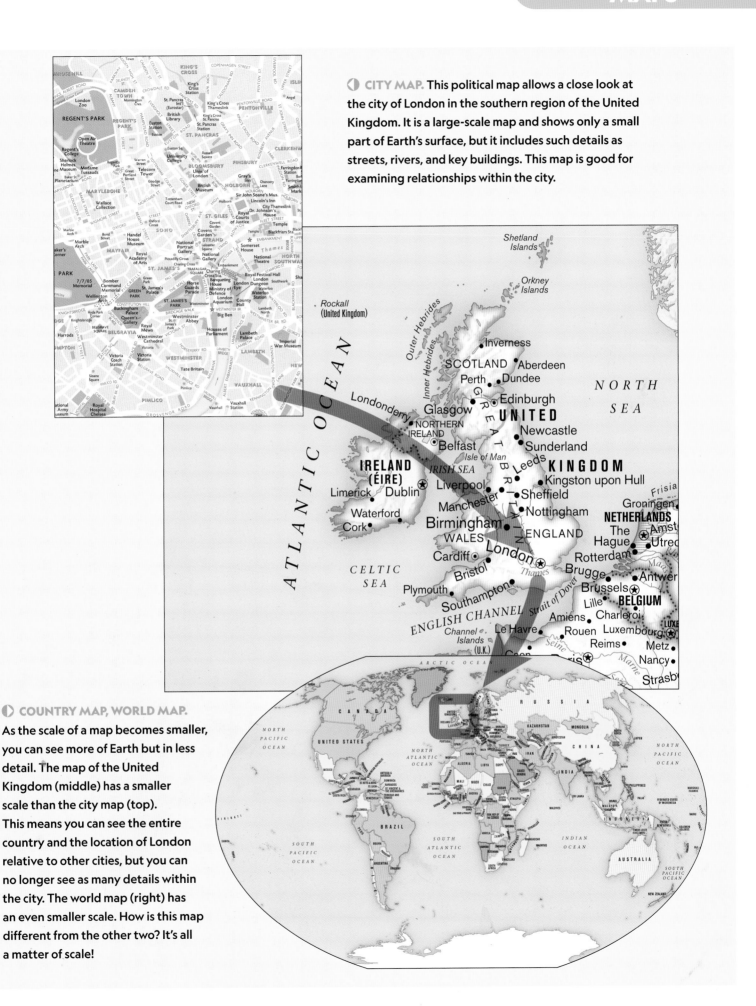

CITY MAP. This political map allows a close look at the city of London in the southern region of the United Kingdom. It is a large-scale map and shows only a small part of Earth's surface, but it includes such details as streets, rivers, and key buildings. This map is good for examining relationships within the city.

COUNTRY MAP, WORLD MAP.

As the scale of a map becomes smaller, you can see more of Earth but in less detail. The map of the United Kingdom (middle) has a smaller scale than the city map (top). This means you can see the entire country and the location of London relative to other cities, but you can no longer see as many details within the city. The world map (right) has an even smaller scale. How is this map different from the other two? It's all a matter of scale!

Kinds of Maps

Maps are special tools that tell a story about Earth. Some maps show physical features, such as mountains or vegetation. Other maps illustrate different human features on Earth—political boundaries, urban centers, and economic systems.

Maps are not perfect. A globe is a scale model of Earth with accurate relative sizes and locations. Because maps are flat, they involve distortions of size, shape, and direction. Also, cartographers—people who create maps—make choices about what information to include. Because of this, it is important to study many different types of maps to learn the complete story of Earth.

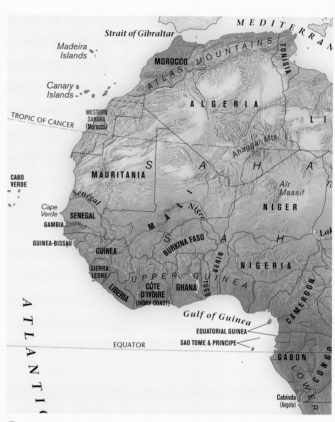

PHYSICAL MAPS. Earth's natural features—landforms, water bodies, and vegetation—are shown on physical maps. The map above uses color and shading to illustrate mountains, lakes, rivers, and deserts in western Africa. Country names and borders are added for reference, but they are not natural features.

MAP PROJECTIONS. To create a map, cartographers transfer an image of the round Earth onto a flat surface, a process called projection. Some types of projection include cylindrical, conic, azimuthal, and interrupted. Each has certain advantages, but all have some distortions. The world maps in the thematic section of this atlas are a projection called Winkel Tripel (shown above), a compromise projection that moderates size and shape distortions. As you use this atlas, look for different map projections on the regional maps, identified below the scale bar.

MAKING MAPS

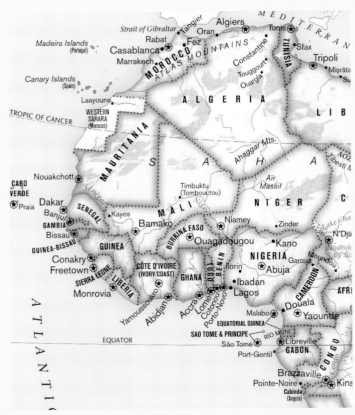

◯ **POLITICAL MAPS.** These maps represent human characteristics of the landscape, such as boundaries, cities, and other place-names. Natural features are added only for reference. On the map above, capital cities are represented with a star inside a circle, while other cities are shown as black dots.

◯ **THEMATIC MAPS.** Patterns related to a particular topic, or theme, such as population distribution, appear on these maps. The map above displays a region's climate zones, which range from tropical wet (bright green) to tropical wet and dry (light green) to semiarid (dark yellow) to arid (light yellow).

Long ago, cartographers worked with pen and ink, carefully handcrafting maps based on explorers' observations and diaries. Today, mapmaking is a high-tech business. Cartographers use Earth data stored in "layers" in a geographic information system (GIS) and special computer programs to create maps that can be easily updated as new information becomes available. These cartographers are making changes to a map in another National Geographic Kids atlas.

Satellites in orbit around Earth act as eyes in the sky, recording data about the planet's land and ocean areas. The data are converted to numbers that are transmitted back to computers that are specially programmed to interpret the data. They record the data in a form that cartographers can use to create maps.

UNDERSTANDING MAPS

How to Read a Map

Every map has a story to tell, but first you have to know how to read the map.

Maps are useful for finding places because every place on Earth has a special address called its absolute location. Imaginary lines, called latitude and longitude, create a grid that makes finding places easy because every spot on Earth has a unique latitude and longitude. In addition, special tools, making use of the Global Positioning System (GPS), communicate with orbiting satellites to determine absolute location.

Maps are also useful for determining distance and direction. The map scale shows the relationship between distance on the map and actual distance on Earth. Since north is not always at the top of every map, a compass rose or arrow is used to indicate direction.

Maps represent other information by using a language of symbols. To find out what each symbol means, you must use the map key. Think of this key as your secret decoder, identifying information represented by each symbol on the map.

◗ LATITUDE AND LONGITUDE. Lines of latitude run west to east parallel to the Equator. They measure distance in degrees from 0° latitude (Equator) to 90°N (North Pole) or to 90°S (South Pole). Lines of longitude run north to south and measure distance in degrees east or west from 0° longitude (prime meridian) to 180° longitude. The prime meridian runs through Greenwich, England.

Latitude

Longitude

◗ ABSOLUTE LOCATION. The imaginary grid composed of lines of latitude and longitude helps us locate places on a map. Suppose you are playing a game of global scavenger hunt. The prize is hidden at absolute location 30°S, 60°W. On the map at right, look south of the Equator to find the line of latitude labeled 30°S and west of 0° longitude to find the line of longitude labeled 60°W. Trace these lines with your fingers until they meet (arrow at right). The prize must be located in central Argentina.

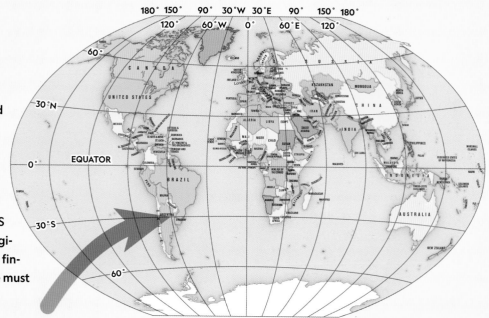

UNDERSTANDING MAPS

SYMBOLS

Points, lines, and areas are the three main types of map symbols. Points, which can be either dots or small icons, represent the location or the number of things, such as cities or landmarks. Lines are used to show boundaries, roads, or rivers and can vary in color and thickness. Area symbols use patterns or color to show regions, such as a sandy area or a neighborhood.

POINT
A point symbol, a black dot, indicates a city, such as Omdurman.

LINE
Sudan's country boundary appears as a line symbol: a dotted line with a colored edge.

AREA
Sandy places, such as parts of the Libyan Desert, are shown by a tan, speckled area.

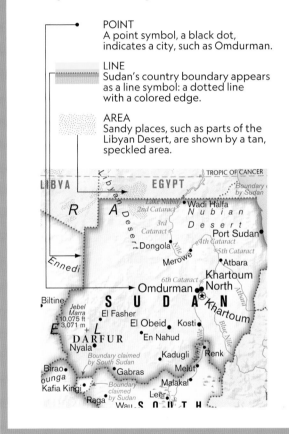

SCALE & DIRECTION

The scale on a map can be shown as a fraction, as words, or as a line or bar. It relates distance on the map to distance in the real world. Sometimes the type of map projection is named below the scale. A map may include an arrow or compass rose to indicate north on the map. Maps in this atlas are oriented north, so they do not use a north indicator.

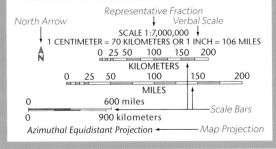

APPLYING WHAT YOU'VE LEARNED.
Now that you know how to read a map, can you find Sapporo in the eastern Asian country of Japan? The index for this atlas says Sapporo is on page 117 B10. Go to page 117, place one finger on the B at the side of the map and another finger on the 10 at the top. Now trace straight across from the B and down from the 10. Sapporo is near where your fingers meet!

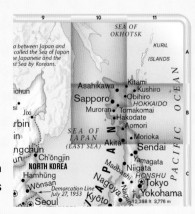

Earth in Space

Earth is part of a cosmic family called the solar system. It is one of the planets that revolves around a giant solar nuclear reactor that we call the sun.

The extreme heat and pressure on the sun cause atoms of hydrogen to combine in a process called fusion, producing new atoms of helium and releasing tremendous amounts of energy. This energy makes life on Earth possible.

Time on Earth is defined by our relationship to the sun. It takes Earth, following a path called an orbit, approximately 365 days—one year—to make one full revolution around the sun. As Earth makes its way around the sun, it also turns on its axis, an imaginary line that passes between the North and South Poles. This motion, called rotation, occurs once every 24 hours and results in day and night.

◗ **TIME ZONES.** Long ago, when people lived in relative isolation, they measured time by the position of the sun. That meant that noon in one place was not the same as noon in a place 100 miles (160 km) to the west. Later, with the development of long-distance railroads, people needed to coordinate time. In 1884, a system of 24 standard time zones was adopted. Each time zone reflects the fact that Earth rotates west to east 15 degrees each hour. Time is counted from the prime meridian (0° longitude).

Callisto

Titan

Triton

Jupiter

Charon

Haumea

Saturn

Uranus

Pluto

Neptune

Makemake

Eris

Note: Art shows relative sizes of the sun and planets, but distances are not to scale.

SOLAR SYSTEM. The sun and its family of planets are located near the outer edge of the Milky Way, a giant spiral galaxy. Earth is the third planet from the sun and one of the four "terrestrial" planets. These planets—Mercury, Venus, Earth, and Mars—are made up of solid rocky material. Beyond these inner planets are the two gas giants, Jupiter and Saturn, and the two ice giants, Uranus and Neptune. Astronomers—scientists who study space—created a category called "dwarf" planets that includes Pluto, Ceres, Eris, Haumea, and Makemake. Astronomers continue to find more possible dwarf planets. Many planets, including Earth, have one or more moons orbiting them. The art above names a few: Io, Callisto, Titan, Triton, and Charon.

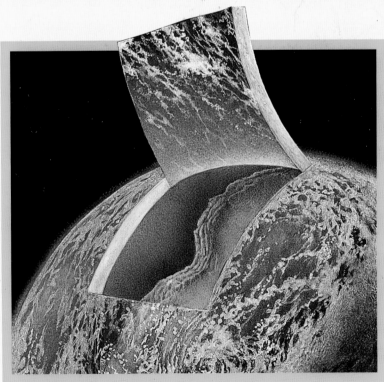

ENVELOPE OF AIR. Earth is enclosed within a thick layer of air called the atmosphere. Made up of a mixture of nitrogen, oxygen, and other gases, the atmosphere provides us with the life-giving air that we breathe. It also protects us from dangerous radiation from the sun. Weather systems move through the atmosphere, redistributing heat and moisture and creating Earth's climates.

Earth in Motion

If we could step into a time machine and travel 240 million years into the past, we probably would not recognize Earth. Back then, most of the landmasses we call continents were joined together in a single giant landmass called Pangaea (below). So how did the continents break away from Pangaea and move to their current positions? The answer lies in a process called plate tectonics. These maps and diagrams tell the story.

A LOOK WITHIN. Earth's crust is a thin shell of solid rock that covers the partially molten rock of the mantle (upper and lower). Currents of heat rising and falling within the mantle break the crust into large pieces called plates. As plates creep across Earth's surface, they reshape its features. Major plates appear on the map at right. Earthquakes and volcanoes are most frequent where plates collide or grind past each other.

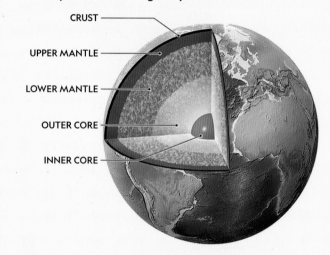

CRUST
UPPER MANTLE
LOWER MANTLE
OUTER CORE
INNER CORE

CONTINENTS ON THE MOVE

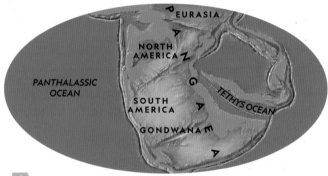

1 PANGAEA. About 240 million years ago, Earth's landmasses were joined together in one supercontinent—Pangaea—that extended from pole to pole.

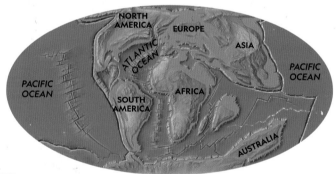

3 EXTINCTION. About 66 million years ago, an asteroid smashed into Earth (red * on map), leading to the extinction of half of all species, including the dinosaurs—one of several major extinctions.

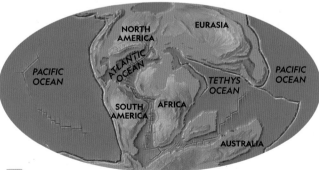

2 BREAKUP. By 94 million years ago, Pangaea had broken into what would become today's continents. Dinosaurs roamed Earth during this period of warmer climates.

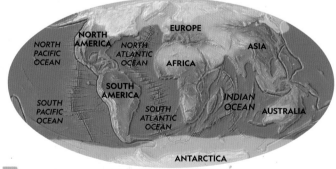

4 ICE AGE. By 18,000 years ago, the continents had drifted close to their present positions, but most far northern and far southern lands were buried beneath huge glaciers.

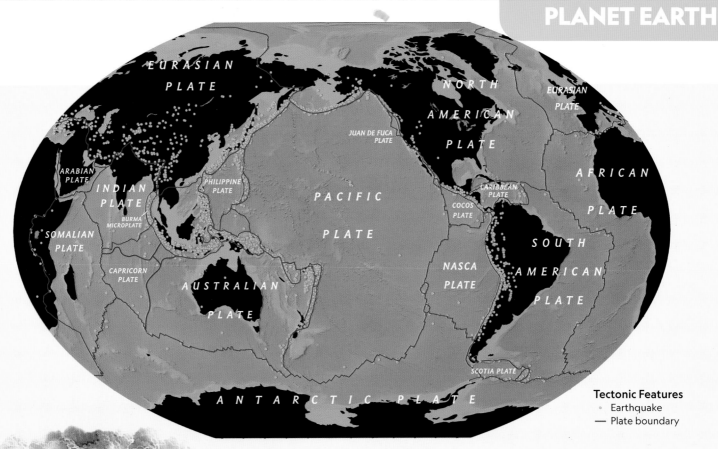

Tectonic Features
- Earthquake
— Plate boundary

Earth Shapers

Earth's features are constantly undergoing change—being built up, destroyed, or just rearranged. Plates are in constant, very slow motion. Some plates collide, others pull apart, and still others slowly grind past each other. As the plates move, mountains are uplifted, volcanoes erupt, and new land is created.

VOLCANOES form when molten rock, called magma, rises to Earth's surface. Some volcanoes occur as one plate pushes beneath another plate. Other volcanoes result when a plate passes over a column of magma, called a hot spot, rising from the mantle.

SUBDUCTION occurs when an oceanic plate dives under a continental plate. This often results in volcanoes and earthquakes, as well as mountain building.

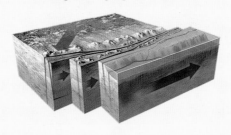

FAULTING happens when two plates grind past each other, creating large cracks along the edges of the plates. A famous fault is the San Andreas, in California, U.S.A., where the Pacific and North American plates meet, causing damaging earthquakes.

SPREADING results when oceanic plates move apart. The ocean floor cracks, magma rises, and new crust is created. The Mid-Atlantic Ridge spreads a few centimeters—about an inch—a year, pushing Europe and North America farther apart.

COLLISION of two continental plates causes plate edges to break and fold, creating mountains, Earth's highest landforms. The Himalaya are the result of the Indian plate colliding with the Eurasian plate, an ongoing process that began 50 million years ago.

The Physical World

Earth is dominated by large landmasses called continents—seven in all—and by an interconnected global ocean that is divided into four parts by the continents. More than 70 percent of Earth's surface is covered by water. Land areas cover the remaining 30 percent.

Different landforms give variety to the surface of the continents. The Rockies and Andes mark the western edge of North and South America, and the Himalaya tower above southern Asia. The Plateau of Tibet forms the rugged core of Asia, while the Northern European Plain extends from the North Sea to the Ural Mountains. Much of Africa is a plateau, and dry plains cover large areas of Australia. In Antarctica, mountains rise more than 16,000 feet (4,877 m) beneath massive ice sheets.

Mountains and trenches make the ocean floors as varied as the surface of any continent (see page 166). The Mid-Atlantic Ridge runs the length of the Atlantic Ocean. In the western Pacific Ocean, trenches drop to depths greater than 36,000 feet (10,972 m).

LAND AND WATER. This world physical map shows Earth's seven continents—North America, South America, Europe, Africa, Asia, Australia, and Antarctica—as well as the four oceans: Pacific, Atlantic, Indian, and Arctic. Some people regard the area from Antarctica to 60°S, where the oceans merge, as a fifth ocean called the Southern Ocean.

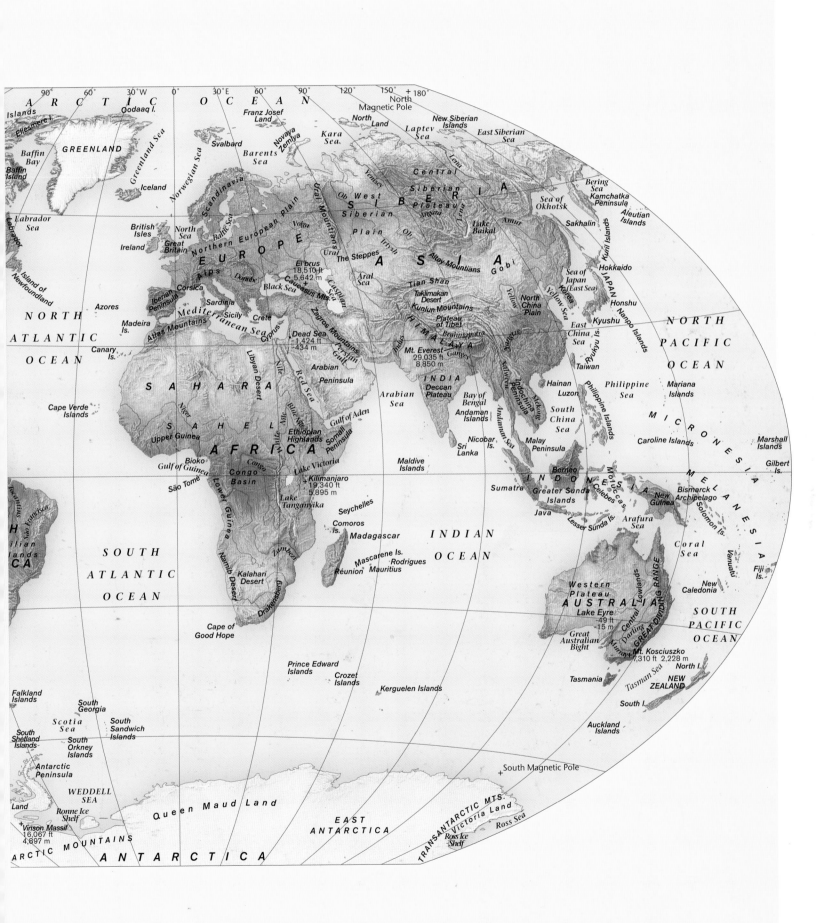

The Land

A closer look at Earth's surface reveals many varied forms and features that make each place unique. This drawing of an imaginary landscape captures 41 natural and human-made features and shows how they relate to each other. For example, a large moving "river" of ice (called a glacier) descends from a high mountain range, and a harbor, built by people, creates safe anchorage for ships.

Such features can be found all over the world because the same forces are at work around the globe. Volcanoes and movement of the plates of Earth's crust are constantly creating and building up new landforms, while external forces such as wind, water, and ice continuously wear down surface features.

Earth is dynamic—constantly changing, never the same.

Dormant volcano
Iceberg
Archipelago
Island
Cape
Strait
Divide
Valley
Sound
Canal
Point
Lagoon
Beach
Bay
Peninsula
Isthmus
Cliff
Breakwater
Reef
Spit
Harbor
Ocean
Gulf

ARCHIPELAGO

Groupings of islands are known as archipelagos. Above, the tropical islands in Ang Thong National Marine Park create an archipelago in Thailand.

CANYON

Steep-sided valleys called canyons are created mainly by running water. Buckskin Gulch (above) is the deepest slot canyon in the American Southwest.

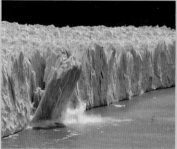

ICEBERG

Icebergs are formed by chunks of ice that break from glaciers into a body of water. Above, a large piece of ice breaks from the Perito Moreno Glacier in Argentina.

OASIS

Occasionally, water rises from deep below a desert, creating an oasis—a fertile area that supports trees and sometimes crops—such as this one in the Sahara desert in Africa.

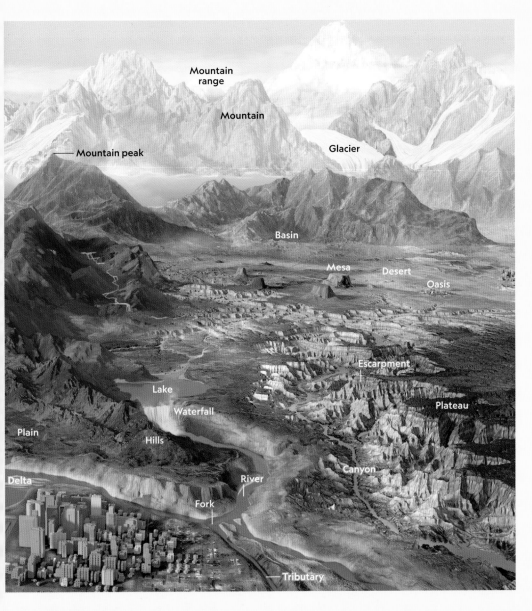

Mountain
range

Mountain

Mountain peak

Glacier

Basin

Mesa

Desert

Oasis

Escarpment

Lake

Plateau

Waterfall

Plain

Hills

Canyon

Delta

River

Fork

Tributary

A NAME FOR EVERY FEATURE.

Land has a vocabulary all its own, each name identifying a specific feature of the landscape. A cape, for example, is a broad chunk of land extending out into the sea. It is not pointed, however, because then it would be a point. Nor does it have a narrow neck. A sizable cape or point with a narrow neck is a peninsula. The narrow neck is an isthmus. Such specific identifiers have proven useful over the centuries. In the early days of exploration, even the simplest maps showed peninsulas, bays, and straits. Sailors used these landmarks to reach safe harbor or to avoid disasters, such as breaking up on a reef.

◁ **EXPLORING THE LANDSCAPE.**

How many of these landscape features have you seen where you live or in your travels to other places?

ISTHMUS

An isthmus, like the one above in Costa Rica, is a narrow piece of land connecting two larger pieces of land. The isthmus at San Juanillo Beach combines two beaches.

GLACIER

Glaciers, such as the Kaskawulsh Glacier in Yukon, Canada (above), move slowly from mountains to the sea. Climate change is causing them to melt.

MESA

A mesa is a flat-topped hill or mountain. The word "mesa" comes from the Spanish word for table. This is a mesa in the Table Mountains in Namibia, Africa.

STRAIT

The coast of the island of Lošinj, Croatia, creates a strait. A strait is a narrow area of water that connects two larger bodies of water.

World Climate

Weather is the condition of the atmosphere—temperature, precipitation, humidity, wind—at a given place at a given time. Climate, however, is the average weather for a particular place over a long period of time. Climate is not a random occurrence. It is a pattern that is controlled by factors such as latitude, elevation, prevailing winds, temperature of ocean currents, and location on land relative to water. Climate is generally constant, but many people are concerned that human activity is causing a change in climate patterns.

THE BASICS

According to the National Oceanic and Atmospheric Administration (NOAA), 2020 was the second warmest year on record over the last 141 years. The 2020 global annual temperature for combined land and ocean surfaces was 1.8°F (.98°C) warmer than the 20th-century average.

Ice cores taken from Antarctica and Greenland allow scientists to gain detailed information about the history of Earth's climate and its atmosphere—especially the presence of greenhouse gases—dating back thousands of years.

According to climatologists—people who study climate—Earth experienced what is called the Little Ice Age, which lasted from the 17th century to the late 19th century. During that time, temperatures were cold enough to cause glaciers to advance.

◉ **CLIMATE GRAPHS.**
Temperature and precipitation data provide a snapshot of the climate of a particular place. This information can be shown in a climate graph, or climograph (below). Average monthly temperatures (scale on the left side of the graphs) are represented by the lines at the tops of the colored areas, while average monthly precipitation totals (scale on the right side of the graphs) are reflected in the bars. For example, the graph for Belém, Brazil, shows a constant warm temperature of about 80°F (27°C) with abundant rainfall year-round. In contrast, the graph for Fairbanks, Alaska, shows a cool, variable temperature with only limited precipitation.

[Map labels: Fairbanks, Subarctic Current, North Pacific Drift, Hawaiian Islands, PACIFIC OCEAN, North Equatorial Current, Equatorial Countercurrent, EQUATOR, South Equatorial Current, ROCKY MOUNTAINS, NORTH AMERICA, Des Moines, California Current, Monterrey, Gulf of Mexico, Gulf Stream, Peru Current, ANDES, AMAZONIA, SOUTH AMERICA]

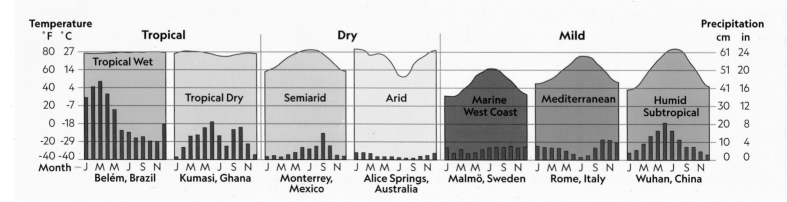

Temperature °F °C	Tropical		Dry		Mild		Precipitation cm in
80 27	Tropical Wet	Tropical Dry	Semiarid	Arid	Marine West Coast	Mediterranean	Humid Subtropical

X-axis: Month J M M J S N for each; Belém, Brazil / Kumasi, Ghana / Monterrey, Mexico / Alice Springs, Australia / Malmö, Sweden / Rome, Italy / Wuhan, China

Temperature scale: 80 27 / 60 14 / 40 4 / 20 -7 / 0 -18 / -20 -29 / -40 -40
Precipitation scale: 61 24 / 51 20 / 41 16 / 30 12 / 20 8 / 10 4 / 0 0

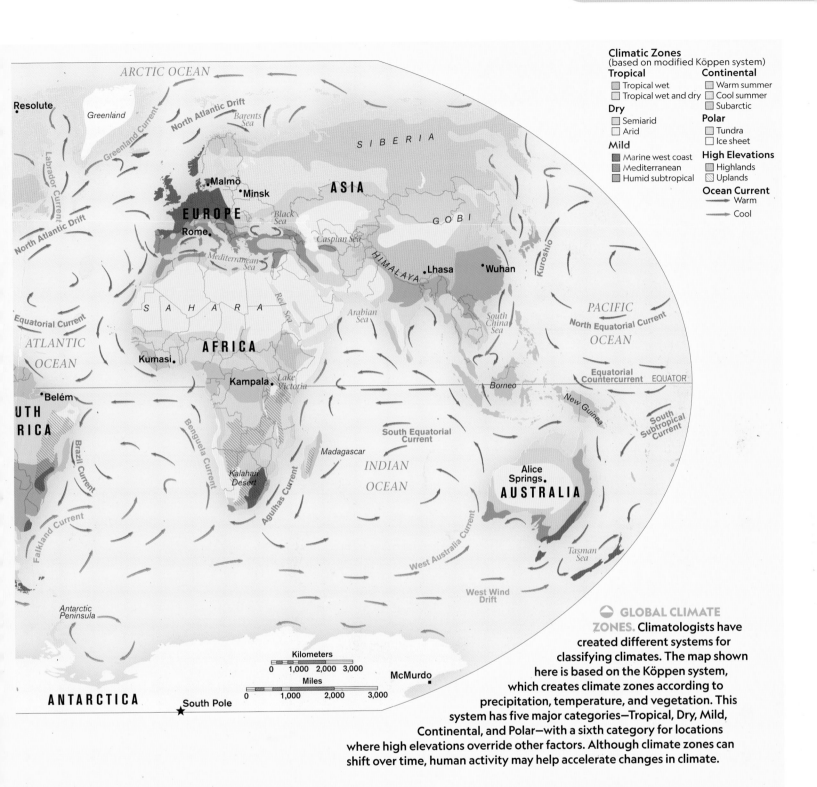

Climatic Zones
(based on modified Köppen system)

Tropical
- Tropical wet
- Tropical wet and dry

Dry
- Semiarid
- Arid

Mild
- Marine west coast
- Mediterranean
- Humid subtropical

Continental
- Warm summer
- Cool summer
- Subarctic

Polar
- Tundra
- Ice sheet

High Elevations
- Highlands
- Uplands

Ocean Current
→ Warm
→ Cool

GLOBAL CLIMATE ZONES. Climatologists have created different systems for classifying climates. The map shown here is based on the Köppen system, which creates climate zones according to precipitation, temperature, and vegetation. This system has five major categories—Tropical, Dry, Mild, Continental, and Polar—with a sixth category for locations where high elevations override other factors. Although climate zones can shift over time, human activity may help accelerate changes in climate.

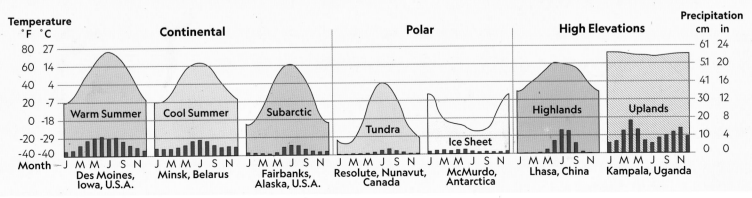

PHYSICAL WORLD

Factors Influencing Climate

Earth's climate is a bit like a big jigsaw puzzle. To understand it, you need to fit all the pieces together, because climate is influenced by a number of different, but interrelated factors. These include latitude, topography (shape of the land), elevation above sea level, wind systems, ocean currents, and distance from large bodies of water. Climate has always affected the way we live, but pollution from industries and motor vehicles is changing Earth's climate.

TOPOGRAPHY. Mountain ranges are natural barriers to the movement of air. In North America, prevailing westerly winds carry air full of moisture from the Pacific Ocean to the West Coast. As air rises over the Coast Ranges, light precipitation falls. Farther inland, the much taller Sierra Nevada range triggers heavy precipitation as air rises higher. On the leeward side of the Sierra Nevada, sinking air warms, water evaporates, and dry "rain shadow" conditions prevail. As winds continue across the interior plateau, the air remains dry because there is no significant source of moisture.

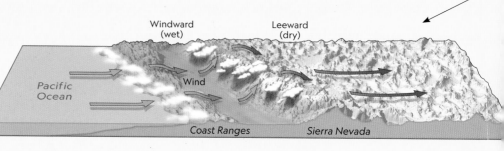

Temperature changes as air moves over mountains

LATITUDE. Energy from the sun drives global climates. Latitude—distance north or south of the Equator—affects the amount of solar energy received. Places near the Equator (e.g., Acajutla, El Salvador, above) have warm temperatures year-round. As distance from the Equator increases (St. Louis, U.S.A., and Resolute, Canada, above), average temperatures decline, and cold winters become more pronounced.

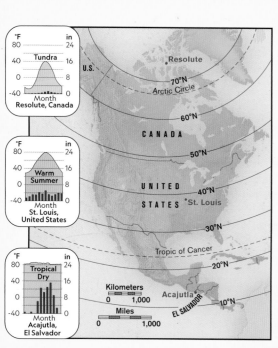

PROXIMITY TO WATER. The distance a location is from water can affect the climate in that location. Using Australia as an example, look at the climographs on the left of the map below. The line graph represents temperature and the bar graph represents precipitation. Gladstone, which is near the coast, receives more precipitation than Alice Springs. Notice that Alice Springs and Longreach are farther from the coast, and both locations have larger differences between the winter and summer temperatures. Locations near large bodies of water tend to be more moderate in their temperature differences between seasons.

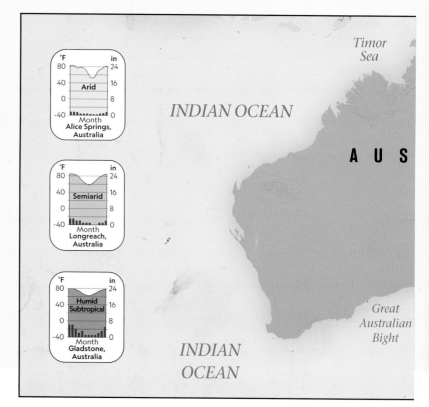

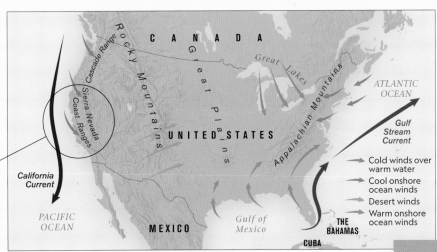

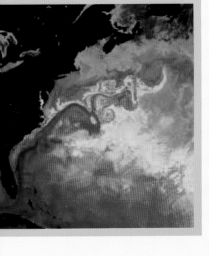

DIGGING OUT. **DIGGING OUT.** Arctic winds roar across Canada, picking up moisture from the Great Lakes (purple arrows on map, left). As the moist air crosses over the frozen land, temperatures fall and heavy precipitation—called lake effect snow—occurs, burying cars and roads, as shown here in Oswego, New York, U.S.A.

WARM CURRENT.
The Gulf Stream, a warm ocean current averaging 50–93 miles (80–150 km) wide, sweeps up the East Coast of North America (red arrow on map above). One branch continues across the North Atlantic Ocean and above the Arctic Circle (map, page 23). In the color-enhanced satellite image (left), the Gulf Stream looks like a dark red river moving up the coast. This "river" of warm water influences climate along its path, bringing moisture and mild temperatures to the East Coast of the United States and causing ice-free ports above the Arctic Circle in Europe.

CLIMATE CHANGE

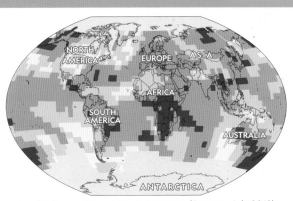

Land & Ocean Temperature Averages (January–July 2019)
No data · Cooler than average · Near average · Warmer than average · Much warmer than average · Record warmest

Earth's climate history is a story of change, with warm periods followed by periods of bitter cold. The early part of the 21st century has seen some of the warmest temperatures ever recorded (map, above). This warming trend is related to human activity and poses many risks to people, including rising sea levels. As average temperatures rise, glaciers melt and ocean waters expand, causing sea levels to rise and flood coastal areas, indicated by the red areas in Florida (below, right).

Current   By 2100

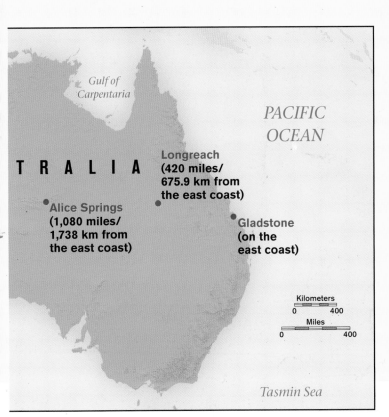

Gulf of Carpentaria

PACIFIC OCEAN

T R A L I A

Longreach (420 miles/ 675.9 km from the east coast)

Alice Springs (1,080 miles/ 1,738 km from the east coast)

Gladstone (on the east coast)

Kilometers 0 400
Miles 0 400

Tasmin Sea

World Vegetation

Natural vegetation—plants that would grow under ideal conditions at a particular place—depends on several factors. The quality and type of soil and climate are key. In fact, vegetation often reflects patterns of climate. (Compare the vegetation map at right with the world climate map on pages 22–23.) Forests thrive in places with ample precipitation; grasses are found where there is less precipitation or only seasonal rainfall; and xerophytes—plants able to survive lengthy periods with little or no water—are found in arid areas that receive very little annual precipitation.

NORTH AMERICA

ATLANTIC OCEAN

PACIFIC OCEAN

SOUTH AMERICA

Kilometers
0   1,000   2,000   3,000

Miles
0   1,000   2,000   3,000

TUNDRA

With only two to three months of above-freezing temperatures, tundra plants are mostly dwarf shrubs, short grasses, mosses, and lichens (above). Much of Russia's Arctic Circle region has tundra vegetation, which turns red as winter approaches.

TEMPERATE CONIFEROUS

Needleleaf trees with cones to protect their seeds from bitter winters grow in cold climates with short summers, such as those in British Columbia, Canada (above). These trees are important in the lumber and papermaking industries.

TEMPERATE GRASSLAND

Grasslands are found in areas where precipitation is too low to support forests. Much of the Pampas grasslands in Patagonia, Chile, is used for ranching. Winds from the Andes mountain range sweep across this region.

DESERT SHRUB

Deserts, areas that receive less than 10 inches (25 cm) of rainfall a year, have vegetation that is specially adapted to survive under dry conditions, such as these dry shrubs growing in South Australia.

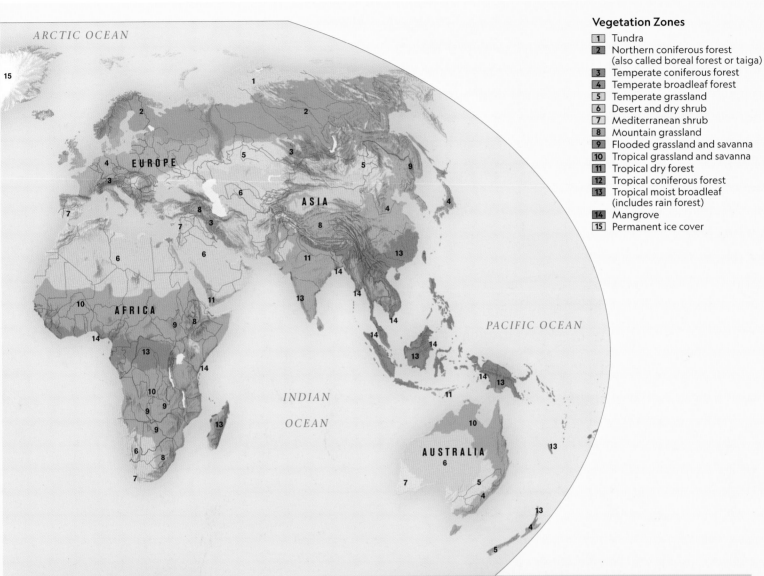

Vegetation Zones

1. Tundra
2. Northern coniferous forest (also called boreal forest or taiga)
3. Temperate coniferous forest
4. Temperate broadleaf forest
5. Temperate grassland
6. Desert and dry shrub
7. Mediterranean shrub
8. Mountain grassland
9. Flooded grassland and savanna
10. Tropical grassland and savanna
11. Tropical dry forest
12. Tropical coniferous forest
13. Tropical moist broadleaf (includes rain forest)
14. Mangrove
15. Permanent ice cover

MEDITERRANEAN SHRUB

The warm, dry summers and mild winters of Greece create an area with plants that can survive low precipitation. The region is known for growing citrus fruits, grapes, figs, and olives.

TROPICAL DRY FOREST

Although the tropical dry forest is warm year-round and receives substantial rainfall, such forests must survive long periods of dry conditions. The Guanacaste region of Costa Rica contains trees that shed their leaves during the dry season.

MANGROVE

Mangroves are found in tidal areas such as in the Caribbean region of Belize. Many species, like sea stars, make their home within the underwater root systems. Mangrove trees prevent erosion in warmer areas that have hurricanes.

CROPLAND

People remove natural vegetation in many places to create fields to grow crops to feed both people and animals. Here, a farmer in the Catskill Mountains of New York, U.S.A., cultivates land that was likely once a temperate forest.

Environmental Hot Spots

People are putting more and more pressure on the environment by dumping pollutants into the air and water and by removing natural vegetation to extract mineral resources or to create cropland for farming. In higher-income countries, industries create waste and pollution; farmers use fertilizers and pesticides that run off into water supplies; and motor vehicles release exhaust fumes into the air. In lower-income countries, forests are cut down for fuel or to clear land for farming; grasslands are turned into deserts as farmers and herders overuse the land; and expanding urban areas face problems of water quality and sanitation.

NORTH AMERICA

New York

Los Angeles

Mexico City

Environmental Stresses
- Megacity with more than 10 million people
- Deforestation
- Desertification
- Major air pollution
- Major human impact to the oceans

Bogota

SOUTH AMERICA

Lima

🌐 **HUMAN FOOTPRINT. This map uses population density, land use, transportation, and energy production and use to identify environmental hot spots—areas of Earth where human impact is greatest.**

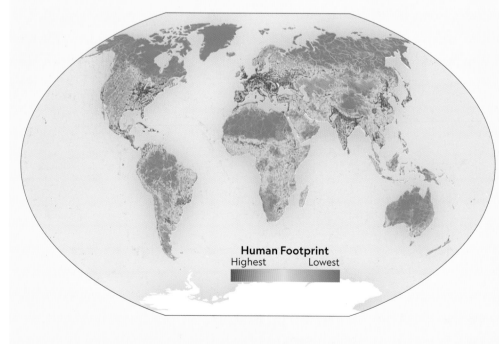

Human Footprint
Highest   Lowest

AIR POLLUTION

Poor air quality is a serious environmental problem. Industrial plants are a major source of pollution. Smoke, which contains particles that combine with moisture in the air to create acid rain, is released from a factory in Poland (above).

EUROPE

Moscow

Paris

Istanbul

ASIA

Beijing Tianjin Tokyo

Osaka

Cairo

Lahore Chongqing Shanghai

Delhi Dhaka Guangzhou Shenzhen

AFRICA Karachi Kolkata

Mumbai Hyderabad Manila

Bengalore Chennai Bangkok

Lagos

Kinshasa

Jakarta

Rio de Janeiro

São Paulo AUSTRALIA

Buenos Aires

Kilometers
0   1,000   2,000   3,000

Miles
0   1,000   2,000   3,000

DEFORESTATION

Loss of forest cover, such as on this hillside in Malaysia, contributes to a buildup of carbon dioxide in the atmosphere, as well as to a loss of biodiversity, or variety of species. These are common problems in the tropics.

DESERTIFICATION

Villagers in Mauritania (above) shovel sand away from their schoolhouse. In semiarid areas, which receive limited and often unreliable rainfall, land that is overgrazed or overcultivated can become desertlike.

OCEAN POLLUTION

Plastic trash, ranging from bottles and bags to microscopic bits, is a serious threat to sea birds and other marine life. Scientists estimate 8.8 million tons (8 million t) of plastic, including this trash off Dakar, Senegal, end up in the oceans every year.

Endangered Species

Earth's environment is made up of a complex system of life-forms ranging from microscopic organisms to giant blue whales. Throughout Earth's history, species such as the dinosaurs have become extinct. Scientists have concluded that in recent years many species are becoming endangered at an increasing rate as humans spread into natural areas for agricultural and urban use and contribute to climate change by using fossil fuels. Loss of species could mean fewer medical discoveries to fight disease and loss of plants and animals that enrich our lives each day.

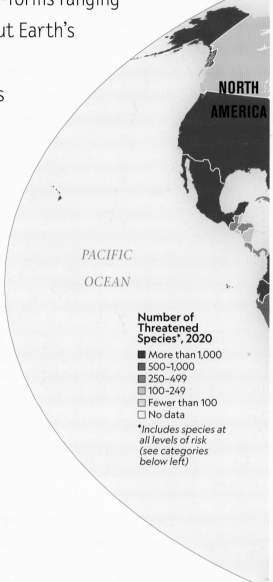

NORTH AMERICA

PACIFIC OCEAN

Number of Threatened Species*, 2020

- ■ More than 1,000
- ■ 500–1,000
- ■ 250–499
- □ 100–249
- □ Fewer than 100
- □ No data

*Includes species at all levels of risk (see categories below left)

SPECIES AT RISK

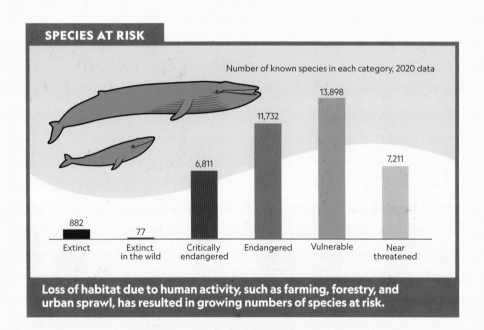

Number of known species in each category, 2020 data

882	77	6,811	11,732	13,898	7,211
Extinct	Extinct in the wild	Critically endangered	Endangered	Vulnerable	Near threatened

Loss of habitat due to human activity, such as farming, forestry, and urban sprawl, has resulted in growing numbers of species at risk.

Extinct*	Extinct in the wild	Critically endangered	Endangered	Vulnerable	Near threatened
no reasonable doubt that the last example of the species has died	best available evidence indicates the species is extinct in its natural habitat, surviving only in captivity	best available evidence indicates the species faces extremely high risk of extinction in the wild	best available evidence indicates the species faces very high risk of extinction in the wild	best available evidence indicates the species faces high risk of becoming endangered in the wild	best available evidence indicates the species is not yet vulnerable, but is likely to be without ongoing conservation action

*Categories and definitions are based on IUCN Red List.

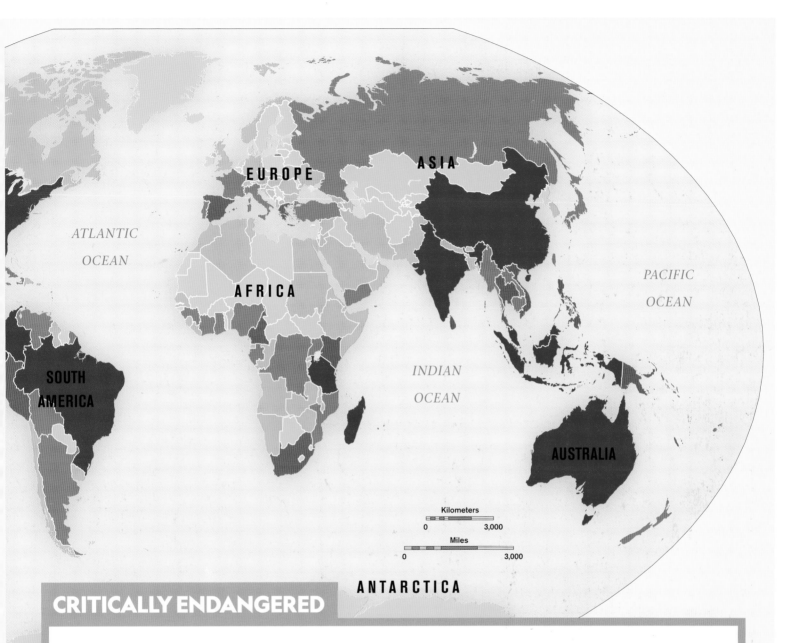

EUROPE

ASIA

ATLANTIC
OCEAN

PACIFIC
OCEAN

AFRICA

INDIAN
OCEAN

SOUTH
AMERICA

AUSTRALIA

Kilometers
0   3,000

Miles
0   3,000

ANTARCTICA

CRITICALLY ENDANGERED

Human activity poses the greatest threat to Earth's rich variety of species. Climate change and loss of habitat put many species at great risk. Experts estimate that species are facing extinction at a greater rate than at any other time in human history. The species shown here were critically endangered as of 2019.

Diademed Sifaka

Eastern Gorilla

Chinese Pangolin

Swift Parrot

Canterbury Knobbled Weevil

Geometric Tortoise

Torrey Pine

Gentiana kurroo

Natural Disasters

Every world region has its share of natural disasters. The Ring of Fire—grinding tectonic plate boundaries that follow the coasts of the Pacific Ocean—shakes with volcanic eruptions and earthquakes (page 17). Coastal areas can be swept away by quake-caused tsunamis. The U.S. heartland endures blizzards in winter and dangerous tornadoes that can strike in spring, summer, or fall. Tropical cyclones batter many coastal areas with ripping winds, torrents of rain, and huge storm surges along their deadly paths.

Natural Disasters
(1900–2019)

← Typical storm track of hurricane, typhoon, or cyclone

▢ "Tornado Alley" (highest concentration of tornadoes worldwide)

· Earthquake greater than 6.5 magnitude

· Tsunami quake epicenter

● Notable tornado

● Notable hurricane, typhoon, or cyclone

▲ Notable volcanic eruption

◓ TORNADO. A funnel cloud moves across open country near Campo, Colorado, U.S.A. More of these storms occur in "Tornado Alley" (see map) than anywhere else on Earth.

◑ RAGING HURRICANE.
In November 2019, Hurricane Dorian roared through Great Abaco Island in the Bahamas (right). With peak sustained winds of 185 miles an hour (298 km/h), the storm destroyed most structures and became one of the most intense hurricanes on record.

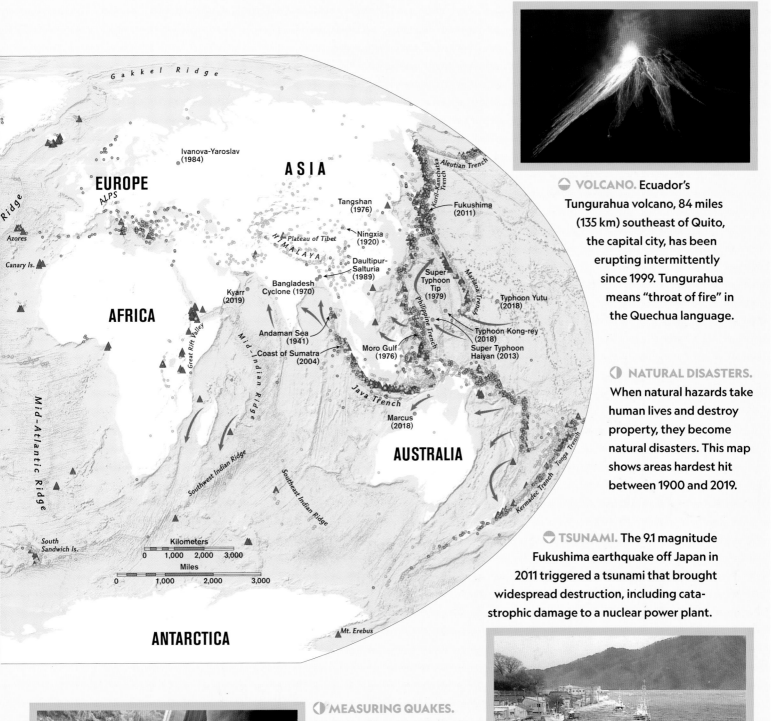

Gakkel Ridge

EUROPE
ALPS

ASIA

Ivanova-Yaroslav
(1984)

Tangshan
(1976)

Plateau of Tibet

Ningxia
(1920)

HIMALAYA

Fukushima
(2011)

Aleutian Trench

Kuril-Kamchatka Trench

Daultipur-
Salturia
(1989)

Kyarr
(2019)

Bangladesh
Cyclone (1970)

Super
Typhoon
Tip
(1979)

Mariana Trench

Typhoon Yutu
(2018)

AFRICA

Andaman Sea
(1941)

Coast of Sumatra
(2004)

Moro Gulf
(1976)

Philippine Trench

Typhoon Kong-rey
(2018)

Super Typhoon
Haiyan (2013)

Ridge

Azores

Canary Is.

Great Rift Valley

Mid-Indian Ridge

Java Trench

Marcus
(2018)

AUSTRALIA

Mid-Atlantic Ridge

Southwest Indian Ridge

Southeast Indian Ridge

Kermadec Trench

Tonga Trench

South
Sandwich Is.

Kilometers
0   1,000   2,000   3,000

Miles
0   1,000   2,000   3,000

Mt. Erebus

ANTARCTICA

◐ **VOLCANO.** Ecuador's
Tungurahua volcano, 84 miles
(135 km) southeast of Quito,
the capital city, has been
erupting intermittently
since 1999. Tungurahua
means "throat of fire" in
the Quechua language.

◑ **NATURAL DISASTERS.**
When natural hazards take
human lives and destroy
property, they become
natural disasters. This map
shows areas hardest hit
between 1900 and 2019.

◐ **TSUNAMI.** The 9.1 magnitude
Fukushima earthquake off Japan in
2011 triggered a tsunami that brought
widespread destruction, including catastrophic damage to a nuclear power plant.

◑ **MEASURING QUAKES.**
Scientists, like this one,
use an instrument called a
seismograph to measure
and record the strength
of tremors caused by
shifts in Earth's crust.

The Political World

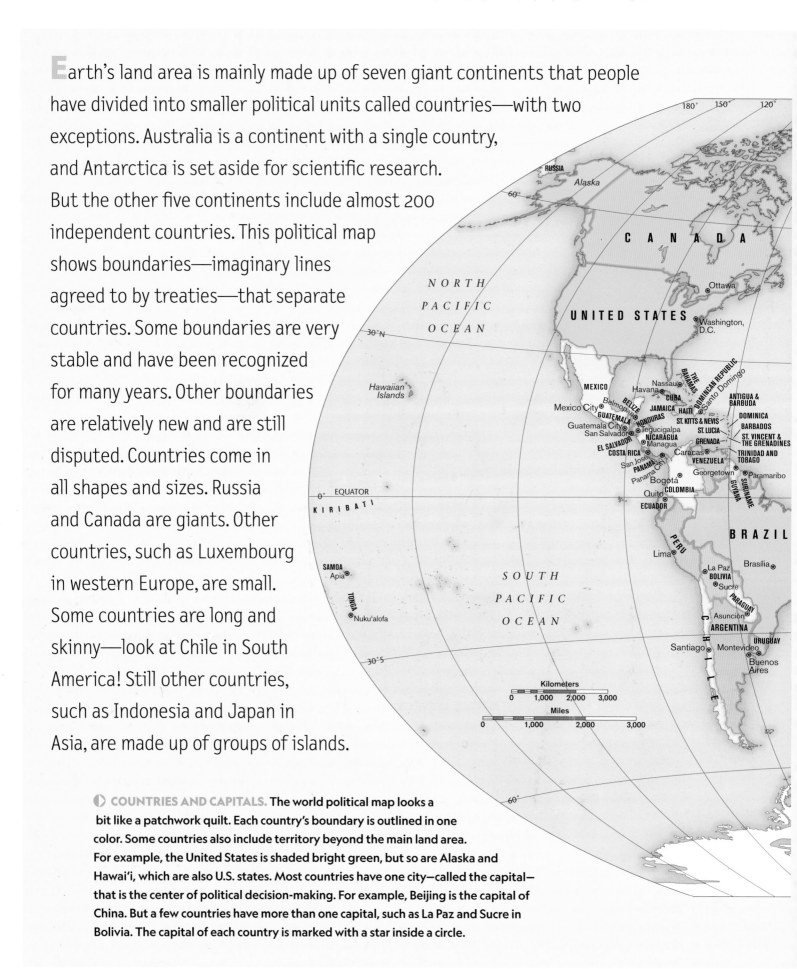

Earth's land area is mainly made up of seven giant continents that people have divided into smaller political units called countries—with two exceptions. Australia is a continent with a single country, and Antarctica is set aside for scientific research. But the other five continents include almost 200 independent countries. This political map shows boundaries—imaginary lines agreed to by treaties—that separate countries. Some boundaries are very stable and have been recognized for many years. Other boundaries are relatively new and are still disputed. Countries come in all shapes and sizes. Russia and Canada are giants. Other countries, such as Luxembourg in western Europe, are small. Some countries are long and skinny—look at Chile in South America! Still other countries, such as Indonesia and Japan in Asia, are made up of groups of islands.

◗ **COUNTRIES AND CAPITALS.** The world political map looks a bit like a patchwork quilt. Each country's boundary is outlined in one color. Some countries also include territory beyond the main land area. For example, the United States is shaded bright green, but so are Alaska and Hawai'i, which are also U.S. states. Most countries have one city—called the capital— that is the center of political decision-making. For example, Beijing is the capital of China. But a few countries have more than one capital, such as La Paz and Sucre in Bolivia. The capital of each country is marked with a star inside a circle.

ARCTIC OCEAN

Greenland
Svalbard

Reykjavik ⊗ ICELAND

RUSSIA

NORWAY SWEDEN FINLAND

Oslo ⊗ ⊗ Helsinki
Copenhagen ⊗ Stockholm ⊗ ESTONIA
LATVIA ⊗ Moscow
UNITED DENMARK LITHUANIA
KINGDOM POLAND BELARUS Minsk ⊗
IRELAND NETH. Berlin ⊗ Warsaw ⊗ Kyiv ⊗
Dublin ⊗ BELG. GERMANY CZECHIA UKRAINE
London ⊗ LUX. Paris ⊗ AUSTRIA SLOVAKIA MOLDOVA
SWITZ. SLOVENIA HUNGARY ROMANIA
FRANCE CROATIA SERBIA CRIMEA
PORTUGAL ITALY BOSN. & HERZE. BULGARIA Ankara ⊗ GEORGIA
Rome ⊗ MONT. KOSOVO N. MACEDONIA TURKEY AZERBAIJAN ARMENIA
Lisbon ⊗ Madrid ⊗ SPAIN ALBANIA GREECE Athens ⊗ CYPRUS SYRIA
Rabat ⊗ Algiers ⊗ Tunis ⊗ MALTA LEBANON IRAQ Baghdad ⊗ IRAN Tehran ⊗
MOROCCO TUNISIA Tripoli ⊗ ISRAEL JORDAN
WESTERN Cairo ⊗ KUWAIT
SAHARA ALGERIA LIBYA EGYPT BAHRAIN QATAR
(Morocco) Riyadh ⊗ SAUDI U.A.E. Muscat ⊗ OMAN
MAURITANIA ARABIA
Nouakchott ⊗ Asmara ⊗ YEMEN
CABO SENEGAL MALI NIGER CHAD Khartoum ⊗ ERITREA Sanaa ⊗
VERDE Dakar ⊗ Niamey ⊗ SUDAN DJIBOUTI
THE GAMBIA BURKINA N'Djamena ⊗ Addis
Bissau ⊗ Bamako ⊗ FASO NIGERIA Ababa ⊗ SOMALILAND
GUINEA-BISSAU Ouagadougou ⊗ Abuja ⊗ CENTRAL SOUTH ETHIOPIA
Conakry ⊗ GUINEA CÔTE BENIN AFRICAN REPUBLIC SUDAN Juba ⊗ SOMALIA
Freetown ⊗ D'IVOIRE GHANA TOGO Bangui ⊗ UGANDA
SIERRA LEONE Abidjan ⊗ Accra ⊗ CAMEROON Yaoundé ⊗ Kampala ⊗ KENYA Mogadishu ⊗
LIBERIA EQUATORIAL Libreville ⊗ CONGO DEM. REP. OF Kigali ⊗ RWANDA Nairobi ⊗
Monrovia ⊗ GUINEA GABON THE CONGO BURUNDI Gitega ⊗
Yamoussoukro ⊗ SAO TOME & PRINCIPE Brazzaville ⊗ Bujumbura ⊗ Dodoma ⊗
Kinshasa ⊗ TANZANIA Dar es Salaam ⊗
Luanda ⊗ Lilongwe ⊗ COMOROS SEYCHELLES Victoria ⊗
ANGOLA ZAMBIA MALAWI Moroni ⊗
Lusaka ⊗ MOZAMBIQUE MADAGASCAR
NAMIBIA ZIMBABWE Antananarivo ⊗
Windhoek ⊗ BOTSWANA Harare ⊗ MAURITIUS
Gaborone ⊗ Maputo ⊗ Port Louis ⊗
(Tshwane) Pretoria ⊗ ESWATINI
Bloemfontein ⊗ (SWAZILAND) LESOTHO
SOUTH
Cape Town ⊗ AFRICA

NORTH
ATLANTIC
OCEAN

SOUTH
ATLANTIC
OCEAN

KAZAKHSTAN
Nur-Sultan (Astana) ⊗ Ulaanbaatar ⊗ MONGOLIA
Tashkent ⊗ Bishkek ⊗ Beijing ⊗ NORTH
UZBEKISTAN KYRGYZSTAN KOREA
TURKMENISTAN Dushanbe ⊗ Pyongyang ⊗ JAPAN
Ashgabat ⊗ TAJIKISTAN SOUTH Seoul ⊗
AFGHANISTAN Kabul ⊗ Islamabad ⊗ CHINA KOREA Tokyo ⊗
PAKISTAN NEPAL Thimphu ⊗
New Delhi ⊗ Kathmandu ⊗ BHUTAN
Dhaka ⊗ BANGLADESH TAIWAN
INDIA MYANMAR Hanoi ⊗
(BURMA) VIETNAM
Nay Pyi Taw ⊗ LAOS Manila ⊗
Vientiane ⊗ THAILAND CAMBODIA PHILIPPINES
Colombo ⊗ Bangkok ⊗ Phnom Penh ⊗
SRI LANKA BRUNEI
Sri Jayewardenepura Kotte ⊗ Bandar Seri Begawan ⊗
Male ⊗ Kuala Lumpur ⊗ MALAYSIA
MALDIVES SINGAPORE

NORTH
PACIFIC
OCEAN

MARSHALL
ISLANDS
Ngerulmud ⊗ Palikir ⊗
PALAU Majuro ⊗
FEDERATED STATES Tarawa ⊗ KIRIBATI
OF MICRONESIA
NAURU ⊗

INDONESIA
Jakarta ⊗ Dili ⊗ PAPUA
TIMOR-LESTE NEW GUINEA
(EAST TIMOR) Port Moresby ⊗ SOLOMON
Honiara ⊗ ISLANDS
TUVALU
Funafuti ⊗
Port-Vila ⊗ FIJI
VANUATU Suva ⊗

INDIAN
OCEAN

AUSTRALIA

Canberra, ⊗
A.C.T.

NEW ZEALAND ⊗
Wellington ⊗

SOUTH
PACIFIC
OCEAN

ANTARCTICA

POLITICAL WORLD

World Population

How big is a billion? It's hard to imagine. But Earth's population is 7.7 billion and rising, with more than a billion living in both China and India. And more than 80 million people are added to the world each year. Most population growth occurs in the lower-income countries in Africa, Asia, North America, and South America, while some countries in Europe are hardly increasing at all. Population changes can create challenges for countries. Fast-growing countries with young populations need food, housing, and schools. Countries with low growth rates and older populations need workers to sustain their economies.

MOST POPULOUS COUNTRIES

(2019 estimates)	
1. China	1,384,689,000
2. India	1,296,834,000
3. United States	329,256,000
4. Indonesia	262,787,000
5. Brazil	208,847,000

MOST CROWDED COUNTRIES

Population Density (People per sq mi/sq km; 2019 estimates)	
1. Monaco	39,000 / 19,500
2. Singapore	22,280 / 8,602
3. Vatican City	5,886 / 2,272
4. Bahrain	4,917 / 1,898
5. Malta	3,680 / 1,420

◗ **DENSITY.** Demographers, people who study population, use density to measure how concentrated population is, but density is just an average. For example, the population density of Egypt is more than 257 people per square mile (99 people per sq km). This incorrectly assumes that the population is evenly spread throughout the country. Actually, most people live along the Nile River. Likewise, Earth's population is not evenly spread across the land. Some places are almost empty, others are very crowded.

NORTH AMERICA

Los Angeles ⊙

Mexico City ⊙

PACIFIC OCEAN

Kilometers
0   1,000   2,000   3,000

Miles
0   1,000   2,000   3,000

◗ **CITY DWELLERS.**
More than half the world's people have shifted from rural areas to urban centers, with some countries adding more than 100 million to their urban populations between 1950 and 2020 (map, right). In higher-income countries, about 75 percent of the population is urban, compared with just 46 percent in lower-income countries. But the fastest growing urban areas are in less developed countries, where thousands flock to cities, such as Dhaka, Bangladesh (photo, far right), in search of a better life. In 2016, there were 34 cities with a population of 10 million or more.

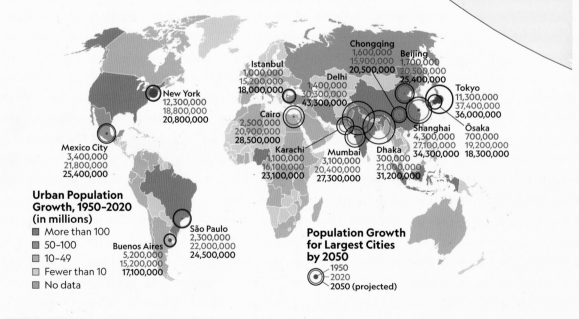

Urban Population Growth, 1950–2020 (in millions)
- More than 100
- 50–100
- 10–49
- Fewer than 10
- No data

Mexico City
3,400,000
21,800,000
25,400,000

New York
12,300,000
18,800,000
20,800,000

Istanbul
1,000,000
15,200,000
18,000,000

Cairo
2,500,000
20,900,000
28,500,000

Delhi
1,400,000
30,300,000
43,300,000

Chongqing
1,600,000
15,900,000
20,500,000

Beijing
1,700,000
20,500,000
25,400,000

Tokyo
11,300,000
37,400,000
36,000,000

Karachi
1,100,000
16,100,000
23,100,000

Mumbai
3,100,000
20,400,000
27,300,000

Dhaka
300,000
21,000,000
31,200,000

Shanghai
4,300,000
27,100,000
34,300,000

Ōsaka
700,000
19,200,000
18,300,000

São Paulo
2,300,000
22,000,000
24,500,000

Buenos Aires
5,200,000
15,200,000
17,100,000

Population Growth for Largest Cities by 2050
- 1950
- 2020
- 2050 (projected)

A.D. 1 50 100 150 200 250 300 350 400 450 500 550 600 650 700 750 800 850
Year

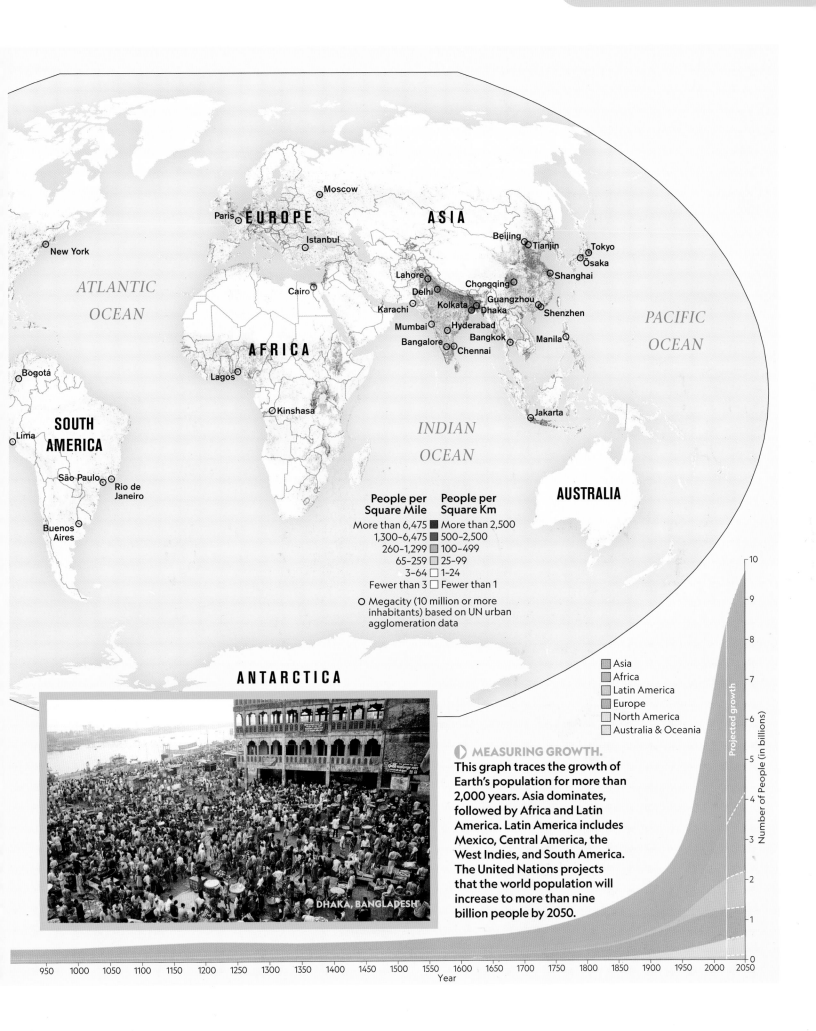

Moscow

Paris ○ EUROPE

Istanbul

ASIA

Beijing ○ Tianjin
Tokyo
Osaka
Shanghai

Lahore
Chongqing
Delhi
Guangzhou
Karachi
Kolkata ○ Dhaka
Shenzhen
Mumbai Hyderabad
Bangalore Bangkok Manila
Chennai

New York

ATLANTIC
OCEAN

Cairo

AFRICA

Lagos

PACIFIC
OCEAN

Bogotá

SOUTH
AMERICA

Lima

Kinshasa

INDIAN
OCEAN

Jakarta

AUSTRALIA

São Paulo
Rio de
Janeiro

Buenos
Aires

People per Square Mile — **People per Square Km**

More than 6,475 ■ More than 2,500
1,300–6,475 ■ 500–2,500
260–1,299 ■ 100–499
65–259 ☐ 25–99
3–64 ☐ 1–24
Fewer than 3 ☐ Fewer than 1

○ Megacity (10 million or more inhabitants) based on UN urban agglomeration data

ANTARCTICA

☐ Asia
☐ Africa
☐ Latin America
☐ Europe
☐ North America
☐ Australia & Oceania

◗ **MEASURING GROWTH.**
This graph traces the growth of Earth's population for more than 2,000 years. Asia dominates, followed by Africa and Latin America. Latin America includes Mexico, Central America, the West Indies, and South America. The United Nations projects that the world population will increase to more than nine billion people by 2050.

DHAKA, BANGLADESH

Projected growth

Number of People (in billions)

10
9
8
7
6
5
4
3
2
1
0

950 1000 1050 1100 1150 1200 1250 1300 1350 1400 1450 1500 1550 1600 1650 1700 1750 1800 1850 1900 1950 2000 2050
Year

Population Trends

Population growth rates are slowing, total fertility rates are declining, and populations are aging. Nevertheless, world population will continue to increase for many years to come because the base population is so large. More than 80 million people are added, on average, to the world's population each year, 90 percent of whom are born in lower-income countries where poverty is greatest. In more affluent countries, life expectancy is higher and populations are aging. It's estimated that by 2050, one-sixth of the world's population will be 65 years of age or older.

POPULATION GROWTH RATE (%)

Lowest (2019 estimates)	
1. Lebanon	-6.7
2. Lithuania	-1.1
3. Latvia	-1.1
4. Moldova	-1.1
5. Bulgaria	-0.7

POPULATION GROWTH RATE (%)

Highest (2019 estimates)	
1. Syria	4.3
2. Niger	3.7
3. Angola	3.4
4. Benin	3.4
5. Uganda	3.3

◑ **POPULATION GROWTH.**

This map shows projected population change (%) from 2015 to 2050. Russia, China, Japan, and much of Europe face a decline in population due to low birth rates and women waiting longer to have children. Countries in most of Africa can expect to see an opposite trend as fertility rates remain high.

NORTH AMERICA

UNITED STATES

United States
80 years
1.8

Projected Population Change (%), 2015–2050

gain {
- More than 100
- 50 to 100
- 0 to 49.9
}

loss {
- -10 to -0.1
- -30 to -10.1
- No data
}

Other Map Symbols
- ■ **Life expectancy** (symbol represents 10 years, both sexes)
- ⚲ **Fertility rate** (average number of children born to women in a given population; symbol represents 1 child)

PACIFIC OCEAN

POPULATION PYRAMIDS

A population pyramid compares population by age and sex and can be used to predict future trends. Countries, such as Nigeria, with high birth rates and high percentages of young people have a pyramid-shaped graph, which suggests continued growth. Countries with low birth rates, such as Italy, have narrow bases with bulges in the higher age brackets, indicating an aging population.

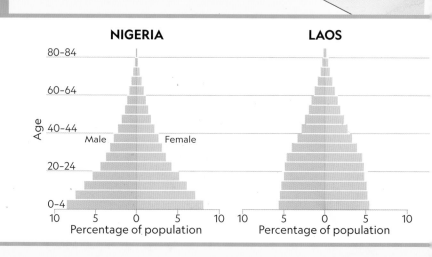

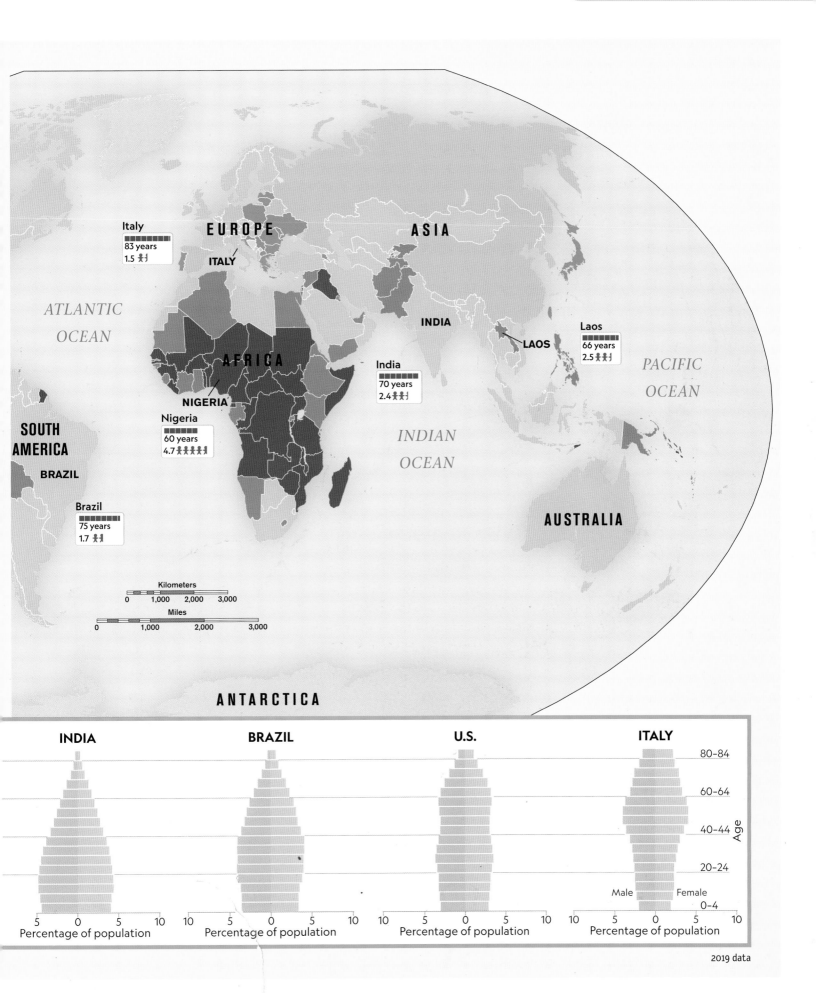

Italy
83 years
1.5

ITALY

EUROPE

ASIA

ATLANTIC
OCEAN

AFRICA

NIGERIA

Nigeria
60 years
4.7

INDIA

India
70 years
2.4

Laos

LAOS

Laos
66 years
2.5

PACIFIC
OCEAN

INDIAN
OCEAN

SOUTH
AMERICA

BRAZIL

Brazil
75 years
1.7

AUSTRALIA

Kilometers
0   1,000   2,000   3,000

Miles
0   1,000   2,000   3,000

ANTARCTICA

INDIA

BRAZIL

U.S.

ITALY

80–84

60–64

40–44

20–24

Age

Male   Female

0–4

5   0   5   10
Percentage of population

10   5   0   5   10
Percentage of population

10   5   0   5   10
Percentage of population

10   5   0   5   10
Percentage of population

2019 data

Migration

Why do people move? Many people move for the same reason that animals migrate. They are looking for food, adequate shelter, safety, and better climate conditions.

The forces that draw people to move into a country are called pull factors. Pull factors are positive forces on migration, such as earning more money, being near family, and having freedom and safety. The forces that make people want to leave a country are called push factors. Push factors are negative forces on migration, such as poverty, unemployment, famine, and conflict or war.

By analyzing the map, you will notice that many countries in North America, Europe, Asia, and Australia are shaded in a darker green. Many of these countries offer freedom and job opportunities for immigrants. You will also notice that the countries of Gabon in Africa, French Guiana in South America, and Kazakhstan in Asia are darker green than the countries around them. These countries have attracted migrants due to the job opportunities found there.

NORTH AMERICA

PACIFIC OCEAN

ATLANTIC OCEAN

SOUTH AMERICA

Kilometers
0   1,000   2,000   3,000

Miles
0   1,000   2,000   3,000

Migrant Population
(percentage of total population)
- More than 25
- 15.1–25
- 5.5–15
- 2.5–5.4
- 1.–2.4
- Less than 1
- No data

◗ **BORDER CROSSING.**
Four countries (Zambia, Namibia, Zimbabwe, and Botswana) meet at the Zambezi River. Most travelers and migrants must wait hours to cross the river. Due to heavy migration, the Kazungula Ferry will soon be replaced by a bridge.

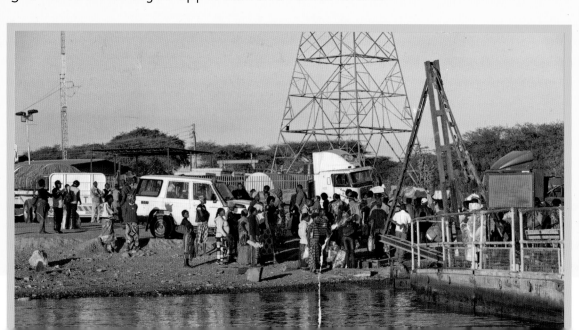

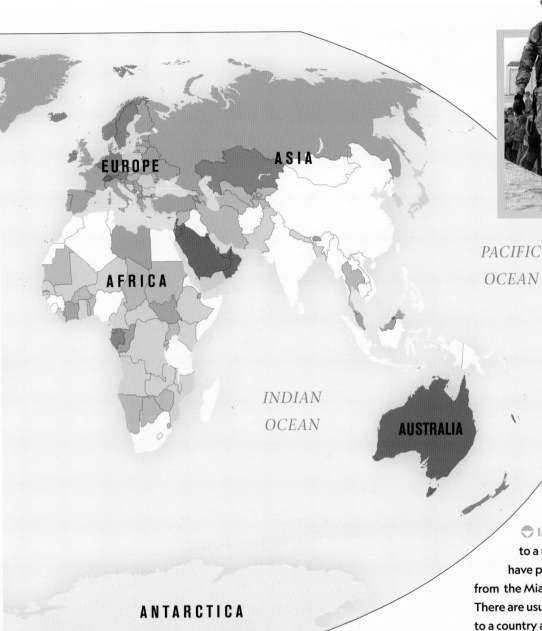

EUROPE

ASIA

AFRICA

PACIFIC
OCEAN

INDIAN
OCEAN

AUSTRALIA

ANTARCTICA

REFUGEES. Civil war in a country can create concerns along the borders with neighboring countries. Due to civil unrest and conflict in surrounding countries, refugees arrive in Ruwaished, Jordan, to escape this upheaval and to seek medical attention.

IMMIGRATION INSPECTION. Traveling to a new country can mean a wait in line to have passports checked, as in the photo below from the Miami International Airport in Florida, U.S.A. There are usually separate lines for citizens returning to a country and citizens of other countries.

MIGRANT WORKERS. In 2015, 36 percent of the Chinese workforce was made up of migrant workers who moved from one place to another within China. Every year, many of these workers leave agricultural areas for jobs in urbanized areas. When these workers return home to celebrate the Chinese New Year, their traveling period, called the Chunyun, is considered the world's largest annual human migration.

POLITICAL WORLD

World Languages

Earth's 7.7 billion people live in 195 independent countries, but they speak more than 7,000 languages. Experts believe that humans may once have spoken as many as 10,000 languages. Some countries, such as Germany, have one official language. Other countries, such as Zimbabwe, have many official languages.

Literacy is the ability to read and write in one's native language. High literacy rates are associated with higher-income countries. But literacy is also a gender issue, since women in lower-income countries often lack access to education.

NORTH
AMERICA

SOUTH
AMERICA

*PACIFIC
OCEAN*

LEADING LANGUAGES

2020 data

Some languages have only a few hundred speakers, but 20 languages stand out with more than 80 million speakers each. Earth's population giant, China, has more than 950 million speakers of Mandarin. Colonial expansion, trade, and migration account for the spread of the other most widely spoken languages. With growing use of the internet, English is becoming the language of the technology age.

Population of first language speakers (in millions)

Language	Speakers
English	1,268
Chinese (Mandarin)	1,120
Hindi	637
Spanish	538
French	277
Arabic	274
Bengali	265
Russian	258
Portuguese	252
Indonesian	199

Languages

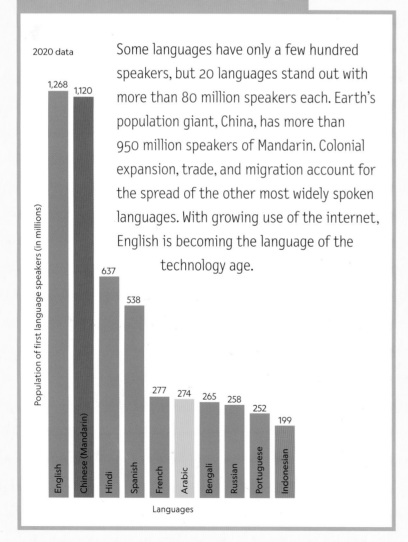

◯ **EDUCATION AND LITERACY. These Nenet boys in Siberia spend hours learning the national language—Russian—but this may result in the loss of their native language. There are more than 7,000 languages spoken on Earth, but by 2100, experts predict that more than half of those may have disappeared.**

& Literacy

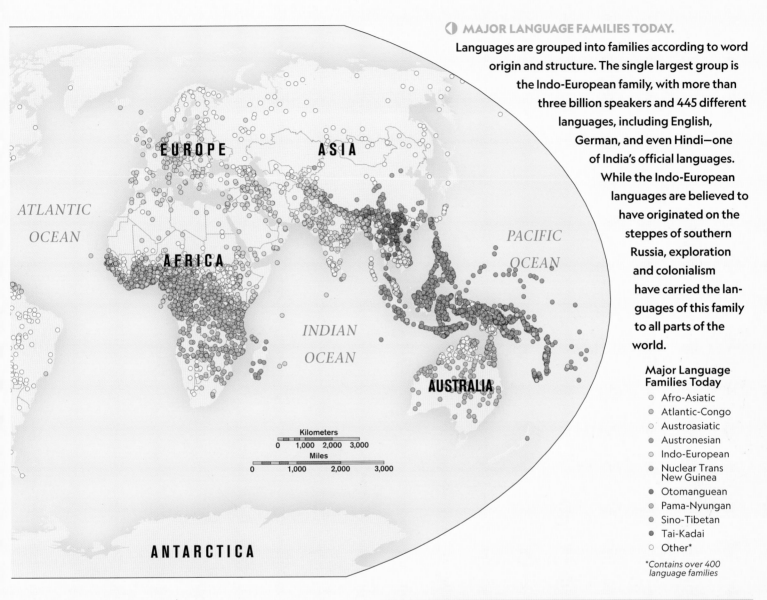

◀ **MAJOR LANGUAGE FAMILIES TODAY.**
Languages are grouped into families according to word origin and structure. The single largest group is the Indo-European family, with more than three billion speakers and 445 different languages, including English, German, and even Hindi—one of India's official languages. While the Indo-European languages are believed to have originated on the steppes of southern Russia, exploration and colonialism have carried the languages of this family to all parts of the world.

Major Language Families Today
- Afro-Asiatic
- Atlantic-Congo
- Austroasiatic
- Austronesian
- Indo-European
- Nuclear Trans New Guinea
- Otomanguean
- Pama-Nyungan
- Sino-Tibetan
- Tai-Kadai
- Other*

*Contains over 400 language families

EUROPE

ASIA

ATLANTIC OCEAN

AFRICA

PACIFIC OCEAN

INDIAN OCEAN

AUSTRALIA

ANTARCTICA

Kilometers
0 1,000 2,000 3,000
Miles
0 1,000 2,000 3,000

◗ **ONE LANGUAGE, TWO FORMS.** Some languages, including Chinese, use characters instead of letters. The Golden Arches provide a clue to the meaning of the characters on the restaurant sign. Many signs, such as the one in the foreground, also show words in pinyin, a spelling system that uses the Western alphabet.

◖ **UNIVERSAL LANGUAGE.** The widespread use of technology—for example, the computer that holds the attention of these girls in Indonesia—has crossed the language barrier. Computers, the internet, and electronic communication devices use a universal language that knows no national borders.

World Religions

Religion takes many forms. Some belief systems, such as Christianity, Islam, and Judaism, are monotheistic, meaning that followers believe in just one supreme being. Others, like Hinduism, Shintoism, and most indigenous belief systems, are polytheistic, meaning that followers believe in many gods.

All of the major religions have their origins in Asia, but they have spread around the world. Christianity, with the largest number of followers, has three main divisions—Roman Catholic, Eastern Orthodox, and Protestant. Islam, with almost one-fourth of all believers, has two main divisions—Sunni and Shia. Together, Hinduism and Buddhism account for more than another one-fifth of believers. Judaism, dating back some 4,000 years, is the oldest of all the major monotheistic religions.

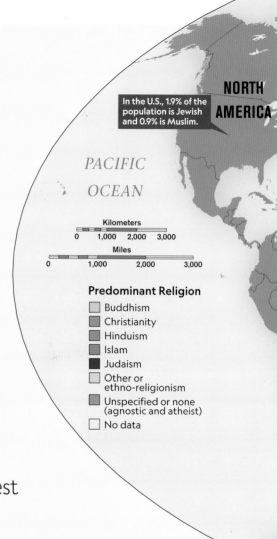

NORTH AMERICA

In the U.S., 1.9% of the population is Jewish and 0.9% is Muslim.

PACIFIC OCEAN

Kilometers
0   1,000   2,000   3,000

Miles
0   1,000   2,000   3,000

Predominant Religion
- Buddhism
- Christianity
- Hinduism
- Islam
- Judaism
- Other or ethno-religionism
- Unspecified or none (agnostic and atheist)
- No data

BUDDHISM

Founded about 2,500 years ago in northern India by a Hindu prince named Gautama Buddha, Buddhism spread throughout eastern and southeastern Asia. Buddhist temples house statues, such as the Mihintale Buddha (above) in Sri Lanka.

CHRISTIANITY

Based on the teachings of Jesus Christ, a Jewish man born some 2,000 years ago in the area of modern-day Israel, Christianity has spread worldwide. Followers in Switzerland (above) participate in a procession with lanterns and crosses.

HINDUISM

Dating back more than 4,000 years, Hinduism is practiced mainly in India. Hindus follow sacred texts known as the Vedas and believe in reincarnation. During the festival of Diwali, Hindus light candles (above) to symbolize the victory of good over evil.

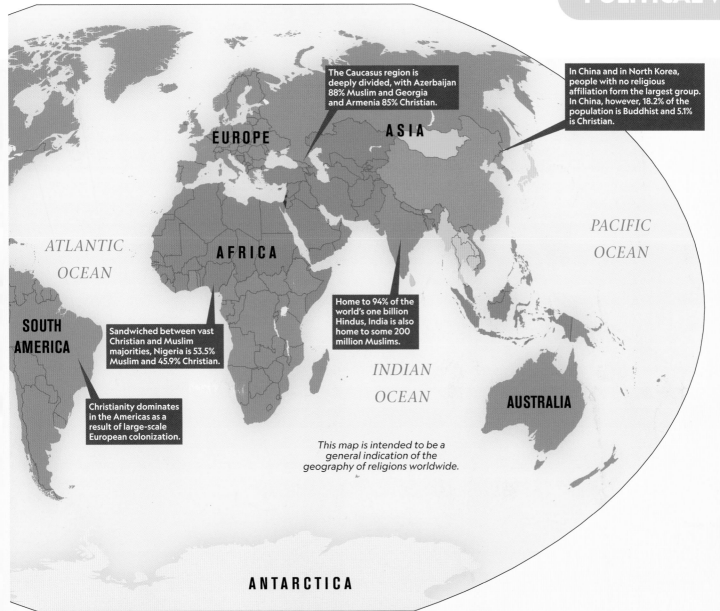

EUROPE

ASIA

The Caucasus region is deeply divided, with Azerbaijan 88% Muslim and Georgia and Armenia 85% Christian.

In China and in North Korea, people with no religious affiliation form the largest group. In China, however, 18.2% of the population is Buddhist and 5.1% is Christian.

ATLANTIC
OCEAN

AFRICA

PACIFIC
OCEAN

SOUTH
AMERICA

Sandwiched between vast Christian and Muslim majorities, Nigeria is 53.5% Muslim and 45.9% Christian.

Home to 94% of the world's one billion Hindus, India is also home to some 200 million Muslims.

INDIAN
OCEAN

AUSTRALIA

Christianity dominates in the Americas as a result of large-scale European colonization.

This map is intended to be a general indication of the geography of religions worldwide.

ANTARCTICA

ISLAM

Muslims believe that the Koran, Islam's sacred book, records the words of Allah (God) as revealed to the Prophet Muhammad around 610 C.E. Believers (above) circle the Kabah in the Haram Mosque in Mecca, Saudi Arabia, the spiritual center of the faith.

JUDAISM

The traditions, laws, and beliefs of Judaism date back some 4,000 years to Abraham, its founder, and to the Torah, the first five books of the Old Testament. Followers pray before the Western Wall (above), which stands below Islam's Dome of the Rock in Jerusalem, Israel.

RELIGIOUS FOLLOWERS

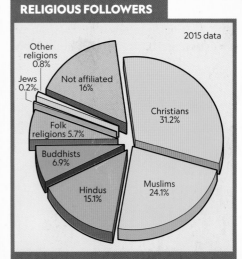

2015 data

Other religions 0.8%

Jews 0.2%

Not affiliated 16%

Christians 31.2%

Folk religions 5.7%

Buddhists 6.9%

Muslims 24.1%

Hindus 15.1%

Most people identify with a major religion. Some are nonreligious.

World Economies

A country's economy can be divided into three parts, or sectors—primary, which includes agriculture, forestry, fishing, and mining; secondary, which includes industry and manufacturing; and tertiary, which includes services ranging from retail sales to mail delivery, to teaching or jobs in medicine. Sometimes a fourth sector, called quaternary, is added. This includes information technology, research, and knowledge creation. The map shows that the economies of the United States, western Europe, and Japan are dominated by service sector jobs. These countries rely heavily on the use of technology and enjoy a high gross domestic product (GDP) per capita—the value of goods and services produced each year, averaged per person in each country. The overall quality of life in these countries is good. In contrast, more than half of the people in Sub-Saharan Africa, South Asia, and Southeast Asia still depend on the primary sector, which generates a low GDP per capita.

UNITED
STATES

PACIFIC

OCEAN

**Dominant Economic Sector
(as a percentage of GDP)**

Agriculture   Industry   Services

70%–100%

50%–69.9%

0%–49.9%

No data

Services   Agriculture

Industry

◐ **INFORMATION.** Computers and other technologies have opened employment opportunities dealing with information and knowledge creation. These college students in the United Kingdom learn skills in an information technology lab that will prepare them for 21st-century jobs.

◔ **INDUSTRY.** A man assembles a hybrid Prius car on an automated assembly line in a Toyota factory in Japan. The manufacture of cars is an important industrial activity and a key part of the global economy.

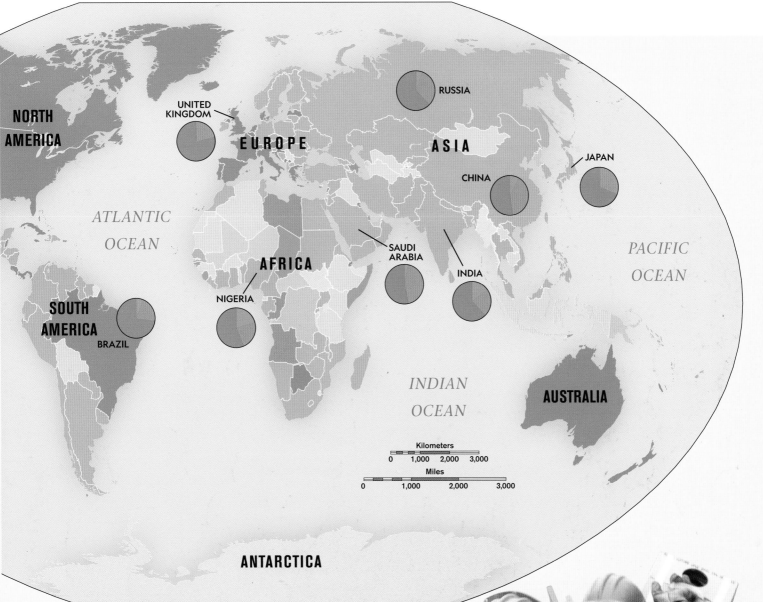

NORTH
AMERICA

UNITED
KINGDOM

EUROPE

RUSSIA

ASIA

JAPAN

CHINA

ATLANTIC
OCEAN

AFRICA

SAUDI
ARABIA

INDIA

PACIFIC
OCEAN

NIGERIA

SOUTH
AMERICA

BRAZIL

INDIAN
OCEAN

AUSTRALIA

Kilometers
0   1,000   2,000   3,000

Miles
0   1,000   2,000   3,000

ANTARCTICA

AGRICULTURE. People in lower-income countries, such as these women in Mozambique, often grow a variety of crops just to support their families. This practice is called subsistence agriculture. In higher-income countries, farmers use machines to produce large quantities of commercial crops.

SERVICES. People employed in the service sector, such as these national forest firefighters in Washington State, U.S.A., use their skills and training to provide services rather than products. Teachers, lawyers, and store clerks, among others, are also part of the service sector.

World Trade

World trade has expanded rapidly since the end of World War II in 1945. In fact, trade has grown faster than world production has. Some countries, such as the United States, China, and Germany, have complex economies that involve trading many different products as well as commercial services, such as financial and information management. But many lower-income countries rely on only a few products—sometimes even just one product—to generate trade income (map, right). Wealthy countries often protect their economies by negotiating agreements and imposing taxes that limit trade in products from other countries. The World Trade Organization works to reduce such trade barriers so that all countries can compete in the global economy.

NORTH AMERICA

PACIFIC OCEAN

Kilometers
0   1,000   2,000   3,000

Miles
0   1,000   2,000   3,000

TOP MERCHANDISE EXPORTERS

(2019 data, billion U.S. dollars)	
1. China	$2,499
2. United States	$1,643
3. Germany	$1,489
4. Netherlands	$709
5. Japan	$705

TOP MERCHANDISE IMPORTERS

(2019 data, billion U.S. dollars)	
1. United States	$2,567
2. China	$2,078
3. Germany	$1,234
4. Japan	$720
5. United Kingdom	$695

TOP COMMERCIAL SERVICE EXPORTERS

(2019 data, billion U.S. dollars)	
1. United States	$853
2. United Kingdom	$414
3. Germany	$340
4. France	$293
5. Ireland	$247

TOP COMMERCIAL SERVICE IMPORTERS

(2019 data, billion U.S. dollars)	
1. United States	$564
2. China	$501
3. Germany	$369
4. Ireland	$331
5. France	$269

◗ TRADE. The map (right) shows the richest and poorest economies around the world. The wealth of an economy can be measured in terms of gross national income (GNI) per person—income derived from all economic activity.

◗ GLOBAL EXCHANGE. The world economy depends on container ports where ships deliver goods for sale or redistribution. Some ports, called transshipment ports, move containers from one form of transportation (such as a ship) to another (such as a truck) so that goods can be delivered to a final destination.

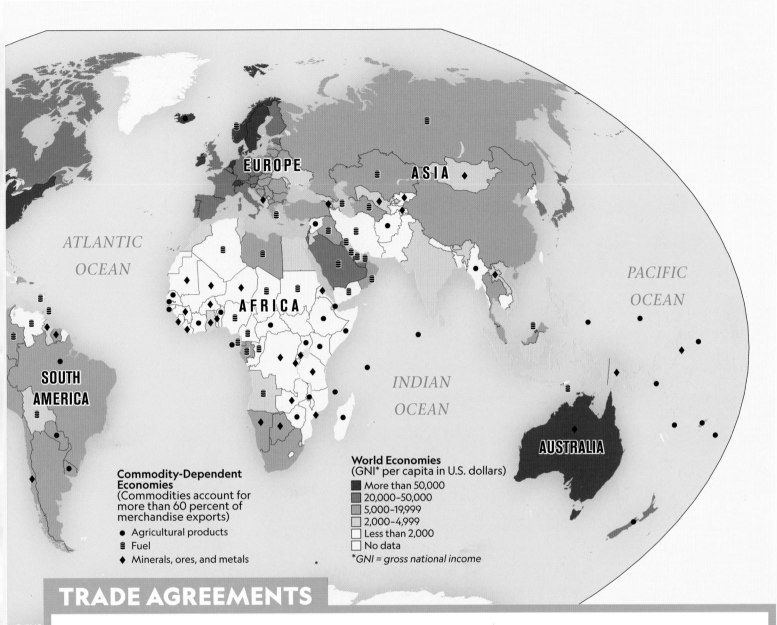

Commodity-Dependent Economies
(Commodities account for more than 60 percent of merchandise exports)

- ● Agricultural products
- ▤ Fuel
- ◆ Minerals, ores, and metals

World Economies
(GNI* per capita in U.S. dollars)

- More than 50,000
- 20,000–50,000
- 5,000–19,999
- 2,000–4,999
- Less than 2,000
- No data

*GNI = gross national income

TRADE AGREEMENTS

Trade within regions is increasing. Neighboring countries agree to offer each other trade benefits that can improve the economy of the whole region. Such agreements allow products, workers, and money to move more easily among the partners. But these agreements may also prevent trade with other countries that may be able to provide products at a lower cost.

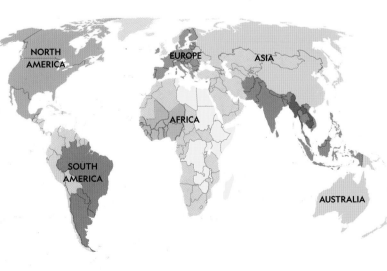

Major Regional Trade Agreements

- ☐ **APEC:** Asia-Pacific Economic Cooperation
- ■ **ASEAN:** Association of Southeast Asian Nations
- ☐ **APEC & ASEAN**
- ☐ **COMESA:** Common Market for Eastern and Southern Africa
- ☐ **ECOWAS:** Economic Community of West African States
- ☐ **EU:** European Union
- ☐ **MERCOSUR:** Southern Common Market
- ☐ **APEC & USMCA:** United States-Mexico-Canada Agreement
- ☐ **SAFTA:** South Asian Free Trade Area

World Water

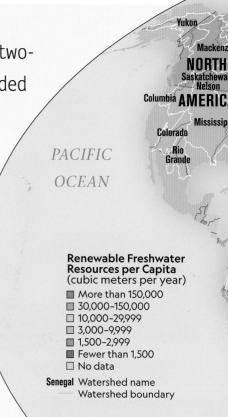

Water is Earth's most precious resource. Although more than two-thirds of the planet is covered by water, freshwater, which is needed by plants and animals—including humans—is only about 2.5 percent of all the water on Earth. Much of this is trapped deep underground or frozen in ice sheets and glaciers. Of the small amount of water that is fresh, less than one percent is available for human use.

The map at right shows each country's access to renewable freshwater supplies. Watersheds are large areas that drain into a particular river or lake. Unfortunately, human activity often puts great stress on watersheds. For example, in Brazil, plans are being made to build large dams on the Amazon. This will alter the natural flow of water in this giant watershed. In the United States, heavy use of chemical fertilizers and pesticides has created toxic runoff that threatens the health of the Mississippi watershed.

Access to clean freshwater is critical for human health. But in many places, safe water is scarce due to population pressure and pollution.

Renewable Freshwater Resources per Capita (cubic meters per year)
- More than 150,000
- 30,000–150,000
- 10,000–29,999
- 3,000–9,999
- 1,500–2,999
- Fewer than 1,500
- No data

Senegal Watershed name
— Watershed boundary

WATER FACTS

Rivers that have been dammed to generate electricity are the source of almost 60 percent of Earth's renewable energy resources.

North America's Great Lakes hold about 20 percent of Earth's available freshwater.

If all the glaciers and ice sheets on Earth's surface melted, they would raise the level of Earth's oceans by about 216 feet (66 m).

If all the world's water could be placed in a gallon jug, the freshwater available for humans to use would equal only about one tablespoon.

🌊 **BIG SPLASH!** Water sports are a favorite recreational activity, especially in hot places such as Albuquerque, New Mexico, U.S.A., where these swimmers cool down in a giant wave pool.

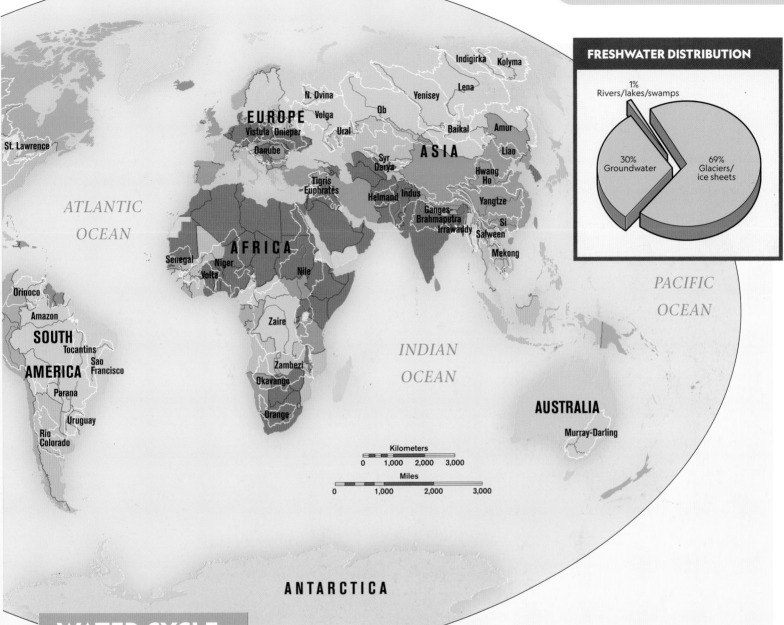

St. Lawrence

EUROPE
Vistula Dnieper
Danube
N. Dvina Volga
Ural
Ob
Yenisey
Indigirka Kolyma
Lena
Baikal
Amur
Liao
ASIA
Syr Darya
Tigris Euphrates
Helmand
Indus
Hwang Ho
Ganges– Brahmaputra
Irrawaddy
Yangtze
Si
Salween
Mekong

ATLANTIC OCEAN

AFRICA
Senegal
Niger
Volta
Nile
Zaire
Zambezi
Okavango
Orange

Orinoco
Amazon
SOUTH AMERICA
Tocantins
Sao Francisco
Parana
Uruguay
Rio Colorado

INDIAN OCEAN

PACIFIC OCEAN

AUSTRALIA
Murray-Darling

ANTARCTICA

Kilometers
0   1,000   2,000   3,000

Miles
0   1,000   2,000   3,000

FRESHWATER DISTRIBUTION

1%
Rivers/lakes/swamps

30%
Groundwater

69%
Glaciers/ ice sheets

WATER CYCLE

The amount of water on Earth has remained more or less constant over the past two billion years— only its form changes. As the sun warms Earth's surface, liquid water is changed to water vapor in a process called evaporation. Plants lose water from their leaves in a process called transpiration. As water vapor rises into the air, it cools and changes again, becoming clouds in a process called condensation. Droplets fall from clouds as precipitation, which travels as groundwater or runoff back to the lakes, rivers, and oceans, where the cycle starts again.

Water vapor becomes clouds

Precipitation falls and runs off into the ground

Lake

Water evaporates

River

Ocean

Groundwater

World Food

Earth produces enough food for all its inhabitants, but not everyone gets enough to eat. Since the 1960s, people in wealthier countries have increased their caloric intake. But many people in poorer countries do not have the same access to food. It's partly a matter of distribution. Agricultural regions (map, right) are unevenly spread around the world, and it is sometimes difficult to move food supplies from areas of surplus to areas of great need. Eastern Africa, in particular, has areas where hunger and malnourishment rob people of healthy, productive lives.

In recent decades, food production has increased, especially production of meats and cereals and the harvesting of fish. As the wealth of a country increases, more people have access to meats, fish, and produce from other regions. Increased production and transportation, along with intensive use of fertilizers and irrigation, create possible threats to the environment.

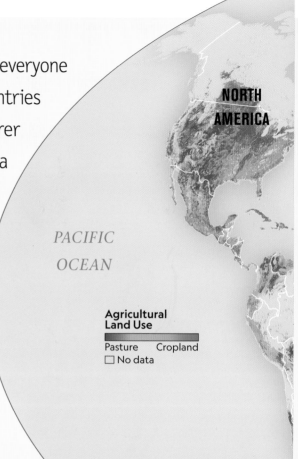

NORTH AMERICA

PACIFIC OCEAN

Agricultural Land Use
Pasture — Cropland
☐ No data

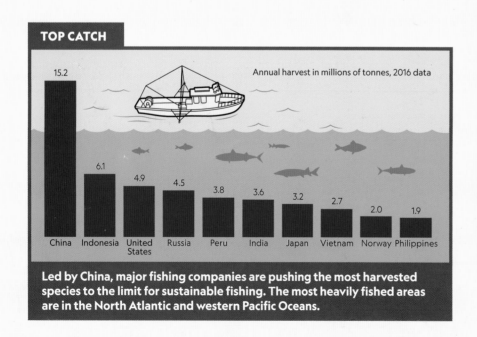

TOP CATCH

Annual harvest in millions of tonnes, 2016 data

15.2 China
6.1 Indonesia
4.9 United States
4.5 Russia
3.8 Peru
3.6 India
3.2 Japan
2.7 Vietnam
2.0 Norway
1.9 Philippines

Led by China, major fishing companies are pushing the most harvested species to the limit for sustainable fishing. The most heavily fished areas are in the North Atlantic and western Pacific Oceans.

⬤ **HEADED TO MARKET.** A woman inspects a batch of bananas at a banana production facility in Basse-Pointe, Martinique.

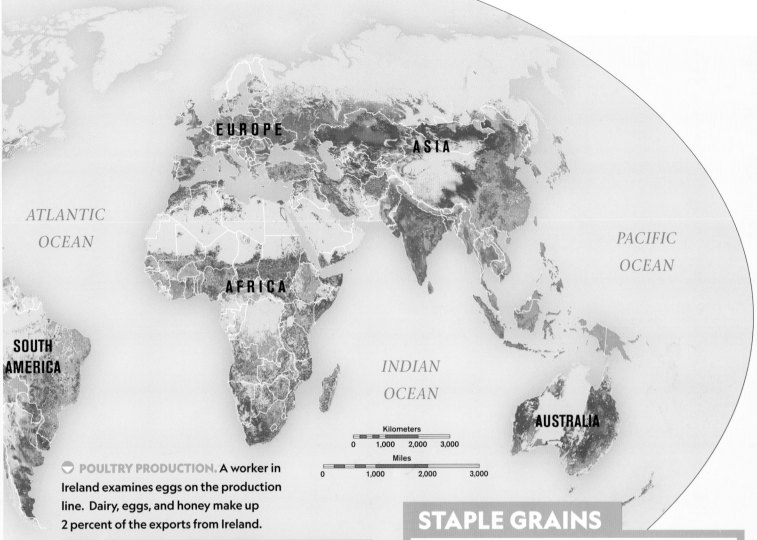

EUROPE

ASIA

ATLANTIC
OCEAN

PACIFIC
OCEAN

AFRICA

SOUTH
AMERICA

INDIAN
OCEAN

AUSTRALIA

Kilometers
0   1,000   2,000   3,000

Miles
0   1,000   2,000   3,000

POULTRY PRODUCTION. A worker in Ireland examines eggs on the production line. Dairy, eggs, and honey make up 2 percent of the exports from Ireland.

CASTING NETS. Fishermen in Orissa, India, cast their nets on the Birupa River. Fish is an important source of protein in their diets. Any surplus catch can be sold in the local market.

STAPLE GRAINS

CORN. A staple in prehistoric Central and South America, corn (or maize) is native to this region. When explorers first arrived in the New World, corn was already a hardy crop in much of North and South America.

WHEAT. One of the two oldest grains (barley is the other), wheat was important in ancient Mediterranean civilizations. Today, it is the most widely cultivated grain. Wheat grows best in temperate climates.

RICE. Originating in Asia many millennia ago, rice is the staple grain for about half the world's people. It is a labor-intensive crop that grows primarily in paddies (flooded fields) and thrives in the hot, humid tropics.

World Energy

Almost everything people do requires energy. But energy comes in different forms. Traditional energy sources, such as burning wood and dried animal dung, are still used by many people in lower-income countries. Industrialized countries and urban centers around the world rely on coal, oil, and natural gas—called fossil fuels because they formed long ago from ancient deposits of decayed plant and animal material. As the map shows, these deposits are unevenly distributed on Earth, and many countries frequently cannot afford them.

Carbon dioxide from the burning of fossil fuels along with other emissions contributes to climate change. Concerned scientists are looking at new ways to harness sources of renewable energy, such as water, wind, sun, and biofuels (wood, plant materials, and garbage).

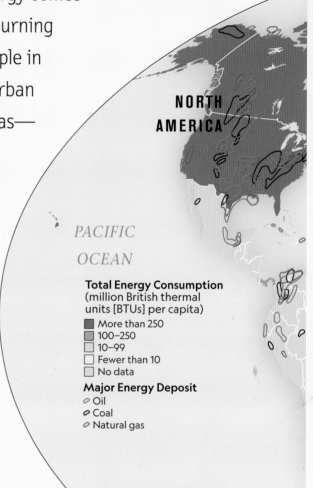

NORTH AMERICA

PACIFIC OCEAN

Total Energy Consumption
(million British thermal units [BTUs] per capita)
- More than 250
- 100–250
- 10–99
- Fewer than 10
- No data

Major Energy Deposit
- Oil
- Coal
- Natural gas

OIL, GAS, AND COAL

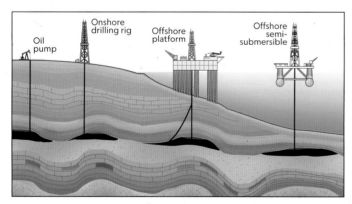

DRILLING FOR OIL AND GAS. The type of equipment used depends on whether the oil or natural gas is in the ground or under the ocean. This illustration shows some of the different kinds of onshore and offshore drilling equipment.

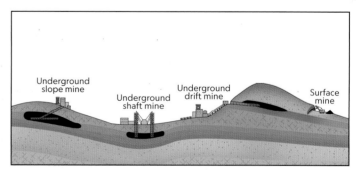

COAL MINING. The mining of coal made possible the industrial revolution, which began in the mid-1700s in England, and coal still remains a major energy source. Work that was once done by people using picks and shovels now relies heavily on mechanized equipment. This diagram shows some of the various kinds of mines currently in use.

POLITICAL WORLD

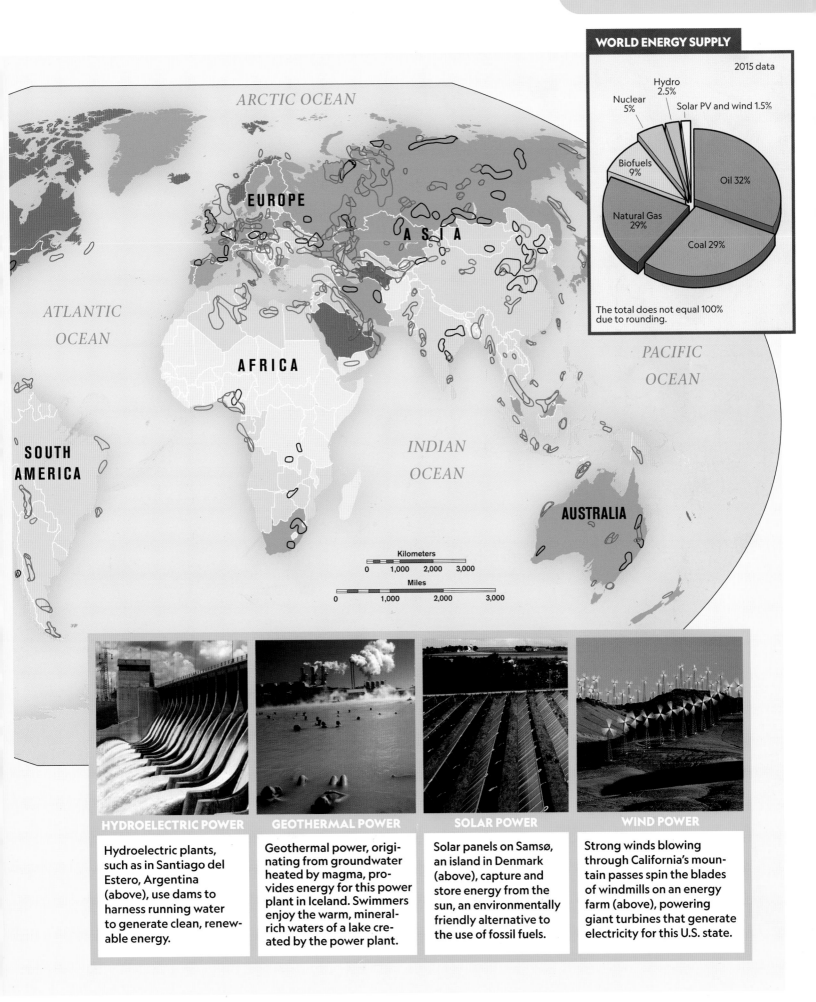

ARCTIC OCEAN

EUROPE

ASIA

ATLANTIC
OCEAN

AFRICA

PACIFIC
OCEAN

INDIAN
OCEAN

SOUTH
AMERICA

AUSTRALIA

Kilometers
0   1,000   2,000   3,000

Miles
0   1,000   2,000   3,000

WORLD ENERGY SUPPLY

2015 data

Hydro
2.5%

Nuclear
5%

Solar PV and wind 1.5%

Biofuels
9%

Oil 32%

Natural Gas
29%

Coal 29%

The total does not equal 100%
due to rounding.

HYDROELECTRIC POWER

Hydroelectric plants, such as in Santiago del Estero, Argentina (above), use dams to harness running water to generate clean, renewable energy.

GEOTHERMAL POWER

Geothermal power, originating from groundwater heated by magma, provides energy for this power plant in Iceland. Swimmers enjoy the warm, mineral-rich waters of a lake created by the power plant.

SOLAR POWER

Solar panels on Samsø, an island in Denmark (above), capture and store energy from the sun, an environmentally friendly alternative to the use of fossil fuels.

WIND POWER

Strong winds blowing through California's mountain passes spin the blades of windmills on an energy farm (above), powering giant turbines that generate electricity for this U.S. state.

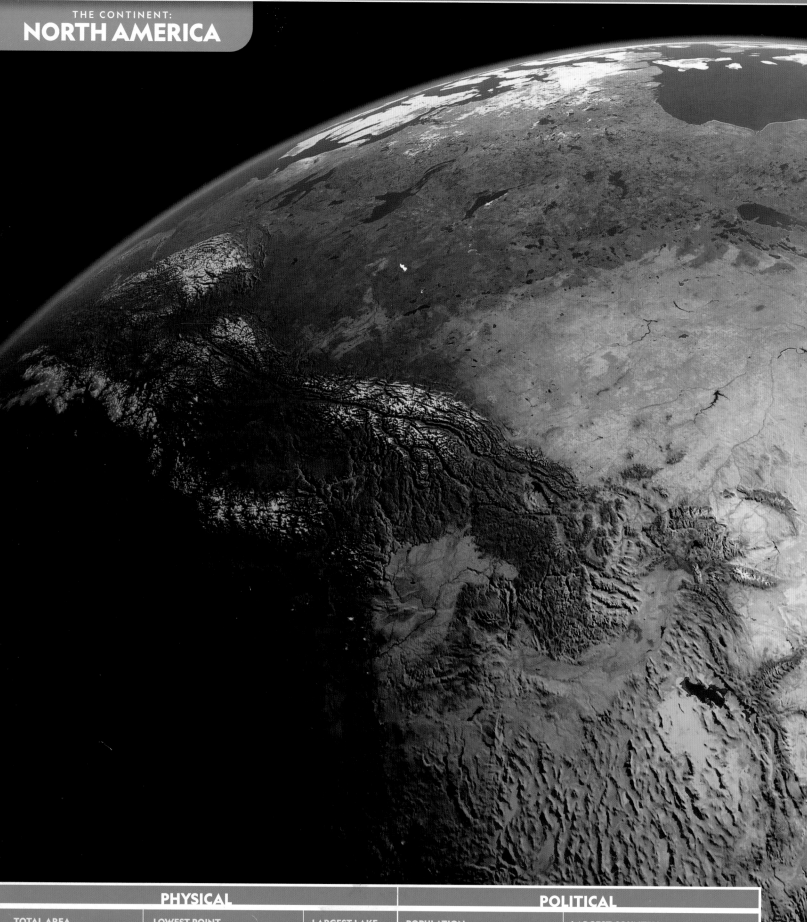

PHYSICAL

TOTAL AREA
9,449,000 sq mi
(24,474,000 sq km)

HIGHEST POINT
Denali (Mount McKinley),
Alaska, U.S.A.
20,310 ft (6,190 m)

LOWEST POINT
Death Valley, California, U.S.A.
-282 ft (-86 m)

LONGEST RIVER
Mississippi-Missouri,
United States
3,710 mi (5,971 km)

LARGEST LAKE
Lake Superior,
U.S.-Canada
31,700 sq mi
(82,100 sq km)

POLITICAL

POPULATION
592,072,000

LARGEST METROPOLITAN AREA
Mexico City, Mexico
Pop. 21,782,000

LARGEST COUNTRY
Canada
3,855,101 sq mi (9,984,670 sq km)

MOST DENSELY POPULATED COUNTRY
Barbados
1,765 people per sq mi
(681 per sq km)

NORTH AMERICA

North America

See inset map on page 66 for the Aleutian Islands and continuation of the Bering Sea.

ASIA

Chukchi Sea

ARCTIC OCEAN

Wandel Sea

Greenland Sea

Jan Mayen

Oodaaq Island
Peary Land
Lincoln Sea

Faroe Islands

Point Barrow

QUEEN ELIZABETH IS.

Knud Rasmussen Land

St. Lawrence Island
Bering Str.

Seward Peninsula
North Slope

Borden Island
Axel Heiberg I.
Ellesmere I.

ICELAND

ARCTIC CIRCLE

Nunivak Island

ALASKA
Brooks Range

Mackenzie King I.
Prince Patrick I.
SVERDRUP ISLANDS
PARRY ISLANDS

GREENLAND

Gunnbjorn +
12,119 feet
3,694 meters

Bristol Bay

Highest point in North America
Denali (Mt. McKinley)
20,310 ft
6,190 m

Beaufort Sea

Banks Island
Melville Island

Devon I.
Somerset I.

Hayes Peninsula

Baffin Bay

Davis Strait

Aleutian Range
Kenai Peninsula

Yukon
Alaska Range

Prince of Wales I.

Boothia Pen.

Qeqertarsuaq

Kodiak I.

Gulf of Alaska

Mt. Logan
19,551 ft
5,959 m

Yukon Plateau

Victoria Island

King William I.

Baffin Island

Prince Charles I.

Cape Farewell

Glacier Bay

Mackenzie Mts.

Great Bear L.

Melville Peninsula

Foxe Basin

Labrador Sea

Alexander Archipelago

Great Slave Lake

Southampton Island

Hudson Strait

Haida Gwaii

Peace

Slave

Ungava Peninsula

Ungava Bay

Vancouver Island

Fraser Plateau

Athabasca

Columbia Mts.

Churchill

Saskatchewan

Nelson

C A N A D A

Hudson Bay

Belcher Islands

James Bay

L A B R A D O R

Laurentide Scarp

Island of Newfoundland

Olympic Peninsula

Columbia

Lake Athabasca

Lake Winnipeg

G R E A T

S H I E L D

Anticosti Island

Avalon Peninsula

Cape Mendocino

Columbia

Missouri

Lake Superior

C A N A D I A N

Gulf of St. Lawrence

Cape Breton Island
Prince Edward Island

Coast Ranges

Cascade Range

Columbia Plateau

Snake

Great Salt Lake

Lake Michigan

Lake Huron

L. Ontario

St. Lawrence

Nova Scotia

Bay of Fundy

Gulf of Maine
Cape Cod

Sierra Nevada

Great Basin

Mt. Whitney
14,494 feet
4,418 meters

Colorado Plateau

Platte

Missouri

CENTRAL LOWLAND

L. Erie

MOUNTAINS

Long Island

ATLANTIC OCEAN

Death Valley
-282 ft -86 m
Lowest point in North America

R O C K Y   M O U N T A I N S

Grand Canyon

Colorado

U N I T E D   S T A T E S

P L A I N S

High Plains

Arkansas

Ozark Plateau

Ohio

APPALACHIAN

Chesapeake Bay
Cape Hatteras

Bermuda Islands

Channel Islands

Red

Mississippi

Guadalupe I.

PACIFIC

Sonoran Desert

Baja California

Gulf of California

Rio Grande

C O A S T A L   P L A I N

Florida

Grand Bahama Island

THE BAHAMAS

TROPIC OF CANCER

Eugenia Point

M E X I C O

Sierra Madre Occidental

Sierra Madre Oriental

Gulf of Mexico

Florida Keys
Straits of Florida

CUBA

W E S T

Virgin Islands

ST. KITTS & NEVIS

OCEAN

False Cape

Cayman Islands

Hispaniola

HAITI

DOMINICAN REPUBLIC

Puerto Rico

Guadeloupe

ANTIGUA & BARBUDA

DOMINICA

Martinique

I N D I E S

Revillagigedo Islands

Pico de Orizaba
18,855 ft
5,747 m

Yucatan Peninsula

Cozumel Island

G R E A T E R

JAMAICA

A N T I L L E S

BARBADOS

ST. LUCIA

Lesser Antilles

ST. VINCENT & THE GRENADINES

GRENADA

TRINIDAD & TOBAGO

Trinidad

BELIZE

C a r i b b e a n

S e a

Map Key
— Country boundary

Clipperton

GUATEMALA

HONDURAS

Sierra Madre del Sur

Gulf of Tehuantepec

Isthmus of Tehuantepec

Sierra Madre

EL SALVADOR

NICARAGUA

Lake Nicaragua

CENTRAL

Mosquito Coast

0   600 miles
0   600 kilometers

Azimuthal Equidistant Projection

AMERICA

COSTA RICA

Isthmus of Panama

PANAMA

Coiba I.

Gulf of Panama

SOUTH AMERICA

Cocos Island

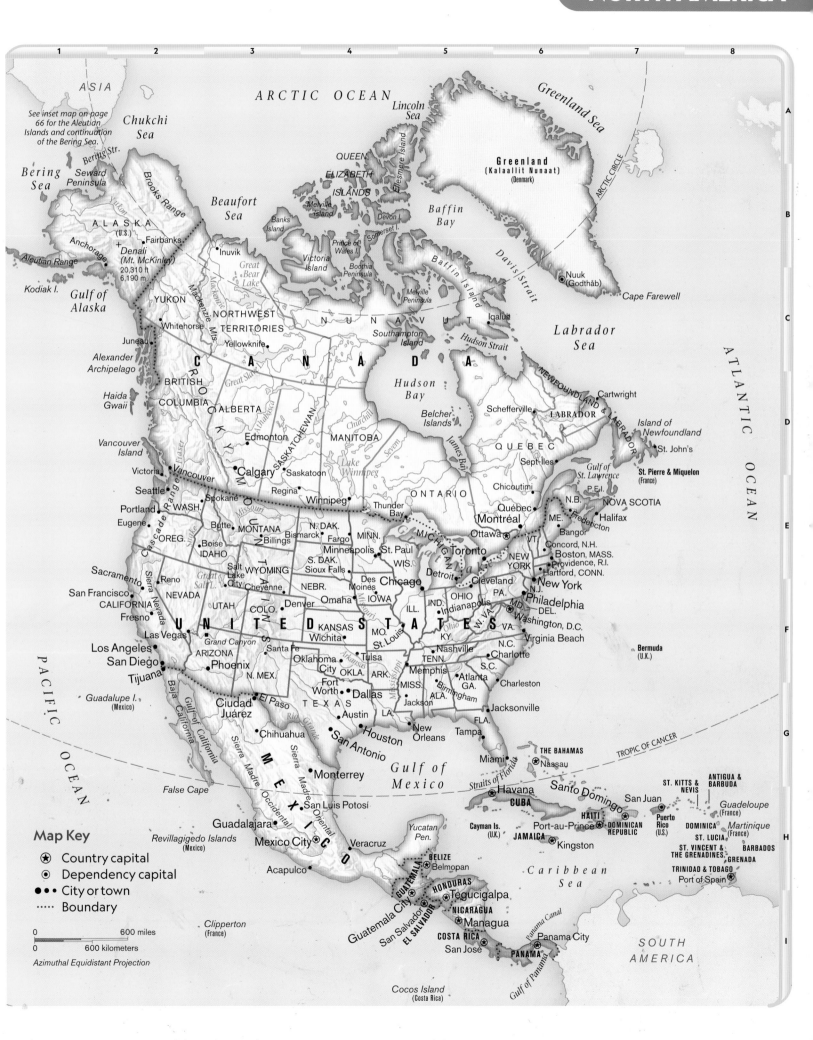

ASIA

See inset map on page 66 for the Aleutian Islands and continuation of the Bering Sea.

Chukchi Sea

ARCTIC OCEAN

Lincoln Sea

Greenland Sea

ARCTIC CIRCLE

Bering Str.

Bering Sea

Seward Peninsula

Brooks Range

Beaufort Sea

QUEEN
ELIZABETH
ISLANDS

Ellesmere Island

Greenland
(Kalaallit Nunaat)
(Denmark)

ALASKA
(U.S.)

Anchorage

Denali
(Mt. McKinley)
20,310 ft
6,190 m

Fairbanks

Inuvik

Melville
Island

Banks
Island

Devon I.

Baffin
Bay

Aleutian Range

Kodiak I.

Gulf of
Alaska

YUKON

Whitehorse

Juneau

Great
Bear
Lake

Prince of
Wales I.

Somerset I.

Victoria
Island

Boothia
Peninsula

NUNAVUT

Melville
Peninsula

Baffin Island

Davis Strait

Nuuk
(Godthåb)

Cape Farewell

NORTHWEST
TERRITORIES

Yellowknife

Southampton
Island

Iqaluit

Labrador
Sea

Alexander
Archipelago

BRITISH
COLUMBIA

CANADA

ROCKY

Great Slave
Lake

Hudson Strait

Haida
Gwaii

ALBERTA

Great Slave
Lake

Hudson
Bay

Cartwright

Schefferville

NEWFOUNDLAND & LABRADOR

LABRADOR

Island of
Newfoundland

Vancouver
Island

Victoria

Vancouver

Seattle

Calgary

Edmonton

SASKATCHEWAN

Saskatoon

MANITOBA

Churchill

Lake
Winnipeg

Belcher
Islands

James Bay

Seven

QUEBEC

Sept-Îles

Chicoutimi

Gulf of
St. Lawrence

P.E.I.

St. John's

St. Pierre & Miquelon
(France)

Portland

Spokane

WASH.

Regina

Winnipeg

Thunder
Bay

ONTARIO

Québec

N.B.

NOVA SCOTIA

Halifax

Eugene

OREG.

Butte

MONTANA

Billings

Bismarck

N. DAK.

Fargo

MINN.

St. Paul

Montréal

Ottawa

MICHIGAN

Toronto

ME.

Fredericton

Bangor

Concord, N.H.

Boston, MASS.

Boise

IDAHO

WYOMING

S. DAK.

Sioux Falls

Minneapolis

WIS.

Detroit

Cleveland

NEW
YORK

VT.

Providence, R.I.

Hartford, CONN.

Sacramento

Reno

Salt
Lake
City

Cheyenne

NEBR.

Des
Moines

IOWA

Chicago

IND.

OHIO

PA.

New York

N.J.

Philadelphia

San Francisco

CALIFORNIA

Fresno

NEVADA

UTAH

COLO.

Denver

Omaha

ILL.

Indianapolis

W. VA.

MD.

Washington, D.C.

DEL.

Las Vegas

Grand Canyon

KANSAS

St. Louis

MO.

KY.

VA.

Virginia Beach

Bermuda
(U.K.)

Los Angeles

San Diego

Tijuana

ARIZONA

Phoenix

N. MEX.

Santa Fe

Wichita

Oklahoma
City

OKLA.

Tulsa

ARK.

Memphis

TENN.

Nashville

N.C.

Charlotte

S.C.

Charleston

Guadalupe I.
(Mexico)

Baja California

Gulf of California

El Paso

Ciudad
Juárez

TEXAS

Fort
Worth

Dallas

Austin

MISS.

Jackson

LA.

ALA.

Birmingham

Atlanta
GA.

Jacksonville

Chihuahua

Rio Grande

San Antonio

Houston

New
Orleans

FLA.

Tampa

UNITED STATES

Sierra Madre

Monterrey

Gulf of
Mexico

Miami

THE BAHAMAS

Nassau

TROPIC OF CANCER

False Cape

San Luis Potosí

Straits of Florida

Havana

Santo Domingo

San Juan

ST. KITTS &
NEVIS

ANTIGUA &
BARBUDA

Guadalajara

MEXICO

CUBA

Port-au-Prince

Cayman Is.
(U.K.)

JAMAICA

HAITI

DOMINICAN
REPUBLIC

Puerto
Rico
(U.S.)

DOMINICA
(France)

Guadeloupe
(France)

Martinique
(France)

ST. LUCIA

Revillagigedo Islands
(Mexico)

Mexico City

Veracruz

Yucatan
Pen.

Kingston

Caribbean
Sea

BARBADOS

ST. VINCENT &
THE GRENADINES

GRENADA

Acapulco

BELIZE

Belmopan

TRINIDAD & TOBAGO

Port of Spain

GUATEMALA

HONDURAS

Tegucigalpa

Clipperton
(France)

Guatemala
City

San Salvador

EL SALVADOR

NICARAGUA

Managua

COSTA RICA

San Jose

PANAMA

Panama Canal

Panama City

Gulf of Panama

SOUTH
AMERICA

Cocos Island
(Costa Rica)

PACIFIC
OCEAN

ATLANTIC
OCEAN

Map Key

⊛ Country capital
⊙ Dependency capital
••• City or town
····· Boundary

0   600 miles
0   600 kilometers

Azimuthal Equidistant Projection

North America

LAND OF CONTRASTS

QUINCEAÑERA IN CUBA. Upon celebrating her 15th birthday, this young lady enjoys her quinceañera in style along the Malecón (roadway) in Havana, Cuba.

From the windswept tundra of Alaska, U.S.A., to the rainforest of Panama, the third largest continent stretches 5,500 miles (8,850 km), spanning natural environments that are home to wildlife from polar bears to jaguars. The continent supports 23 countries and 592 million people who live primarily near the coasts and inland water sources. Culturally, the region reflects a mix of people who can trace their ancestry to indigenous people, West African countries, European countries, and elsewhere. Economically, the region's resources have enhanced the growth of North America's countries, as well as provided job opportunities for its people.

DRESSED TO CELEBRATE. This boy in Mexico's southern state of Chiapas wears traditional clothing, including a charro-style tie with the colors of the Mexican flag and a sombrero used to shade his face from the sun.

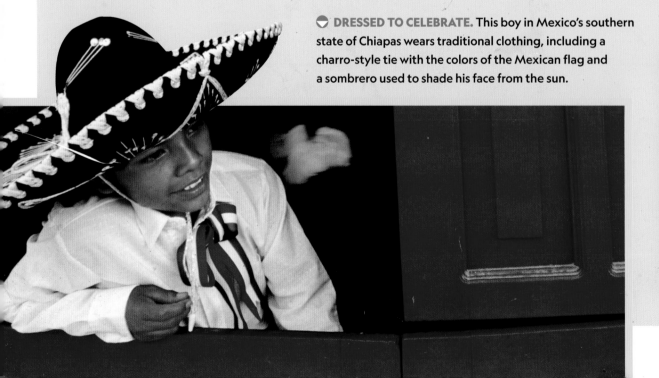

◐ **HOLD TIGHT.** These daring rafters run the roaring rapids of the Kicking Horse River in British Columbia, Canada's westernmost province. Rivers tumbling down the steep slopes of the Rocky Mountains provide many recreational opportunities.

◐ **STREET MUSIC.**
People from around the world visit New Orleans, Louisiana, U.S.A., to hear jazz musicians fill the air with their music.

◐ **COYOTE CALL.**
A coyote sends its mournful howl into the Arizona skies. Members of the dog family, coyotes originated in the southwestern United States but are now found throughout North America—even in urban areas.

more about
North America

◓ **HIGH FLIER.** A young Kutchin boy sails off a snowbank on snowshoes in Canada's Yukon. The Kutchin, an Athabascan tribe, live in the forested lands of eastern Alaska and western Canada. The name Kutchin means "people."

◓ **DWELLINGS FROM THE PAST.** Between 1000 and 1300 C.E., native people known as ancestral Puebloans built cliff dwellings called pueblos, such as this one in Mesa Verde, Colorado, U.S.A.

◓ **MAYA TREASURE.** The Pyramid of the Magician marks the ruins of Uxmal on the Yucatan Peninsula. At least five million people of Maya descent still live in southern Mexico and Central America.

◑ **FROZEN SUMMER.** Because Greenland lies so far north, even summers there are cold. Here, local people navigate their boat among icebergs in waters off the village of Aappilattoq.

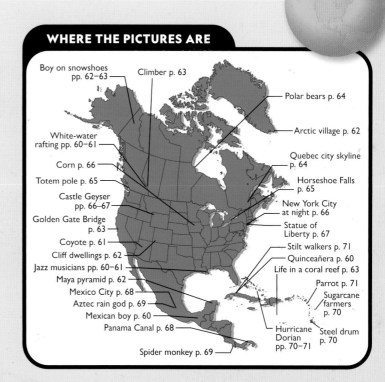

WHERE THE PICTURES ARE

Boy on snowshoes pp. 62–63
Climber p. 63
Polar bears p. 64
Arctic village p. 62
White-water rafting pp. 60–61
Quebec city skyline p. 64
Corn p. 66
Horseshoe Falls p. 65
Totem pole p. 65
New York City at night p. 66
Castle Geyser pp. 66–67
Statue of Liberty p. 67
Golden Gate Bridge p. 63
Coyote p. 61
Stilt walkers p. 71
Cliff dwellings p. 62
Quinceañera p. 60
Jazz musicians pp. 60–61
Life in a coral reef p. 63
Maya pyramid p. 62
Parrot p. 71
Mexico City p. 68
Sugarcane farmers p. 70
Aztec rain god p. 69
Mexican boy p. 60
Steel drum p. 70
Panama Canal p. 68
Hurricane Dorian pp. 70–71
Spider monkey p. 69

⬆ **SWIMMING FREE.** A variety of fish swim among colorful corals in the clear blue waters of the Caribbean Sea. Tropical waters are the habitat for many species of fish.

⬇ **DON'T LOOK DOWN.** Clinging to a rock face, an adventurous climber demonstrates great skill as she scales a steep cliff in Banff National Park in Alberta, Canada. Covering more than 2,500 square miles (6,475 sq km) in the Canadian Rockies, Banff is a major tourist attraction.

⬆ **WESTERN GATEWAY.** The Golden Gate Bridge marks the entrance to San Francisco Bay, U.S.A. Beyond the bridge, captured above, is the California port city that shares a name with the bay.

THE CONTINENT:
NORTH AMERICA

Canada

1   2

Topped only by Russia in area, Canada has just 36 million people. That's less than the population of the U.S. state of California. Ancient rocks yield abundant minerals. Lakes and rivers in Quebec are tapped for hydropower, and wheat farming and cattle ranching thrive across the western Prairie Provinces. Vast forests attract loggers, and mountain slopes provide a playground for nature lovers. Enormous deposits of oil sands are converted into barrels of oil, exposing the fragile tundra and waterways to possible contamination and habitat disruption. Most Canadians live within a hundred miles (161 km) of the U.S. border in cities, such as Asian-influenced Vancouver, ethnically diverse Toronto, national capital Ottawa, and French-speaking Montreal.

THE BASICS

STATS

Area
3,855,101 sq mi
(9,984,670 sq km)

Population
35,882,000

Predominant languages
English, French (both official)

Predominant religion
Christianity

GDP per capita
$48,300

Life expectancy
82 years

GEO WHIZ

Nunavut, Canada's newest territory, has issued license plates shaped like a polar bear for cars, motorcycles, and snowmobiles.

Canada's government is a parliamentary democracy that governs under a constitutional monarch, Britain's Queen Elizabeth II.

Canada's Bay of Fundy, located between the eastern provinces of New Brunswick and Nova Scotia, has the highest tides in the world, with a tidal range reaching up to 53 feet (16 m).

Geologists believe the impact of a meteorite may have created Quebec's Réservoir Manicouagan more than 200 million years ago.

SILENT WATCHERS. Polar bears, North America's largest land carnivores, are adapted to the extreme Arctic environment around Cape Churchill in northern Manitoba. An estimated 16,000 polar bears live in Canada.

LONGEST COASTLINE

Country	Coastline
Canada	151,023 miles (243,042 km)
Indonesia	33,998 miles (54,716 km)
Russia	23,397 miles (37,653 km)
Philippines	22,549 miles (36,289 km)
Japan	18,486 miles (29,751 km)
Australia	16,006 miles (25,760 km)
Norway	15,626 miles (25,148 km)
United States	12,380 miles (19,924 km)
New Zealand	9,404 miles (15,134 km)
China	9,010 miles (14,500 km)

Canada has the longest coastline in the world, and at more than 150,000 miles (243,000 km) it far surpasses the length of coastline of any other country.

ALASKA (U.S.)

Tuktoyaktuk

Inuvik

MACKENZIE MOUNTAINS

Yukon

YUKON

SELWYN MTS

Mt. Logan
19,551 ft.
5,959 m

St. Elias Mts.

Haines
Junction

Whitehorse

PACIFIC OCEAN

ROCKY MOUNTAINS

C

Prince
Rupert

HAIDA
GWAII

Dawson
Creek

BRITISH

Prince George

Grande
Prairie

COLUMBIA

Campbell
River

Fraser

BANFF
NAT.
PARK

Vancouver
Island

Kamloops

Columbia

Nanaimo

Kelowna

Victoria

Vancouver

FRENCH ENCLAVE. Château Frontenac sparkles in Quebec City's nighttime skyline. Settled by the French in the early 1600s, the province of Quebec has maintained close ties to its French heritage.

KNOWING WHO WE ARE. Native people of the Pacific Northwest preserve family stories and legends in massive carved poles called totems.

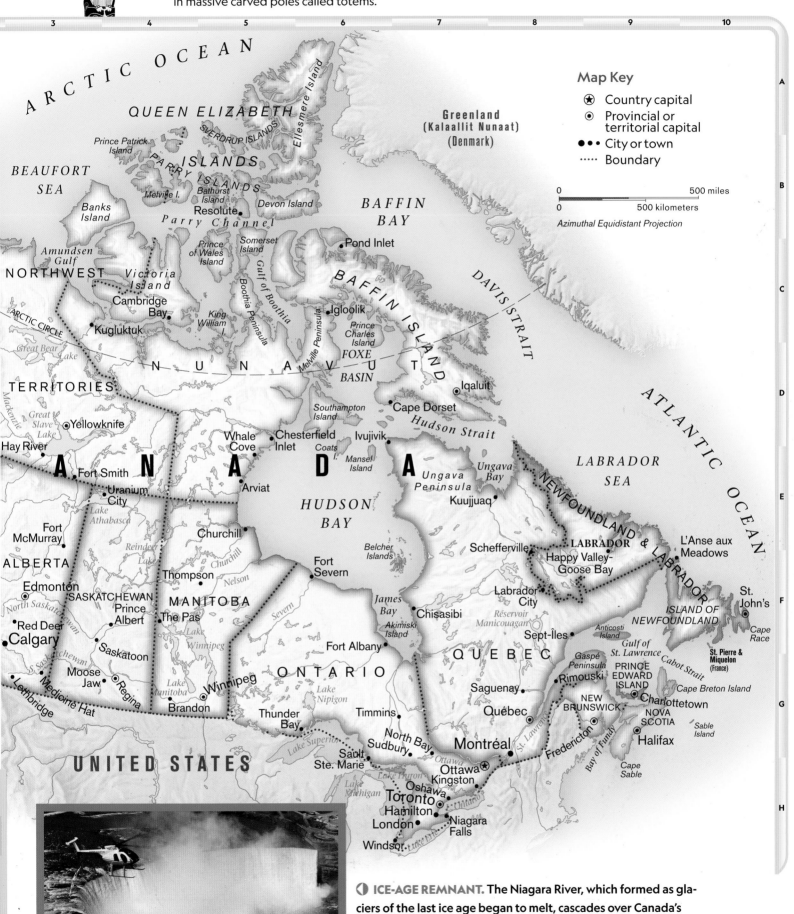

Map Key

⊛ Country capital
⊙ Provincial or territorial capital
●•• City or town
····· Boundary

0 — 500 miles
0 — 500 kilometers
Azimuthal Equidistant Projection

ARCTIC OCEAN
QUEEN ELIZABETH
Prince Patrick Island
SVERDRUP ISLANDS
Ellesmere Island
ISLANDS
BEAUFORT SEA
Melville I.
Bathurst Island
Devon Island
PARRY ISLANDS
Banks Island
Resolute
Parry Channel
Greenland (Kalaallit Nunaat) (Denmark)
BAFFIN BAY
Amundsen Gulf
Victoria Island
Prince of Wales Island
Somerset Island
Pond Inlet
NORTHWEST
Cambridge Bay
King William I.
Boothia Peninsula
Gulf of Boothia
Igloolik
BAFFIN ISLAND
DAVIS STRAIT
ARCTIC CIRCLE
Kugluktuk
Melville Peninsula
Prince Charles Island
N U N A V U T
FOXE BASIN
Iqaluit
Great Bear Lake
Cape Dorset
ATLANTIC OCEAN
TERRITORIES
Southampton Island
Hudson Strait
Mackenzie
Great Slave Lake
Yellowknife
Whale Cove
Chesterfield Inlet
Coats I.
Ivujivik
Hay River
C A N A D A
Mansel Island
LABRADOR SEA
Fort Smith
Arviat
Ungava Peninsula
Ungava Bay
Uranium City
HUDSON BAY
Kuujjuaq
NEWFOUNDLAND & LABRADOR
Lake Athabasca
Fort McMurray
Reindeer Lake
Churchill
Belcher Islands
Schefferville
LABRADOR
L'Anse aux Meadows
ALBERTA
Churchill
Fort Severn
Happy Valley-Goose Bay
Edmonton
Thompson
Nelson
Labrador City
St. John's
SASKATCHEWAN
MANITOBA
James Bay
Chisasibi
Réservoir Manicouagan
ISLAND OF NEWFOUNDLAND
Red Deer
Prince Albert
The Pas
Akimiski Island
Sept-Îles
Cape Race
Calgary
North Saskatchewan
Lake Winnipeg
Fort Albany
Anticosti Island
St. Pierre & Miquelon (France)
Saskatoon
Lake Manitoba
ONTARIO
QUEBEC
Gaspé Peninsula
Gulf of St. Lawrence
Cape Breton Island
Moose Jaw
Regina
Lake Nipigon
Saguenay
Rimouski
PRINCE EDWARD ISLAND
Medicine Hat
Winnipeg
Timmins
Québec
NEW BRUNSWICK
Charlottetown
Lethbridge
Brandon
Thunder Bay
North Bay
Sudbury
St. Lawrence
Fredericton
NOVA SCOTIA
Sable Island
UNITED STATES
Lake Superior
Sault Ste. Marie
Ottawa
Montréal
Bay of Fundy
Halifax
Lake Huron
Kingston
Oshawa
Cape Sable
Lake Michigan
Toronto
Hamilton
London
Niagara Falls
Windsor
Lake Ontario

ICE-AGE REMNANT. The Niagara River, which formed as glaciers of the last ice age began to melt, cascades over Canada's Horseshoe Falls. The falls, which stretch across the border between Canada and the United States, are a major tourist attraction.

United States

THE BASICS

STATS

Area
3,796,741 sq mi
(9,833,517 sq km)

Population
329,256,000

Predominant languages
English, Spanish

Predominant religion
Christianity

GDP per capita
$59,500

Life expectancy
80 years

GEO WHIZ

Florida is known as the lightning capital of the United States. Breezes from the Gulf of Mexico and Atlantic Ocean collide over the warm Florida peninsula to create thunderstorms and the lightning associated with them.

Hawai'i is politically part of the United States but geographically part of Polynesia, a cultural region of Oceania (pages 156–157).

Lake Michigan is the only one of the Great Lakes located entirely within the United States. Each of the other four lakes spans the U.S.-Canada border.

From "sea to shining sea" the United States is blessed with a rich bounty of natural resources. Mineral treasures abound—oil, coal, iron, and gold—and its croplands are among the most productive in the world. Americans have used this storehouse of raw materials to build an economic base unmatched by that of any other country. An array of high-tech businesses populates the Sunbelt of the South and West. By combining its natural riches and the creative ideas of its ethnically diverse population, this land of opportunity has become a leading global power.

STAPLE CROP.
In 2020, 92 million acres (37 million ha) of corn were planted in the U.S. Most of the crop is used as livestock feed.

WORLD CITY. The lights of Manhattan glitter around New York City's Chrysler Building. The city's influence as a financial and cultural center extends across the United States and around the world.

LETTING OFF STEAM. Castle Geyser in Wyoming is just one of many active geological features in Yellowstone National Park. The park is part of a region that sits on top of a major tectonic hot spot.

LADY LIBERTY. The Statue of Liberty, in New York City's harbor, has become a symbol of hope for millions of immigrants coming to the United States.

0 — 200 miles
0 — 200 kilometers
Albers Conic Equal-Area Projection

Map Key
★ Country capital
◎ State capital
● City or town
···· Boundary

C A N A D A

MEXICO

Kaua'i
Ni'ihau
H A W A I ' I
O'ahu
Moloka'i
Honolulu   Lāna'i   Maui
Kaho'olawe
Principal   Hawai'i
Hawaiian Islands
0 — 150 mi
0 — 150 km
PACIFIC OCEAN

See map on page 34 for position of Alaska and Hawai'i.

GULF OF MEXICO

ATLANTIC OCEAN

THE BAHAMAS

NATION OF IMMIGRANTS

Number of immigrants obtaining legal permanent resident status in 2018

160,132	75,159	61,848	57,286	56,761	44,776
Mexico	Cuba	China	Dominican Republic	India	Philippines

From its founding, the United States has attracted people from other lands. Today, most immigrants come from the Americas and Asia.

Mexico & Central America

THE BASICS

STATS

Largest country
Mexico
758,449 sq mi
(1,964,375 sq km)

Smallest country
El Salvador
8,124 sq mi (21,041 sq km)

Most populous country
Mexico
125,959,000

Least populous country
Belize
386,000

Predominant languages
English, Spanish, Mayan,
indigenous languages

Predominant religion
Christianity

Highest GDP per capita
Panama
$25,400

Lowest GDP per capita
Honduras
$5,600

Highest life expectancy
Costa Rica, Panama
79 years

Lowest life expectancy
Belize
69 years

GEO WHIZ

Mexico takes its name from the word Mexica, another name for the Aztec, an indigenous people who ruled the land before it fell to the Spanish in 1521.

Coral colonies growing along much of the coast of Belize form the longest barrier reef in the Western Hemisphere.

Thumb-size vampire bats live throughout Central America.

◉ **VITAL LINK.** More than 17,000 oil tankers, cruise ships, and cargo vessels pass through the Panama Canal yearly, avoiding a long trip around South America.

False Cape

Mexico and most Central American countries share a mountain range, a legacy of powerful First People empires, and an influence from Spanish colonization. Deforestation has destroyed much of the rainforest in the region. Mexico dwarfs its seven Central American neighbors in area, population, and natural resources. Its economy boasts a rich diversity of agricultural crops, highly productive oil fields, and a growing manufacturing base, as well as strong trade with the United States and Canada. Overall, Central American countries rely on agricultural products such as bananas and coffee, though tourism is increasing. Opportunities for jobs and education and concerns over violence increase migration from Central American countries to the northern countries of Mexico and the United States.

◖ **URBAN OASIS.** Throughout Mexico City, traditional and modern structures create a vibrant cityscape. After an earthquake in 1985, developers built the Santa Fe neighborhood and La Mexicana Park. To maximize land use, both areas were constructed on a former landfill area.

◖ **MYTHS AND LEGENDS.** The powerful Aztec Empire dominated much of Mexico and Central America from 1427 to 1521.

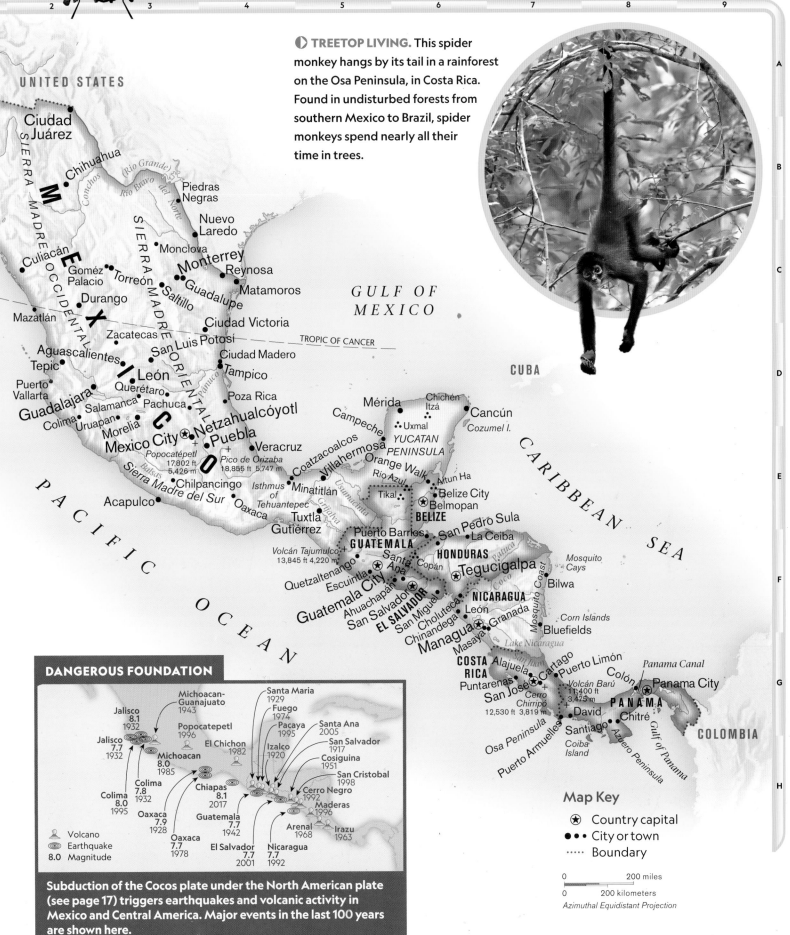

◖ **TREETOP LIVING.** This spider monkey hangs by its tail in a rainforest on the Osa Peninsula, in Costa Rica. Found in undisturbed forests from southern Mexico to Brazil, spider monkeys spend nearly all their time in trees.

UNITED STATES

Ciudad Juárez
SIERRA MADRE OCCIDENTAL
Chihuahua
(Rio Grande)
Conchos
Río Bravo del Norte
Piedras Negras
Nuevo Laredo
Monclova
Culiacán
Goméz Palacio
Torreón
Monterrey
Reynosa
Durango
Saltillo
Guadalupe
Matamoros
Mazatlán
Zacatecas
Ciudad Victoria
TROPIC OF CANCER
Aguascalientes
San Luis Potosí
Ciudad Madero
Tepic
Tampico
Puerto Vallarta
León
Querétaro
Poza Rica
Pánuco
Guadalajara
Salamanca
Pachuca
Netzahualcóyotl
Colima
Uruapan
Morelia
Mexico City
Puebla
Veracruz
Popocatépetl 17,802 ft 5,426 m
Pico de Orizaba 18,855 ft 5,747 m
Balsas
Chilpancingo
Sierra Madre del Sur
Isthmus of Tehuantepec
Minatitlán
Acapulco
Oaxaca

M E X I C O

GULF OF MEXICO

CUBA

Mérida
Chichén Itzá
Cancún
Cozumel I.
Campeche
Uxmal
YUCATAN PENINSULA
Villahermosa
Coatzacoalcos
Orange Walk
Río Azul
Altun Ha
Usumacinta
Tikal
Belize City
Tuxtla Gutiérrez
Grijalva
Belmopan
BELIZE
Volcán Tajumulco 13,845 ft 4,220 m
Puerto Barrios
San Pedro Sula
GUATEMALA
Santa Ana
Copán
La Ceiba
HONDURAS
Quetzaltenango
Escuintla
Tegucigalpa
Mosquito Cays
Guatemala City
Ahuachapán
San Salvador
San Miguel
León
NICARAGUA
Patuca
Bilwa
EL SALVADOR
Choluteca
Coco
Mosquito Coast
Chinandega
Masaya
Granada
Corn Islands
Managua
Lake Nicaragua
Bluefields
COSTA RICA
Alajuela
San Juan
Cartago
Puerto Limón
Panama Canal
Puntarenas
Colón
Panama City
San José
Volcán Barú 11,400 ft 3,475 m
Cerro Chirripó 12,530 ft 3,819 m
PANAMA
Osa Peninsula
David
Chitré
Santiago
COLOMBIA
Puerto Armuelles
Coiba Island
Azuero Peninsula
Gulf of Panama

PACIFIC OCEAN

CARIBBEAN SEA

DANGEROUS FOUNDATION

Jalisco 8.1 1932
Michoacan-Guanajuato 1943
Santa Maria 1929
Jalisco 7.7 1932
Popocatepetl 1996
Fuego 1974
El Chichon 1982
Pacaya 1995
Santa Ana 2005
Michoacan 8.0 1985
Izalco 1920
San Salvador 1917
Colima 7.8 1932
Chiapas 8.1 2017
Cosiguina 1951
Colima 8.0 1995
San Cristobal 1998
Oaxaca 7.9 1928
Guatemala 7.7 1942
Cerro Negro 1992
Oaxaca 7.7 1978
El Salvador 7.7 2001
Arenal 1968
Maderas 1996
Irazu 1963
Nicaragua 7.7 1992

⛰ Volcano
◎ Earthquake
8.0 Magnitude

Subduction of the Cocos plate under the North American plate (see page 17) triggers earthquakes and volcanic activity in Mexico and Central America. Major events in the last 100 years are shown here.

Map Key

⊛ Country capital
●●● City or town
····· Boundary

0 ——— 200 miles
0 ——— 200 kilometers
Azimuthal Equidistant Projection

West Indies & The Bahamas

THE BASICS

STATS

Largest country
Cuba
42,803 sq mi (110,860 sq km)

Smallest country
St. Kitts & Nevis
101 sq mi (261 sq km)

Most populous country
Cuba
11,116,000

Least populous country
St. Kitts & Nevis
53,000

Predominant languages
Spanish, English, French, Creole

Predominant religion
Christianity

Highest GDP per capita
Trinidad & Tobago
$31,400

Lowest GDP per capita
Haiti
$1,800

Highest life expectancy
Cuba
79 years

Lowest life expectancy
Haiti
64 years

GEO WHIZ

Pico Duarte (10,417 ft/3,175 m), on Hispaniola, is the highest peak in the Caribbean.

Parrotfish are the reason that the Caribbean has white sand beaches. Parrotfish spend their days grinding up coral with their strong teeth. Their poop comes out as sand. One fish can produce hundreds of pounds of sand a year.

RHYTHM OF THE TROPICS.
When traditional drums were banned in Trinidad in 1884, plantation workers looked for new instruments, including 55-gallon (208-L) oil drums, which were the origin of today's steel drums, or "pans."

This region of tropical islands stretches from the Bahamas, off the eastern coast of Florida, to Trinidad and Tobago, off the northern coast of South America. The Greater Antilles—Cuba, Jamaica, Hispaniola, and U.S. territory Puerto Rico—account for nearly 90 percent of the region's land area and most of its 42 million people. An archipelago of smaller islands called the Lesser Antilles, plus the Bahamas, make up the rest of this region. Lush vegetation, warm waters, and scenic beaches attract tourists from across the globe. While these visitors bring much needed income, poverty is still a concern in the region.

WHITE GOLD. Sugarcane is an important economic resource throughout the Caribbean. This woman carries freshly cut cane on her head in a field in Barbados.

FUN IN THE SUN

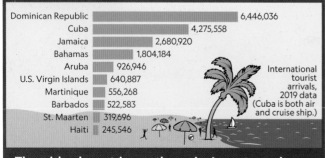

Country	International tourist arrivals
Dominican Republic	6,446,036
Cuba	4,275,558
Jamaica	2,680,920
Bahamas	1,804,184
Aruba	926,946
U.S. Virgin Islands	640,887
Martinique	556,268
Barbados	522,583
St. Maarten	319,696
Haiti	245,546

International tourist arrivals, 2019 data (Cuba is both air and cruise ship.)

These island countries are the region's most popular destinations for tourists seeking sandy beaches, blue waters, and warm breezes.

◑ **RARE BIRD.** The red-necked Amazon, or Jaco, parrot is found only on the island of Dominica, where it lives on flowers, seeds, and fruits.

Map Key
- ⍟ Country capital
- ⊙ Dependency capital
- ••• City or town
- ····· Boundary

UNITED STATES
GULF OF MEXICO
Grand Bahama Island
Abaco I.
Eleuthera I.
Cat I.
⍟ Nassau
San Salvador
Straits of Florida
Andros I.
Long I.
TROPIC OF CANCER
Acklins I.
ATLANTIC OCEAN
THE BAHAMAS
Havana ⍟ • Matanzas • Santa Clara
• Pinar del Río
C U B A
Cienfuegos
Ciego de Ávila
Holguín
Sancti Spíritus
Camagüey
Las Tunas
Manzanillo
Santiago de Cuba
Guantánamo
Great Inagua I.
Caicos Islands
Turks & Caicos Islands (U.K.)
Turks Islands
Cap-Haïtien
Puerto Plata
Hispaniola
Santo Domingo
St. Thomas
Virgin Islands (U.S. & U.K.)
Anguilla (U.K.)
St. Martin (France) SINT MAARTEN (Neth.)
St. Barthélemy (France)
Isle of Youth
GREATER
Little Cayman
Cayman Islands (U.K.)
Grand Cayman
Montego Bay
Spanish Town ⍟
Kingston
JAMAICA
HAITI
Port-au-Prince
Santiago
Pico Duarte +10,417 ft 3,175 m
DOMINICAN REPUBLIC
Barahona
ANTILLES
San Juan
Ponce
Puerto Rico (U.S.)
(NETH.) Saba.
(NETH.) St. Eustatius
Basseterre
ST. KITTS & NEVIS
(U.K.) Montserrat
Roseau
ANTIGUA AND BARBUDA
⍟ St. John's
Guadeloupe (France)
• Marie-Galante (France)
DOMINICA
Martinique (France)
Leeward Islands
Castries ⍟ ST. LUCIA
Kingstown ⍟
ST. VINCENT & THE GRENADINES
St. George's ⍟ GRENADA
⍟ Bridgetown
BARBADOS
Windward Is.
CARIBBEAN SEA
LESSER ANTILLES
ARUBA (Neth.)
Bonaire (Neth.)
CURAÇAO (Netherlands)
Tobago
TRINIDAD & TOBAGO
Port of Spain ⍟
Trinidad
COLOMBIA
VENEZUELA

0 ⊢⊣ 200 miles
0 ⊢⊣ 200 kilometers
Azimuthal Equidistant Projection

◑ **NATURAL DISASTERS.** Hurricanes, such as Dorian in 2019, are a reminder of the forces of nature affecting the West Indies and the Bahamas. Islands in the region range in elevation from 0 to 10,000 feet (3,048 m), making them vulnerable to flooding and damage.

⬤ **CELEBRATION.** Stilt walkers in brightly colored costumes tower above this street in Old Havana, Cuba, during the annual celebration of Carnival. Introduced by Catholic colonizers from Spain, this festival occurs prior to the beginning of the religious season of Lent.

THE CONTINENT:
SOUTH AMERICA

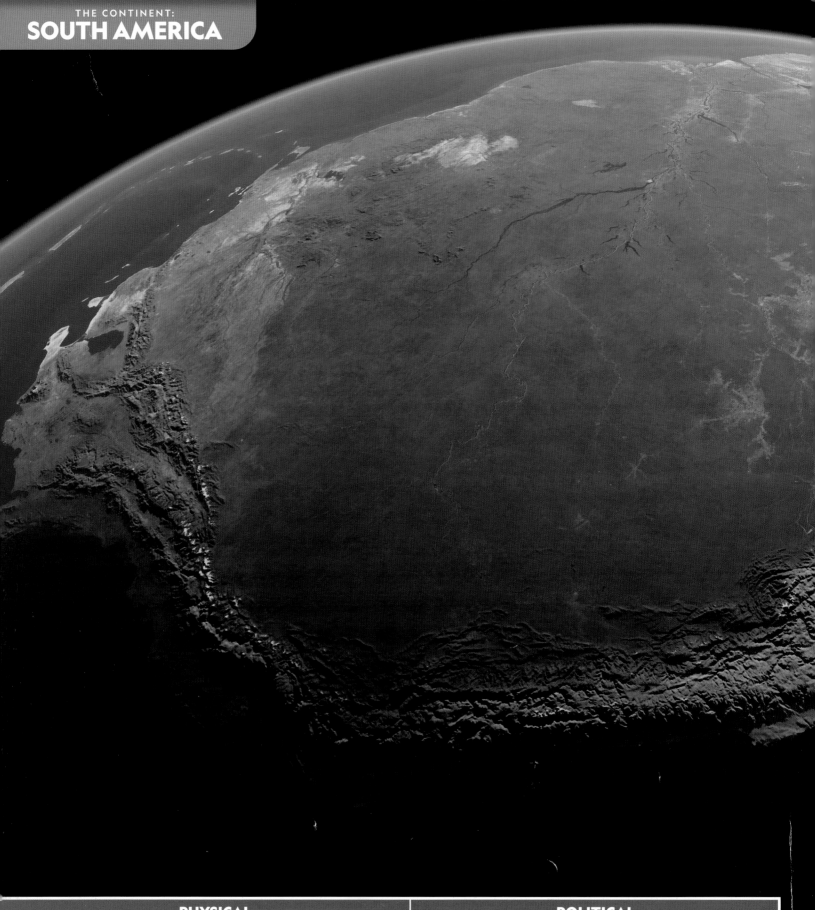

PHYSICAL			POLITICAL	
TOTAL AREA 6,880,000 sq mi (17,819,000 sq km)	**LOWEST POINT** Laguna del Carbón, Argentina -344 ft (-105 m)	**LARGEST LAKE** Lake Titicaca, Bolivia-Peru 3,200 sq mi (8,300 sq km)	**POPULATION** 430,760,000	**LARGEST COUNTRY** Brazil 3,287,611 sq mi (8,514,877 sq km)
HIGHEST POINT Cerro Aconcagua, Argentina 22,831 ft (6,959 m)	**LONGEST RIVER** Amazon 4,150 mi (6,679 km)		**LARGEST METROPOLITAN AREA** São Paulo, Brazil Pop. 22,043,000	**MOST DENSELY POPULATED COUNTRY** Ecuador 150.7 people per sq mi (58.1 per sq km)

SOUTH AMERICA

South America

NORTH
AMERICA

CARIBBEAN SEA

Lake
Maracaibo

Orinoco

L
L
A
N
O
S

VENEZUELA

Total drop
3,212 ft 979 m

Angel Falls

GUYANA
HIGHLANDS

GUYANA

SURINAME

French
Guiana
(France)

Malpelo
Island

COLOMBIA

ANDES

A   M   A   Z   O   N

Negro

Amazon

EQUATOR

Marajó
Island

Galápagos
Islands

ECUADOR

Marañón

Amazon

S
e
l
v
a
s

B   A   S   I   N

Purus

Ucayali

Madeira

Tapajós

Teles Pires

Xingu

Tocantins

São Francisco

PERU

PACIFIC

OCEAN

Lake
Titicaca

Altiplano

BOLIVIA

Pantanal

Paraguay

B   R   A   Z   I   L

BRAZILIAN

H I G H L A N D S

Atacama Desert

Salar de Uyuni

PARAGUAY

Gran Chaco

Iguazú
Falls

TROPIC OF CAPRICORN

San Félix Island

San Ambrosio Island

Paraná

Uruguay

ATLANTIC

OCEAN

Cerro
Aconcagua
22,831 ft
6,959 m

Highest point in
South America

Juan Fernández Islands

A
N
D
E
S

A   R   G   E   N   T   I   N   A

PAMPAS

URUGUAY

River Plate

Negro

Valdés Peninsula

Isla Grande
de Chiloé

P
A
T
A
G
O
N
I
A

Taitao
Peninsula

Gulf of
San Jorge

Lowest point in
South America

Wellington Island

Laguna del Carbón
-344 ft -105 m

FALKLAND ISLANDS
(ISLAS MALVINAS)

Strait of Magellan

TIERRA DEL FUEGO

Cape Horn

South Georgia

Map Key

— Country boundary

0   600 miles

0   600 kilometers

Azimuthal Equidistant Projection

CARIBBEAN SEA

NORTH
AMERICA

Santa Marta
Barranquilla
Cartagena
Maracaibo
Lake
Maracaibo
Barquisimeto
Caracas
Maracay
Ciudad Guayana
Valencia
Orinoco
Cúcuta
San Cristóbal
Bucaramanga
VENEZUELA
Georgetown
Medellín
Angel Falls
GUYANA
Paramaribo
Manizales
Bogotá
GUIANA
SURINAME
Cayenne
Ibagué
COLOMBIA
HIGHLANDS
French
Guiana
(France)
Cali
Boa Vista
Amapá
Malpelo Island
(Colombia)
Boundary claimed
by Venezuela
Boundary claimed
by Suriname
EQUATOR
Esmeraldas
Pasto
A
M
A
Z
O
N
Marajó
Island
Quito
Negro
Belém
São Luís
ECUADOR
Manaus
Santarém
Parnaíba
Galápagos
Islands
(Ecuador)
Guayaquil
Iquitos
Amazon (Solimões)
Fortaleza
Cuenca
Marañón
Madeira
Marabá
Teresina
S
Tapajós
Piura
e
l
v
a
s
Natal
Chiclayo
B
A
S
I
N
Rio
Branco
Porto Velho
Xingu
João Pessoa
Campina Grande
Trujillo
Purus
Teles Pires
Recife
Chimbote
Ucayali
B   R   A   Z   I   L
Maceió
Callao
P
E
R
U
Machu Picchu
Tocantins
Aracaju
Feira de Santana
Lima
Cusco
BRAZILIAN
Salvador
(Bahia)
Ayacucho
Titicaca
Trinidad
Ilhéus
Arequipa
La Paz
BOLIVIA
Brasília
São Francisco
HIGHLANDS
Cochabamba
Santa Cruz
Goiânia
Oruro
Sucre
Uberlândia
Ariça
Altiplano
Uberaba
Governador Valadares
Salar
de Uyuni
Campo
Grande
Belo Horizonte
Iquique
Tarija
São José do
Rio Preto
Ribeirão Preto
Paraguay
PARAGUAY
Campinas
Nova Iguaçu
Londrina
TROPIC OF CAPRICORN
Antofagasta
Salta
Campinas
São Paulo
Rio de Janeiro
San Félix Island
(Chile)
San Ambrosio Island
Gran Chaco
Asunción
(Paraguay)
Iguazú Falls
Santos
Curitiba
La Serena
Paraná
Resistencia
Corrientes
Passo
Fundo
Florianópolis
Cerro
Aconcagua
22,831 ft
6,959 m
Córdoba
Uruguaiana
Santa
Maria
Porto Alegre
Valparaíso
Mendoza
Santa Fe
URUGUAY
Santiago
A
R
G
E
N
T
I
N
A
Rosario
Buenos
Aires
Montevideo
Juan Fernández Islands
(Chile)
Talca
P A M P A
River Plate
La Plata
Concepción
Mar del Plata
Temuco
Negro
Bahía Blanca
Puerto Montt
Viedma
Isla Grande
de Chiloé
Valdés Peninsula
Taitao
Peninsula
Comodoro Rivadavia
Gulf of San Jorge
Laguna del Carbón
-344 ft -105 m
Wellington I.
PATAGONIA
Río Gallegos
Stanley
Falkland Islands (Islas Malvinas)
(United Kingdom)
Claimed by Argentina
Strait of Magellan
Punta Arenas
TIERRA DEL FUEGO
Ushuaia
Cape Horn
South Georgia
(U.K.)

PACIFIC
OCEAN

ATLANTIC
OCEAN

Map Key
⊛ Country capital
⊙ Dependency capital
••• City or town
····· Boundary
····· Claimed boundary

0 ————— 600 miles
0 ————— 600 kilometers
Azimuthal Equidistant Projection

South America

A MIX OF OLD AND NEW

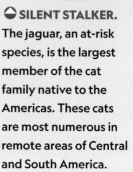

South America stretches from the warm waters of the Caribbean to the frigid ocean near Antarctica. Draining a third of the continent, the mighty Amazon carries more water than the world's next 10 biggest rivers combined. Its basin contains the planet's largest rainforest. The Andes tower along the continent's western edge from Colombia to southern Chile. The Incas, an indigenous civilization, had the largest empire in the Americas, helping influence culture in the Andes region prior to the Spanish and Portuguese colonial period. Centuries of ethnic blending have woven indigenous, European, African, and Asian heritage into South America's rich cultural fabric.

⬤ **SILENT STALKER.** The jaguar, an at-risk species, is the largest member of the cat family native to the Americas. These cats are most numerous in remote areas of Central and South America.

◑ **ROYAL CITY.** Built between 1460 and 1470, Machu Picchu reveals the Inca's skill as stone masons. Massive blocks of granite were carved so carefully that all seams fit tightly without the use of mortar.

⬤ **SOUTHERN METROPOLIS.** A 1,300-foot (396-m)-high block of granite called Sugarloaf dominates the harbor of Brazil's second largest city, Rio de Janeiro. Rio was Brazil's capital until 1960 and remains the country's most popular tourist destination.

◑ **NATURAL HERITAGE.**
Extending 1.7 miles (2.7 km) along the border between Brazil and Argentina, Iguazú Falls is clouded in mist as the water drops 296 feet (90 m) into the Iguazú River. Iguazú means "great water" in the local Guaraní language.

◑ **MOUNTAIN BUDDIES.**
An Aymara woman, with her llama, wears the fedora (hat) and shawl distinctive of her culture in the Andes of Peru.

more about
South America

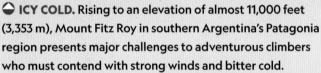

◖ **STAYING WARM.** The Falkland Islands are home to hundreds of thousands of southern rockhopper penguins. This colony makes up about a third of all rockhoppers found in the world. Seven species of penguins live in South America.

◖ **ICY COLD.** Rising to an elevation of almost 11,000 feet (3,353 m), Mount Fitz Roy in southern Argentina's Patagonia region presents major challenges to adventurous climbers who must contend with strong winds and bitter cold.

◖ **QUIET VIGIL.** A Panare Indian sits beside a rushing stream in Venezuela, ready to catch a fish with his spear. The Panare Indians are part of Venezuela's relatively isolated indigenous groups, who make up less than 3 percent of the total population.

⬤ **JUICY HARVEST.** In Santiago, Chile, grapes hang in heavy clusters ready for harvest. A leading exporter of table grapes, Chile is the major supplier of these grapes for the United States and European Union during their winter months.

WHERE THE PICTURES ARE

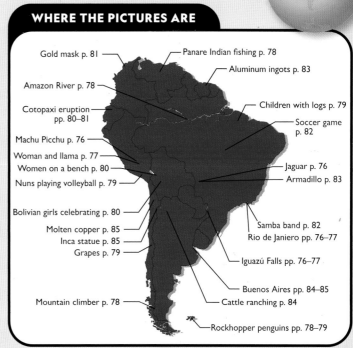

Gold mask p. 81
Panare Indian fishing p. 78
Aluminum ingots p. 83
Amazon River p. 78
Children with logs p. 79
Cotopaxi eruption pp. 80–81
Soccer game p. 82
Machu Picchu p. 76
Woman and llama p. 77
Women on a bench p. 80
Jaguar p. 76
Armadillo p. 83
Nuns playing volleyball p. 79
Bolivian girls celebrating p. 80
Molten copper p. 85
Samba band p. 82
Inca statue p. 85
Rio de Janiero pp. 76–77
Grapes p. 79
Iguazú Falls pp. 76–77
Buenos Aires pp. 84–85
Mountain climber p. 78
Cattle ranching p. 84
Rockhopper penguins pp. 78–79

⬤ **BREAK TIME.** Colonization of South America by Spain and Portugal in the 16th century brought a new religion—Roman Catholicism—to the region. Here, Catholic nuns in Arequipa, Peru, take a break from prayers to engage in a game of volleyball.

⬤ **ENVIRONMENTAL TRAGEDY.** These giants of the rainforest dwarf two children in the Amazon village of Paragominas in Brazil. Harvesting such trees provides income for villagers but poses a serious long-term threat to the environment.

◑ **THE AMAZON RIVER.** Flowing through the Amazon rainforest, the Amazon River in Brazil fills with sediment during the heavy rains. Due to the thick rainforest and lack of roads, the river is the main source of transportation in the region.

THE CONTINENT:
SOUTH AMERICA

Northwestern South America

THE BASICS

STATS

Largest country
Peru 496,224 sq mi
(1,285,216 sq km)

Smallest country
Ecuador
109,483 sq mi (283,561 sq km)

Most populous country
Colombia 48,169,000

Least populous country
Bolivia 11,306,000

Predominant languages
Spanish, indigenous languages, English

Predominant religion
Christianity

Highest GDP per capita
Colombia $14,500

Lowest GDP per capita
Bolivia $7,500

Highest life expectancy
Ecuador 77 years

Lowest life expectancy
Bolivia 69 years

GEO WHIZ

On the llanos of Venezuela, capybaras, the world's largest rodents, are hunted by anacondas. These snakes can weigh as much as 550 pounds (250 kg).

Colombia is the source of some of the world's finest emeralds, a gemstone sacred to the Inca. Mines once operated by the Inca still yield quality stones.

Marine iguanas live only on Ecuador's Galápagos Islands.

UP HIGH. La Paz, Bolivia, is located at 11,942 feet (3,639 m) above sea level with summer temperatures ranging from 40 to 60°F (4 to 15°C). Two women enjoy a sunny afternoon while they read the newspaper and eat a snack.

Like a huge letter "C," five countries crest the continent's northwest— Venezuela, Colombia, Ecuador, Peru, and Bolivia. Each has a seacoast, except for landlocked Bolivia. Dominated by the volcano-studded Andes range, the region contains huge rainforests in the upper Amazon and Orinoco River basins. Colombia and Venezuela share an extensive tropical grassland called Los Llanos. Cattle ranching in the region, along with oil and coffee production, are the main economic activities. Due to poverty and politics, the region often experiences civil unrest and demonstrations.

FOLKLORE CENTER. Founded as a mining town, Oruro, Bolivia, is a UNESCO World Heritage site. Each November, people there celebrate traditional Andean culture with ancient dances, music, and rituals.

INDIGENOUS PEOPLE

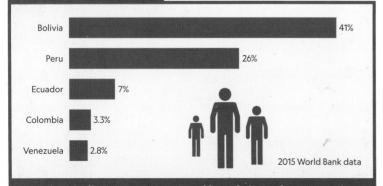

Bolivia — 41%
Peru — 26%
Ecuador — 7%
Colombia — 3.3%
Venezuela — 2.8%

2015 World Bank data

American Indians are concentrated largely in Andean countries. Almost half of Bolivia's population is made up of these indigenous people.

VOLCANIC REGIONS. Living in the Andes mountain range amid volcanoes means that residents must be aware of potential eruptions. In 2015, residents of Quito, Ecuador, could see the eruption of nearby Cotopaxi.

◖ ANCIENT ARTISANS. Early cultures of Colombia left no great stone monuments, but distinguished themselves with fine gold work, such as this mask.

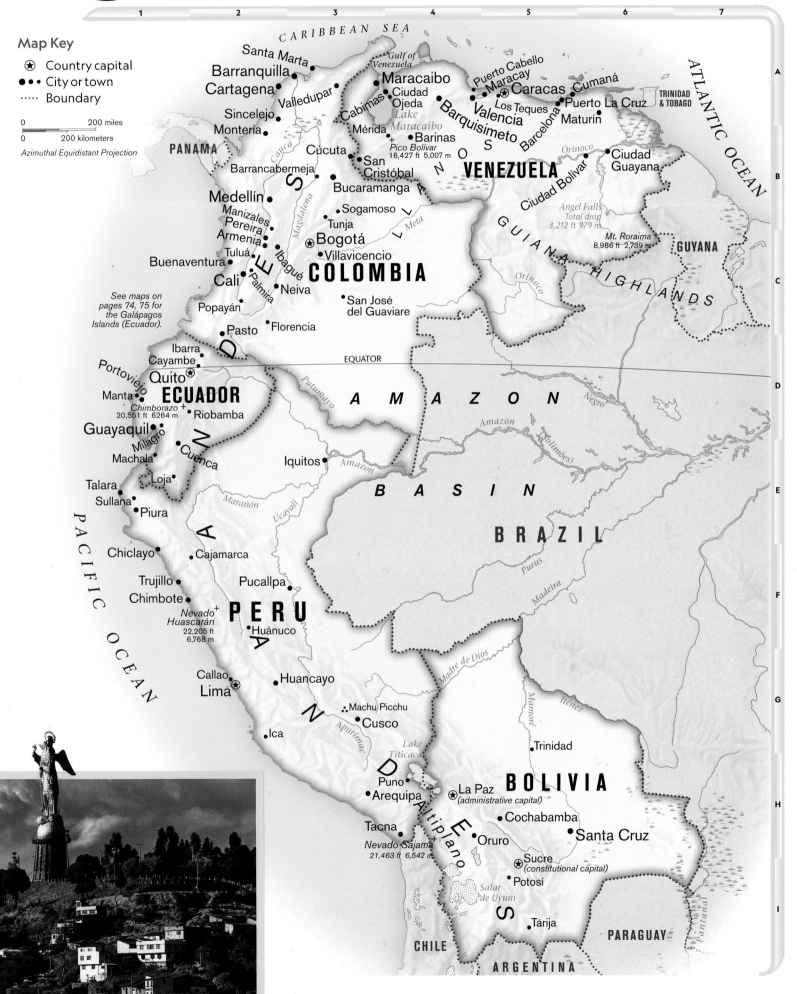

Map Key

⊛ Country capital

••• City or town

‥‥‥ Boundary

0 — 200 miles
0 — 200 kilometers

Azimuthal Equidistant Projection

CARIBBEAN SEA

Santa Marta
Barranquilla
Cartagena
Valledupar
Sincelejo
Montería

PANAMA

Gulf of Venezuela
Maracaibo
Ciudad Ojeda
Cabimas
Lake Maracaibo
Mérida
Cúcuta
San Cristóbal

Puerto Cabello
Maracay
Caracas Cumaná
Los Teques ⊛
Valencia Barcelona Puerto La Cruz
Barquisimeto Maturín
Barinas
Pico Bolívar
16,427 ft 5,007 m

VENEZUELA

TRINIDAD & TOBAGO

ATLANTIC OCEAN

Barrancabermeja

Medellín
Manizales
Pereira
Armenia
Tuluá
Ibagué
Buenaventura
Cali
Palmira
Neiva
Popayán

Bucaramanga
Sogamoso
Tunja
Bogotá ⊛
Villavicencio

COLOMBIA

San José del Guaviare

Florencia

Ciudad Bolívar
Ciudad Guayana

GUIANA HIGHLANDS

Angel Falls
Total drop
3,212 ft 979 m

Mt. Roraima
8,986 ft 2,739 m

GUYANA

Orinoco

See maps on pages 74, 75 for the Galápagos Islands (Ecuador).

Pasto
Ibarra
Cayambe
Portoviejo
Quito ⊛
Manta
Chimborazo
20,551 ft 6264 m
Riobamba
Guayaquil
Milagro
Machala
Cuenca
Talara
Loja
Sullana
Piura

ECUADOR

EQUATOR

Putumayo

AMAZON

BASIN

BRAZIL

Amazon

Negro

Iquitos
Marañón
Ucayali

Amazon

Chiclayo
Cajamarca
Trujillo
Pucallpa
Chimbote
Nevado Huascarán
22,205 ft
6,768 m

PERU

Purus

Madeira

Huánuco

PACIFIC OCEAN

Callao
Lima ⊛
Huancayo

Machu Picchu
Cusco

Madre de Dios

Trinidad

Mamoré
Iténez

Ica

Apurímac

Lake Titicaca

Puno
Arequipa

La Paz
(administrative capital) ⊛

BOLIVIA

Cochabamba
Santa Cruz
Oruro

ALTIPLANO

Tacna
Nevado Sajama
21,463 ft 6,542 m

Sucre ⊛
(constitutional capital)
Potosí

Salar de Uyuni

Tárija

ANDES

Pantanal

CHILE

PARAGUAY

ARGENTINA

THE CONTINENT:
SOUTH AMERICA

Northeastern South America

THE BASICS

STATS

Largest country
Brazil
3,287,611 sq mi (8,514,877 sq km)

Smallest country
Suriname
63,251 sq mi (163,820 sq km)

Most populous country
Brazil 208,847,000

Least populous country
Suriname 598,000

Predominant languages
Portuguese, English, Dutch, Hindi

Predominant religions
Christianity, Hinduism, Islam

Highest GDP per capita
Brazil $15,600

Lowest GDP per capita
Guyana $8,200

Highest life expectancy
Brazil 74 years

Lowest life expectancy
Guyana 68 years

GEO WHIZ

Guyana's roughly 300 species of catfish are hunted for the international aquarium trade.

Brazil's Pantanal is the world's largest freshwater wetland.

Paramaribo, Suriname's capital, is a mix of Dutch, Hindu, Chinese, East Indian, and Javanese cultures. Dutch is the only official language.

GOAL! Fans of soccer cheer on the women from Brazil and Jamaica in the 2019 FIFA Women's World Cup in Grenoble, France.

Brazil dominates the region as well as the continent in size and population. It is the world's fifth largest country in area, and it is home to about half of South America's 430 million people. São Paulo and Rio de Janeiro are among the world's largest cities, and the country's vast agricultural lands make it a top global exporter of coffee, soybeans, beef, orange juice, and sugar. The Amazon rainforest, once a dense wilderness of unmatched biodiversity, is now threatened by farmers, loggers, and miners. Lands colonized by the British, Dutch, and French make up sparsely settled Guyana and Suriname as well as French Guiana, a French overseas department. Formerly known as the Guianas, these lands are populated by people of African, South Asian, and European heritage.

VAST WATERSHED

The United States and South America are shown at the same scale.

Amazon Basin

SOUTH AMERICA

The Amazon River basin includes 2.4 million square miles (6.1 million sq km). It would cover much of the contiguous, or lower 48, U.S. states.

NATIONAL RHYTHM. Samba, often called Brazil's national music, combines the music traditions of the country's populations—Amerindian, Portuguese, and African. Here, a samba band practices on Rio de Janeiro's Ipanema Beach.

◐ **THE SIX-BANDED ARMADILLO,** found throughout the dry grassland areas of the region, lives on plants and insects. Unlike others of its species, it remains active during the day.

Map Key

✪ Country capital
••• City or town
····· Boundary
····· Claimed boundary

| 0 | | 400 miles |
| 0 | | 400 kilometers |

Azimuthal Equidistant Projection

ATLANTIC OCEAN

VENEZUELA
Georgetown
Paramaribo
GUYANA
SURINAME
Cayenne
French Guiana (France)
GUIANA HIGHLANDS
Boa Vista
COLOMBIA
Boundary claimed by Venezuela
Boundary claimed by Suriname
Macapá
Pico da Neblina 9,826 ft 2,995 m
EQUATOR
Negro
Itacoatiara
Amazon
Marajó Island
Belém
São Luís
Parnaíba
Putumayo
Amazon (Solimões)
Manaus
Altamira
Paragominas
Codó
Sobral
Fortaleza
A M A Z O N
Tefé
Coari
Parintins
Santarém
Tucuruí
Caxias
Teresina
Amazon
Madeira
Tapajós
Marabá
Imperatriz
Natal
B A S I N
Araguaína
Crato
João Pessoa
Cruzeiro do Sul
Purus
Olinda
Jaboatão
Recife
S e l v a s
Porto Velho
B R A Z I L
Petrolina
Arapiraca
Maceió
PERU
Rio Branco
Ariquemes
Gurupi
Palmas
Aracaju
Ji-Paraná
Barreiras
Feira de Santana
Alagoinhas
Madre de Dios
Alvorado
B R A Z I L I A N
Guaporé
Várzea Grande
Cuiabá
Brasília
Jequié
Salvador (Bahia)
Itabuna
Juruena
Rondonópolis
São Francisco
Vitória da Conquista
Ilhéus
Mamoré
Lake Titicaca
Goiânia
Anápolis
H I G H L A N D S
BOLIVIA
Uberlândia
Teófilo Otoni
Governador Valadares
Belo Horizonte
Linhares
São José do Rio Preto
Ribeirão Preto
Vitória
Campo Grande
São José dos Campos
Nova Iguaçu
Juiz de Fora
Vila Velha
Duque de Caxias
CHILE
Paraná
São Paulo
Niterói
TROPIC OF CAPRICORN
Santo André
Santos
Guaratinguetá
Rio de Janeiro
P A R A G U A Y
Londrina
Iguazú Falls
Paraná
Curitiba
Paranaguá
ARGENTINA
Joinville
Uruguay
Florianópolis
Caxias do Sul
Criciúma
Santa Maria
Novo Hamburgo
Canoas
Porto Alegre
Patos Lagoon
Pelotas
URUGUAY

◐ **BAUXITE TO ALUMINUM.** By exploiting rich deposits of bauxite, the ore from which aluminum is made, and inexpensive hydropower, Suriname produces aluminum ingots, such as these headed for global markets.

THE BASICS

STATS

Largest country
Argentina
1,073,518 sq mi (2,780,400 sq km)

Smallest country
Uruguay
68,037 sq mi (176,215 sq km)

Most populous country
Argentina 44,694,000

Least populous country
Uruguay 3,369,000

Predominant languages
Spanish, Guaraní, English, Italian, German, French

Predominant religion
Christianity

Highest GDP per capita
Chile $24,500

Lowest GDP per capita
Paraguay $9,800

Highest life expectancy
Chile 79 years

Lowest life expectancy
Argentina, Paraguay, Uruguay
77 years

GEO WHIZ

The Itaipú Dam, which spans the Paraná River between Paraguay and Brazil, is currently the world's second largest operating hydroelectric power plant.

Guanacos, llama-like animals that live mainly in the Patagonia region of Argentina and Chile, keep enemies at bay by spitting at them.

Southern South America

Four countries make up this region, which is sometimes called the Southern Cone because of its shape. Long north-south distances in Chile and Argentina result in varied environments. Chile's Atacama Desert in the north contrasts with much cooler, moister lands in the country's south, where there are fjords and glaciers. Almost half of Chileans live in and around the country's booming capital, Santiago. Similarly, most neighboring Argentinians live in the central Pampas region, where wheat and cattle flourish on the fertile plains. Farther south lie the arid, windswept plateaus of Patagonia. Landlocked Paraguay is small in comparison, less urbanized, and one of South America's poorest countries. Uruguay is smaller still, but it possesses a strong agricultural economy, including cattle- and sheep-raising.

◑ **COWBOYS OF THE PAMPAS.** Cattle are herded by gauchos, the Argentine term for cowboys. The country's pampas, extensive grass-covered plains, support grain and cattle production on ranches called estancias.

◑ **GATEWAY CITY.** Skyscrapers in the modern skyline rise above Buenos Aires, capital of Argentina and second largest metropolitan area in South America. Situated on the Rio de la Plata, the city was established in 1536 by Spanish explorers. Its port is one of the busiest in South America.

WORLD BEEF EXPORTS

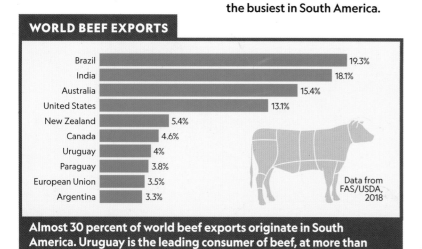

Country	Percentage
Brazil	19.3%
India	18.1%
Australia	15.4%
United States	13.1%
New Zealand	5.4%
Canada	4.6%
Uruguay	4%
Paraguay	3.8%
European Union	3.5%
Argentina	3.3%

Data from FAS/USDA, 2018

Almost 30 percent of world beef exports originate in South America. Uruguay is the leading consumer of beef, at more than 124 pounds (56 kg) per capita annually.

◗ **INCA TREASURE.** Near the frozen summit of Argentina's Cerro Llullaillaco, archaeologists uncovered well-preserved Inca mummies and 20 clothed statues, such as this one.

◗ **DESERT RICHES.** Molten copper is poured into molds at a refinery near Chuquicamata, a mine that has operated since 1910 in Chile's Atacama Desert. Chile produces 28 percent of the world's copper.

PERU

BOLIVIA

Arica

Iquique

Chuquicamata
Calama

Antofagasta

Copiapó

Catamarca

La Rioja

La Serena
Coquimbo

San
Juan

Viña del Mar
Valparaíso

Santiago

Rancagua

Curicó

Talca

Chillán

Concepción

Los Ángeles

Temuco

Valdivia

Osorno

Puerto Montt

Isla Grande
de Chiloé

PACIFIC OCEAN

Wellington
Island

Punta Arenas

Ushuaia

Cape Horn

Cerro Llullaillaco
22,057 ft
6,723 m

San Salvador
de Jujuy

Salta

San Miguel
de Tucumán

Santiago
del Estero

Córdoba

Cerro Aconcagua
22,831 ft 6,959 m

Río Cuarto

Mendoza

Godoy Cruz

San Luis

Neuquén

Colorado

Negro

ARGENTINA

PATAGONIA

PAMPAS

GRAN CHACO

Puerto
Bahía Negra

La Esmeralda

PARAGUAY

Asunción
(Paraguay)

Formosa

Resistencia

Villarrica

Corrientes

Concordia

Santa Fe

Paraná

Rosario

San Nicolás

Buenos Aires

San Justo
La Plata

Bahía
Blanca

San Matías Gulf

Valdés
Peninsula

Comodoro Rivadavia
Gulf of San Jorge

Laguna
del Carbón
-344 ft -105 m

Río Gallegos

Strait of Magellan

TIERRA DEL
FUEGO

BRAZIL

TROPIC OF CAPRICORN

Concepción

Ciudad
del Este
Itaipú Dam

Iguazú
Falls

Posadas

Paraná

Uruguay

Rivera

Patos
Lagoon

Salto

URUGUAY

River Plate

Montevideo

Mar del Plata

ATLANTIC OCEAN

Map Key

★ Country capital
◎ Dependency capital
•••• City or town
..... Boundary

0   200 miles
0   200 kilometers

Azimuthal Equidistant Projection

Falkland Islands
(Islas Malvinas)
(United Kingdom)
*Claimed by
Argentina*

◎ Stanley

Atacama Desert

ANDES

CHILE

THE CONTINENT:
EUROPE

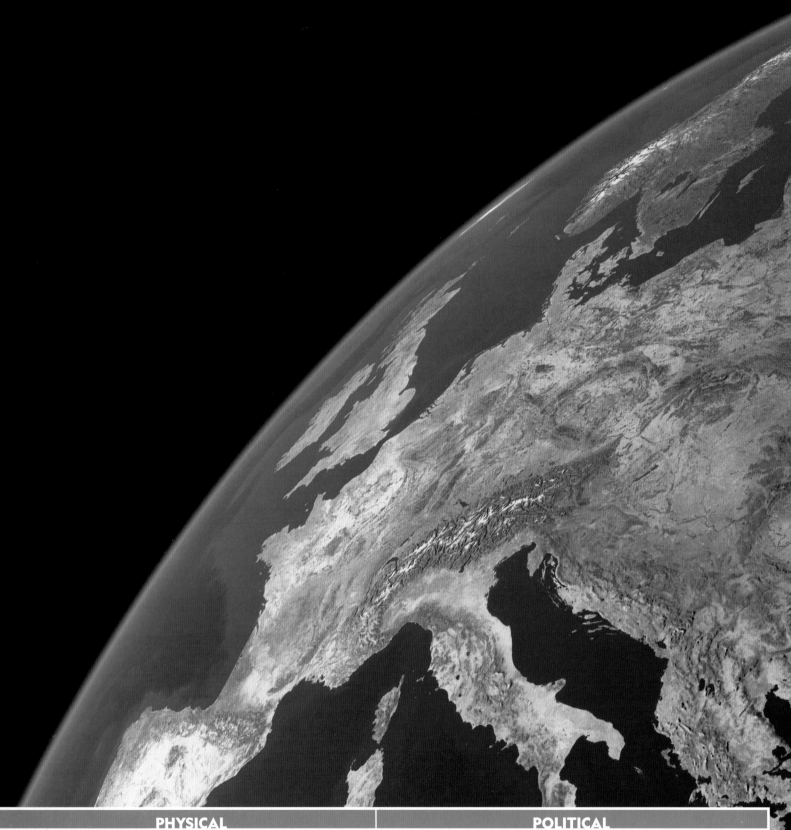

PHYSICAL			POLITICAL	
TOTAL AREA 3,841,000 sq mi (9,947,000 sq km)	**LOWEST POINT** Caspian Sea -92 ft (-28 m)	**LARGEST LAKE** **ENTIRELY IN EUROPE** Ladoga, Russia 6,800 sq mi (17,700 sq km)	**POPULATION** 747,636,000	**LARGEST COUNTRY ENTIRELY IN EUROPE** France 248,573 sq mi (643,801 sq km)
HIGHEST POINT El'brus, Russia 18,510 ft (5,642 m)	**LONGEST RIVER** Volga, Russia 2,290 mi (3,685 km)		**LARGEST METROPOLITAN AREA** Moscow, Russia Pop. 12,410,000	**MOST DENSELY POPULATED COUNTRY** Monaco 39,000 people per sq mi (19,500 per sq km)

EUROPE

Europe

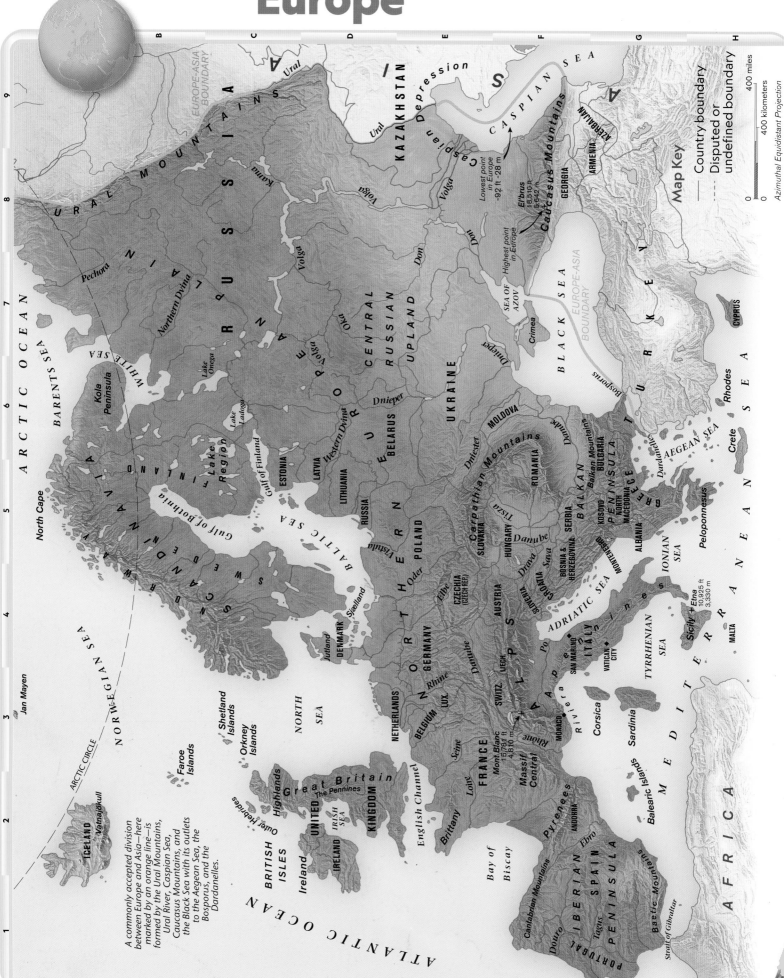

A commonly accepted division between Europe and Asia—here marked by an orange line—is formed by the Ural Mountains, Ural River, Caspian Sea, Caucasus Mountains, and the Black Sea with its outlets to the Aegean Sea, the Bosporus, and the Dardanelles.

Map Key

— Country boundary

---- Disputed or undefined boundary

Azimuthal Equidistant Projection

400 miles

400 kilometers

ARCTIC OCEAN

URAL MOUNTAINS

EUROPE-ASIA BOUNDARY

KAZAKHSTAN

Ural

Ural

Volga

Caspian Depression

Lowest point in Europe -92 ft -28 m

CASPIAN SEA

S I A

Caucasus Mountains

Elbrus 18,510 ft 5,642 m

Highest point in Europe

GEORGIA

AZERBAIJAN

ARMENIA

A S I A

TURKEY

CYPRUS

Pechora

Northern Dvina

Kama

Volga

Don

Don

Volga

SEA OF AZOV

Crimea

BLACK SEA

EUROPE-ASIA BOUNDARY

Bosporus

R U S S I A

BARENTS SEA

WHITE SEA

Kola Peninsula

Lake Onega

Oka

Volga

C E N T R A L   R U S S I A N   U P L A N D

Dnieper

UKRAINE

Dnieper

Dniester

MOLDOVA

Danube

Carpathian Mountains

ROMANIA

Balkan Mountains

BULGARIA

AEGEAN SEA

Crete

Rhodes

North Cape

Lake Ladoga

Lake Region

Gulf of Finland

ESTONIA

LATVIA

Western Dvina

LITHUANIA

RUSSIA

BELARUS

N O R T H E R N

Vistula

Oder

POLAND

Tisza

SLOVAKIA

HUNGARY

Danube

Drava

Sava

SERBIA

KOSOVO

NORTH MACEDONIA

MONTENEGRO

ALBANIA

B A L K A N   P E N I N S U L A

G R E E C E

Peloponnesus

IONIAN SEA

Dardanelles

ARCTIC OCEAN

NORWEGIAN SEA

ARCTIC CIRCLE

North Cape

F I N L A N D

S C A N D I N A V I A

S W E D E N

N O R W A Y

Gulf of Bothnia

BALTIC SEA

Elbe

CZECHIA (CZECH REP.)

AUSTRIA

SLOVENIA

CROATIA

BOSNIA & HERZEGOVINA

ADRIATIC SEA

Jan Mayen

ICELAND

Vatnajökull

Shetland Islands

Orkney Islands

Faroe Islands

Outer Hebrides

Highlands

Great Britain

The Pennines

UNITED KINGDOM

BRITISH ISLES

Ireland

IRELAND

IRISH SEA

Sjælland

Jutland

DENMARK

NETHERLANDS

GERMANY

Rhine

BELGIUM

LUX.

Danube

SWITZ.

LIECH.

A L P S

Mont Blanc 15,781 ft 4,810 m

Po

Apennines

SAN MARINO

ITALY

VATICAN CITY

MONACO

Riviera

Corsica

Sardinia

TYRRHENIAN SEA

Sicily

Etna 10,925 ft 3,330 m

MALTA

M E D I T E R R A N E A N   S E A

ATLANTIC OCEAN

NORTH SEA

English Channel

Brittany

Seine

Loire

FRANCE

Massif Central

Rhône

Bay of Biscay

Pyrenees

ANDORRA

Cantabrian Mountains

Douro

Tagus

SPAIN

PORTUGAL

I B E R I A N   P E N I N S U L A

Ebro

Sistema Bética

Baetic Mountains

Strait of Gibraltar

Balearic Islands

A F R I C A

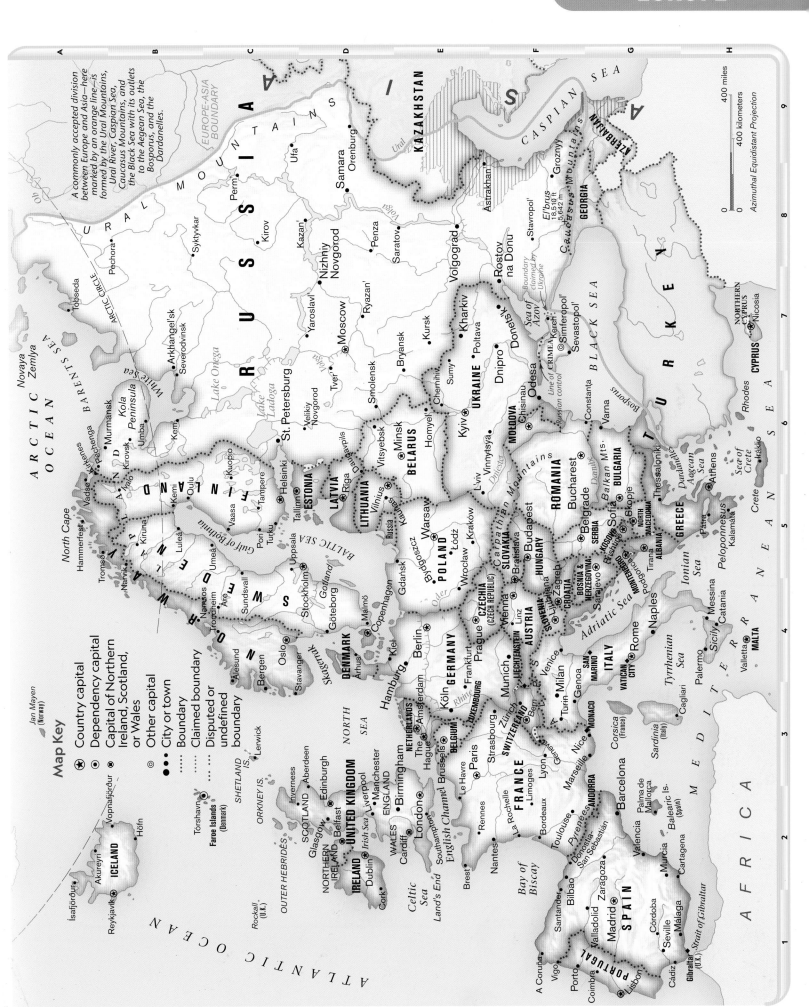

A commonly accepted division between Europe and Asia—here marked by an orange line—is formed by the Ural Mountains, Ural River, Caspian Sea, Caucasus Mountains, and the Black Sea with its outlets to the Aegean Sea, the Bosporus, and the Dardanelles.

EUROPE-ASIA BOUNDARY

400 miles
400 kilometers
Azimuthal Equidistant Projection

Map Key

✪ Country capital
◉ Dependency capital
⊛ Capital of Northern Ireland, Scotland, or Wales
◎ Other capital
● City or town
····· Boundary
•••• Claimed boundary
····· Disputed or undefined boundary

ARCTIC OCEAN

URAL MOUNTAINS

R U S S I A

KAZAKHSTAN

CASPIAN SEA

AZERBAIJAN

GEORGIA

Caucasus Mountains
El'brus 18,510 ft 5,642 m

Novaya Zemlya
BARENTS SEA
White Sea
Lake Onega
Lake Ladoga

Pechora
Tobseda
ARCTIC CIRCLE
Pechenga
Arkhangel'sk
Severodvinsk
Murmansk
Kola Peninsula
Umba
Kem'
Kirovsk
Apatity
Vadsø
Kirkenes
Hammerfest
Tromsø
Narvik
North Cape

Perm'
Ufa
Syktyvkar
Kirov
Kazan'
Orenburg
Samara
Ural
Orsk
Astrakhan'
Saratov
Penza
Nizhniy Novgorod
Yaroslavl'
Volga
Moscow
Ryazan'
Tver'
Veliky Novgorod
St. Petersburg
Kursk
Bryansk
Smolensk
Volgograd
Rostov na Donu
Stavropol'
Grozny
Kharkiv
Poltava

Boundary claimed by Ukraine

Sea of Azov
CRIMEA Kerch
Simferopol'
Sevastopol'
Line of Russian control

BLACK SEA

Bosporus

T U R K E N
TURKEY

NORTHERN CYPRUS
Nicosia
CYPRUS

Rhodes
Crete
Sea of Crete
Iráklio
AEGEAN SEA

FINLAND
Oulu
Kemi
Tornio
Kiruna
Luleå
Kuopio
Tampere
Helsinki
Vaasa
Pori
Turku
Uppsala
Gulf of Bothnia

ESTONIA
Tallinn
Daugavpils
LATVIA
Riga
LITHUANIA
Vilnius
Russia
BELARUS
Minsk
Vitsyebsk
Homyel'
UKRAINE
Kyiv
Vinnytsya
Chernihiv
Sumy
Donetsk
Dnipro
Odesa
MOLDOVA
Chişinău
Lviv
Dnister
Dniester

S W E D E N
N O R W A Y
Trondheim
Namsos
Ålesund
Bergen
Stavanger
Oslo
Skagerrak
Sundsvall
Åre
Umeå
Stockholm
Göteborg
Gotland
BALTIC SEA
Öland
Malmö
Copenhagen
DENMARK
Århus
Kiel
Gdansk
Bydgoszcz
POLAND
Warsaw
Łódź
Wrocław
Kraków
Oder
Odra

Jan Mayen (Norway)
ICELAND
Reykjavík
Ísafjörður
Akureyri
Vopnafjörður
Höfn

ATLANTIC OCEAN

Faroe Islands (Denmark)
Tórshavn
SHETLAND IS.
Lerwick
ORKNEY IS.
OUTER HEBRIDES
SCOTLAND
Inverness
Aberdeen
Glasgow
Edinburgh
UNITED KINGDOM
NORTHERN IRELAND
Belfast
IRELAND
Dublin
Cork
Rockall (U.K.)
Celtic Sea
Irish Sea
ENGLAND
Manchester
Liverpool
Birmingham
WALES
Cardiff
London
Land's End
English Channel
Southampton
NORTH SEA

Rennes
Brest
Nantes
Bay of Biscay
La Rochelle
FRANCE
Paris
Le Havre
Strasbourg
Bordeaux
Limoges
Lyon
Toulouse
Pyrenees
ANDORRA
Marseille
Nice
MONACO
Donostia-San Sebastián
Bilbao
A Coruña
Vigo
Porto
PORTUGAL
Coimbra
Lisbon
SPAIN
Madrid
Valladolid
Zaragoza
Barcelona
Palma de Mallorca
Valencia
Murcia
Cartagena
Córdoba
Seville
Málaga
Cádiz
Gibraltar (U.K.)
Strait of Gibraltar
Balearic Is. (Spain)
Santander

NETHERLANDS
Amsterdam
The Hague
BELGIUM
Brussels
LUXEMBOURG
GERMANY
Berlin
Hamburg
Köln
Frankfurt
Munich
Prague
CZECHIA (CZECH REPUBLIC)
LIECHTENSTEIN
SWITZERLAND
Zürich
Bern
Geneva
Linz
Wien
AUSTRIA
SLOVAKIA
Bratislava
HUNGARY
Budapest
SLOVENIA
Ljubljana
Zagreb
CROATIA
Venice
Milan
Turin
Genoa
ITALY
Rome
VATICAN CITY
SAN MARINO
Naples
Corsica (France)
Sardinia (Italy)
Cagliari
Tyrrhenian Sea
Sicily
Palermo
Catania
Messina
MALTA
Valletta
Rhine
Danube
Carpathian Mountains
ROMANIA
Bucharest
Belgrade
SERBIA
BOSNIA & HERZEGOVINA
Sarajevo
MONTENEGRO
Podgorica
KOSOVO
Priština
NORTH MACEDONIA
Skopje
BULGARIA
Sofia
Balkan Mts.
Varna
Constanţa
ALBANIA
Tirana
GREECE
Thessaloníki
Athens
Pátra
Kalamáta
Peloponnesus
Ionian Sea
Adriatic Sea
MEDITERRANEAN SEA

AFRICA

A F R I C A

Europe

SMALL SPACES, DIVERSE PLACES

WIND POWER.
A traditional windmill stands silent in Spain, as most electricity comes from nonrenewable sources. Modern windmills, along with hydroelectricity and solar, provide 49 percent of Spain's renewable energy.

Acluster of islands and peninsulas jutting west from Asia, Europe is bordered by two oceans and more than a dozen seas, which are linked to inland areas by canals and navigable rivers such as the Rhine and Danube. The fertile Northern European Plain sweeps west from the Urals. Rugged uplands form part of Europe's western coast, while the Alps shield Mediterranean lands from frigid northern winds. Here, first Greek and then Roman civilizations laid Europe's cultural foundation. Its colonial powers built wealth from vast empires, while its inventors and thinkers influenced world industry, economy, and politics. Today, the European Union seeks to achieve political and economic cooperation among member countries.

CHEERY GREETINGS. Laughing children clown for the camera in Klaipėda, Lithuania. The city is the northernmost ice-free port on the eastern coast of the Baltic Sea.

🌐 **NOTRE DAME.** In 2019, stunned citizens of Paris, France, and the world watched as the centuries-old cathedral burned during renovations. It is currently undergoing restoration supported by donations.

🌐 **ROCKY SENTINEL.** Towering 14,692 feet (4,478 m) in elevation, the Matterhorn, on the border between Switzerland and Italy, is one of Europe's most famous mountains. Frequent avalanches on its steep slopes pose challenges for mountain climbers.

🌐 **WINDOW ON THE PAST.** The brightly painted houses of Nyhavn (New Harbor), once the homes and warehouses of wealthy Copenhagen merchants, are now shops and restaurants and one of the most popular tourist attractions in Denmark's capital city.

THE CONTINENT:
EUROPE

more about
Europe

◔ **AGELESS TIME.** This famous astronomical clock, built in 1410 in Prague, Czechia, has an astronomical dial on top of a calendar dial. Together, the dials keep track of time as well as the movement of the sun, moon, and stars.

◑ **CLIFF DWELLERS.** The town of Positano clings to the rocky hillside along Italy's Amalfi coast. In the mid-19th century, more than half the town's population emigrated, mainly to the United States. The economy today is based on tourism.

◔ **SEABIRDS OF THE NORTH.** Colorful Atlantic puffins perch on a grass-covered cliff in Iceland, Europe's westernmost country. These birds are skilled fishers but have difficulty becoming airborne and often crash as they attempt to land.

◔ **FAMILY BUSINESS.** A father and son monitor and gather cherry tomatoes on their farm in Portugal. In the most recent agricultural census (2009), 90 percent of Portugal's farms were family-owned, with most of the work being completed by family members.

GLIMPSE OF THE PAST. Rome's Colosseum is a silent reminder of a once powerful empire that stretched from the British Isles to Persia (now Iran). The concrete, stone, and brick structure could seat as many as 50,000 people.

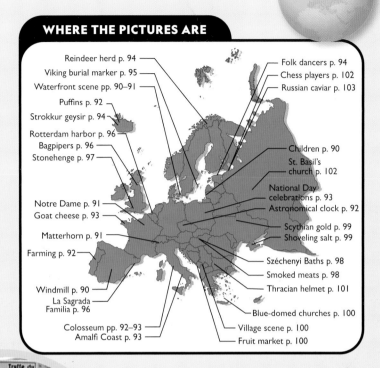

WHERE THE PICTURES ARE

Reindeer herd p. 94
Viking burial marker p. 95
Waterfront scene pp. 90–91
Puffins p. 92
Strokkur geysir p. 94
Rotterdam harbor p. 96
Bagpipers p. 96
Stonehenge p. 97
Notre Dame p. 91
Goat cheese p. 93
Matterhorn p. 91
Farming p. 92
Windmill p. 90
La Sagrada Familia p. 96
Colosseum pp. 92–93
Amalfi Coast p. 93

Folk dancers p. 94
Chess players p. 102
Russian caviar p. 103
Children p. 90
St. Basil's church p. 102
National Day celebrations p. 93
Astronomical clock p. 92
Scythian gold p. 99
Shoveling salt p. 99
Széchenyi Baths p. 98
Smoked meats p. 98
Thracian helmet p. 101
Blue-domed churches p. 100
Village scene p. 100
Fruit market p. 100

LUNCHTIME! Varieties of creamy, fresh goat cheese are displayed in a market in the Brittany region of northern France.

NATIONAL PRIDE. Women carry banners in a parade marking Poland's National Day. Celebrated each year on May 3, it is the anniversary of the 1997 proclamation of the Polish Constitution.

THE CONTINENT: EUROPE

Northern Europe

THE BASICS

STATS

Largest country
Sweden
173,860 sq mi (450,295 sq km)

Smallest country
Denmark
16,639 sq mi (43,094 sq km)

Most populous country
Sweden 10,041,000

Least populous country
Iceland 344,000

Predominant languages
Swedish, Danish, Finnish, Norwegian, Lithuanian, Latvian, Estonian, Russian, Icelandic

Predominant religion
Christianity

Highest GDP per capita
Norway $71,800

Lowest GDP per capita
Latvia $27,600

Highest life expectancy
Iceland 83 years

Lowest life expectancy
Latvia, Lithuania 75 years

GEO WHIZ

Vatnajökull, in Iceland, is the largest glacier in Europe.

The inventors of LEGO blocks opened their first business in 1932 in Billund, Denmark, manufacturing stools and wooden toys.

In Tromsø, Norway, which is north of the Arctic Circle, the sun does not rise from November to January.

This region lies in latitudes similar to Canada's Hudson Bay, but the warm North Atlantic Drift current moderates temperatures from volcanically active Iceland to Denmark and Norway. Sparsely populated but mostly urban, northern Europe is home to slightly more than 33 million people. The region's better farmlands lie in southern Sweden and Denmark's lowlands. Forested Finland shares a border with Russia. Estonia, Latvia, and Lithuania—the so-called Baltic States—are former republics of the Soviet Union.

● **NORDIC HERDERS.** The Sami, indigenous people of northern Europe, herd their reindeer across the borders of Norway, Sweden, Finland, and Russia. Some use snowmobiles instead of horses.

◗ **STROKKUR GEYSIR.** The word "geysir" comes from the Icelandic verb, *geysa,* which means "to gush." Every 5 to 10 minutes, to the delight of tourists, Strokkur in Iceland erupts. From 2011 to 2018, Iceland experienced a huge increase in tourism, leading to concerns for natural areas.

◗ **COLORFUL TRADITION.**
Costumed folk dancers perform traditional dances at an open-air museum in Tallinn, Estonia's capital city.

NORTHERN FISHERIES

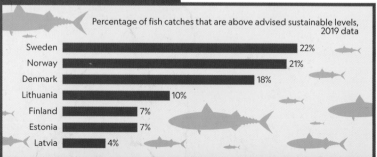

Percentage of fish catches that are above advised sustainable levels, 2019 data

Sweden	22%
Norway	21%
Denmark	18%
Lithuania	10%
Finland	7%
Estonia	7%
Latvia	4%

Profits from the fishing industry conflict with conservation interests to protect the North Sea from overfishing.

MARKER FROM THE PAST. This stone memorial in Sweden marks the burial site of Viking warriors. Although known for their fierce raids, Vikings were mainly farmers and traders.

ARCTIC CIRCLE

Ísafjörður
Akureyri
Neskaupstaður
ICELAND
Reykjavík
Kópavogur
Keflavík
Vatnajökull
Höfn

See maps on pages 88, 89 for position.

0   200 miles
0   300 kilometers

Svalbard (Norway)
See map on page 35 for position.

North East Land

Spitsbergen
Longyearbyen
Edgeøya

0   200 miles
0   300 kilometers

Map Key
⊛ Country capital
⊙ Dependency capital
•••• City or town
•••• Boundary

0   100 miles
0   100 kilometers
Azimuthal Equidistant Projection

North Cape
ARCTIC OCEAN
BARENTS SEA

Sørøya
Hammerfest

Tromsø
LOFOTEN
VESTERÅLEN
Vestfjorden
Bodø

L A P L A N D

Ivalo

Kiruna
+Kebnekaise
6,880 ft
2,097 m

F I N L A N D

ARCTIC CIRCLE

Rovaniemi
Kemi
Torneälven

Luleå
Oulu
Oulujoki

Skellefteå
Raahe
Kajaani
Nurmes

Umeå
Kokkola
Jakobstad
Kuopio
Joensuu

Vaasa
Lake Region
Savonlinna

Norrland
Örnsköldsvik
Ångermanälven
Umeälven

Östersund
Sundsvall
Jyväskylä
Mikkeli
Imatra

S W E D E N
N O R W A Y

Gulf of Bothnia

Tampere
Lappeenranta
Pori
Lahti
Rauma

ATLANTIC OCEAN

Trondheim
Trondheimsfjorden
Ålesund

Galdhøpiggen
8,100 ft
2,469 m +
Glåma
Ljusnan

Falun
Gävle
Turku
Helsinki
Espoo
ÅLAND ISLANDS

Bergen
Hønefoss
Drammen
Oslo

Svealand
Uppsala
Klarälven
Västerås

Haugesund
Stavanger
Skien
Karlstad
Örebro
Stockholm
Mälaren

Tallinn
Narva

Fredrikstad
Vänern
Norrköping

E S T O N I A
Hiiumaa
Lake Peipus

Kristiansand
Skagerrak
Linköping
Vättern
Gotland
Pärnu
Tartu

Göteborg
Jönköping
Borås
Visby
Saaremaa
Gulf of Riga
Valmiera

G ö t a l a n d
Öland
Ventspils
Rīga
Rēzekne

Ålborg
Kattegat
L A T V I A
Jelgava
Daugavpils
Daugava

NORTH SEA
Århus
JUTLAND
Helsingborg
Šiauliai
Panevėžys

Esbjerg
DENMARK
Odense
Fyn
Sjælland
Malmö
Copenhagen
Bornholm
Klaipėda
Neman
LITHUANIA
Kaunas

Russia
Vilnius
B E L A R U S

G E R M A N Y   **P O L A N D**

NORWEGIAN SEA
B A L T I C   S E A
Lake Ladoga
R U S S I A

THE CONTINENT:
EUROPE

THE BASICS

STATS

Largest country
France
248,573 sq mi (643,801 sq km)

Smallest country
Vatican City
0.17 sq mi (0.44 sq km)

Most populous country
Germany 80,458,000

Least populous country
Vatican City 1,000

Predominant languages
German, French, English, Italian, Spanish, Dutch, Portuguese

Predominant religion
Christianity

Highest GDP per capita
Liechtenstein $139,100

Lowest GDP per capita
Portugal $30,400

Highest life expectancy
Monaco 89 years

Lowest life expectancy
Portugal 79 years

GEO WHIZ

Turiasaurus riodevensis is the largest dinosaur ever found in Europe. The fossil was discovered in northern Spain in 2006.

Mount Etna, on Sicily, is known as the home of Zeus, ruler of all Greek gods. It is also Europe's highest active volcano.

Using imported diamonds, Antwerp, Belgium, is the center of the world's diamond-cutting industry.

Western Europe

Eighteen countries crowd this diverse region, which has enjoyed a central role in world affairs for centuries. Over time, bitter rivals have become allies, with today's European Union growing out of the need to rebuild economic and political stability after World War II. Fertile soil in the many river valleys across the Northern European Plain and on Mediterranean hillsides gives rise to abundant harvests of a wide variety of crops. France leads in agricultural production and area, while Germany is the most populous country.

⬧ **MONUMENT TO FAITH.** The towering spires of La Sagrada Familia (The Holy Family) rise above Barcelona, Spain. This massive Roman Catholic church has been under construction for more than a century.

⬧ **MODERN SPAN.**
Tall red arches support the Willem Bridge across the Maas River in Rotterdam, Netherlands. The Maas, which flows into the North Sea, is a major trade and transport artery, linking the Netherlands to the rest of Europe.

⬧ **HIGHLAND TUNE.** Bagpipers in formal dress parade through the streets of Edinburgh, Scotland, in the United Kingdom. Bagpipes may have arrived centuries ago with Roman invaders, but today they are most associated with the Scottish Highlands.

HOW BIG IS A COUNTRY?

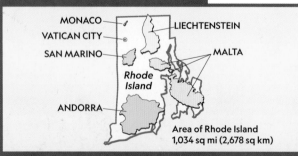

MONACO
VATICAN CITY
SAN MARINO
Rhode Island
ANDORRA
LIECHTENSTEIN
MALTA

Area of Rhode Island
1,034 sq mi (2,678 sq km)

Europe's six smallest countries (for areas, see pages 176–185) would fit inside Rhode Island, the smallest U.S. state, with room to spare.

◑ **CELTIC POWER.** These rock pillars, part of Stonehenge in southern England, United Kingdom, were placed more than 5,000 years ago and may be associated with sun worship.

0   200 miles
0   200 kilometers
Azimuthal Equidistant Projection

Map Key

⊛ Country capital

⊗ Capital of Northern
Ireland, Scotland,
or Wales

••• City or town

····· Boundary

FINLAND

ESTONIA

N O R W A Y

S W E D E N

Shetland
Islands

Orkney
Islands

Rockall
(United Kingdom)

A T L A N T I C   O C E A N

Outer Hebrides

Inner Hebrides

Inverness

SCOTLAND   Aberdeen

Perth   Dundee

Edinburgh

Glasgow

NORTHERN
IRELAND

⊗ Belfast

Londonderry

IRELAND
(ÉIRE)

Limerick   Dublin ⊛

Waterford

Cork

IRISH SEA

Isle of Man

Liverpool

Manchester

Birmingham

WALES

Cardiff ⊗

Bristol

Plymouth

Southampton

CELTIC
SEA

UNITED

Newcastle

Sunderland

Leeds

KINGDOM

Kingston upon Hull

Sheffield

Nottingham

ENGLAND

London ⊛

Thames

G R E A T   B R I T A I N

N O R T H
S E A

DENMARK

BALTIC SEA

Kiel   Rostock

Lübeck

Hamburg

Oldenburg   Bremen   Berlin ⊛

Groningen

Frisian Islands

NETHERLANDS

Amsterdam
(official capital)

The Hague
(administrative capital)   Utrecht

Rotterdam

Brugge   Antwerp

Brussels ⊛

BELGIUM

Lille   Charleroi

Hannover

Bielefeld   Magdeburg

Leipzig

Dortmund   Erfurt

Essen

Köln   GERMANY   Dresden

Bonn   Frankfurt   Chemnitz

LUXEMBOURG ⊛   Mainz

Luxembourg   Mannheim   Nürnberg

POLAND

CZECHIA
(CZECH REPUBLIC)

SLOVAKIA

ENGLISH CHANNEL   Strait of Dover

Channel
Islands
(U.K.)

Amiens

Rouen

Reims

Le Havre

Caen

Brest

Rennes   Le Mans

Angers

Nantes

Paris ⊛

Orléans

Tours

Seine

Marne

Seine

Metz   Nancy

Strasbourg

Karlsruhe   Stuttgart   Augsburg

Freiburg

Mulhouse   Basel

Munich

Besançon

Dijon

Lausanne

Geneva

Zürich

Bern ⊛

SWITZERLAND

LIECHTENSTEIN

Innsbruck

Linz

Vienna ⊛

Salzburg

AUSTRIA

Graz

HUNGARY

Bolzano

Trento

SLOVENIA

Trieste

CROATIA

SERBIA

Danube

Rhine

Mont
Blanc
15,781 ft
4,810 m

Matterhorn
14,692 ft
4,478 m

FRANCE

Limoges

Clermont-Ferrand

MASSIF
CENTRAL

Bordeaux

Vichy

Lyon

St.-Étienne

Nîmes

Avignon

Aix-en-Provence

Nice

Montpellier

Marseille

Toulon

MONACO

Verona

Milan

Turin

Modena

Genoa

Ferrara

Bologna

Florence

Pisa

Perugia

LIGURIAN
SEA

Padova

Venice

SAN MARINO

Ancona

ADRIATIC
SEA

BOSNIA &
HERZEGOVINA

MONTENEGRO

ALBANIA

A L P S

Po

A P E N N I N E S

B A Y   O F
B I S C A Y

Donostia-San Sebastián

A Coruña   Gijón   Santander   Bilbao

Oviedo

Santiago de
Compostela

Vigo   León

Braga   Burgos

Porto

Bragança

Viseu

Coimbra

PORTUGAL

Lisbon ⊛

Setúbal

Vitoria-
Gasteiz

Valladolid

Salamanca

Madrid ⊛

Toledo

Badajoz

SIERRA MORENA

Córdoba

Seville

Huelva

Jerez

Cádiz

Algeciras   Gibraltar (U.K.)

Ceuta
(Spain)

Strait of Gibraltar

MOROCCO

Melilla
(Spain)

ALBORAN
SEA

Tagus

Guadiana

Duero

Douro

Ebro

PYRENEES

Pamplona

ANDORRA

Zaragoza

Andorra la Vella

Lleida

Tarragona

SPAIN

Castelló
de la Plana

Valencia

Albacete

Murcia

Alicante

Cartagena

Granada

Jaén

Málaga

Almería

Perpignan

Sabadell

Martaró

Barcelona

BALEARIC SEA

Minorca

Palma de
Mallorca

Majorca

BALEARIC ISLANDS

Toulouse

Gatonne

Loire

Loire

Rhône

CORSICA

Ajaccio

Bastia

Sassari

Cagliari

SARDINIA

TYRRHENIAN
SEA

VATICAN
CITY

Rome ⊛

Naples

Vesuvius
4,203 ft
1,281 m

Terni

Pescara

Foggia   Bari

Salerno

Taranto

Lecce

Gulf of
Taranto

Cosenza

IONIAN
SEA

ITALY

Messina

Mt. Etna
10,925 ft
3,330 m

Palermo

Marsala

SICILY

Reggio di
Calabria

Taormina

Catania

Syracuse

M E D I T E R R A N E A N   S E A

ALGERIA

TUNISIA

MALTA

Valletta

ITALY

THE CONTINENT:
EUROPE

THE BASICS

STATS

Largest country
Ukraine
233,032 sq mi (603,550 sq km)

Smallest country
Moldova
13,070 sq mi (33,851 sq km)

Most populous country
Ukraine 43,952,000

Least populous country
Moldova 3,438,000

Predominant languages
Ukrainian, Russian, Polish, Hungarian, Czech, Belarusian, Slovak, Moldovan

Predominant religions
Christianity, Judaism, Islam

Highest GDP per capita
Czechia $35,500

Lowest GDP per capita
Moldova $5,700

Highest life expectancy
Czechia 79 years

Lowest life expectancy
Moldova 71 years

GEO WHIZ

The Wieliczka salt mine is known as the underground salt cathedral of Poland. It features historical, religious, and mythical figures, chambers, a chapel, and an exhibit about how salt is mined—all carved in salt!

Budapest became a united city in 1873 after Count István Széchenyi built a bridge connecting Buda on the west bank of the Danube River and Pest on the east bank.

The Pinsk Marshes, one of Europe's largest wetlands, are still contaminated by radioactive waste from a 1986 nuclear reactor explosion in Chernobyl, Ukraine.

Eastern Europe

◔ **TIME TO EAT.**
Smoked sausages and bacon, ready for purchase in the market, are an important part of the diet in the countries of eastern Europe.

Eastern Europe stretches from the Baltic Sea southeast to the Black Sea. Before 1991, the former republics of Ukraine, Belarus, and Moldova were controlled by the Soviet Union, with the region's other countries heavily influenced by it. Kaliningrad, a small region of Russia separated from the main country, lies just north of Poland. Much of the region has a continental climate similar to that of the U.S. Midwest. Nearly the size of Texas, Ukraine is the region's largest country in both population and area. Like Poland, it holds rich agricultural and industrial resources. Warsaw is the region's largest city, while historic Prague and Budapest are popular tourist stops. With the exceptions of Hungarians and Moldovans, most people in these lands are linked by branches of Slavic language and ethnicity.

◑ **HEALING WATERS.**
Budapest's Széchenyi Baths, built between 1909 and 1913, are famous for their thermal waters, discovered in 1879. A total of 15 baths, as well as saunas and steam rooms, are housed in buildings decorated with sculptures and mosaics by Hungary's leading artists.

BALTIC

Koszalin

Szczecin

Gorzów
Wielkopolski

Poznań

Zielona
Góra

P O

Kalisz

Legnica

Wrocław

Walbrzych

Opole

GERMANY

Liberec

Prague

Pilsen

C Z E C H I A
(CZECH REPUBLIC)

Ostrava

Olomouc

České
Budějovice

Brno

Danube

S L

Bratislava

AUSTRIA

Győr

Székesfehérvár

H U

SLOVENIA

Pécs

Drava

Danube

CROATIA

ANCIENT GOLD. Scythians, who occupied the area from what is now Ukraine into Russia from the third century B.C.E. to the second century C.E., crafted this gold collar.

MOUNTAIN OF SALT. Workers shovel salt in Ukraine, where the mineral is a symbol of friendship.

LATVIA

SEA

LITHUANIA

Russia

Gdynia
Gdańsk

Olsztyn

Bydgoszcz
Toruń

Białystok

Vistula

Hrodna

Barysaw

Vitsyebsk

Orsha

Mahilyow

Minsk

B E L A R U S

Baranavichy

Babruysk

Homyel'

L A N D

Warsaw

Brest

Pinsk

Pinsk Marshes

Mazyr

Dnieper

Łódź

Radom

Częstochowa
Kielce

Bytom
Katowice
Tychy Kraków
Tarnów

Vistula

Lublin

Luts'k

Rivne

Chernihiv

Chernobyl'

Sumy

R U S S I A

Rzeszów

L'viv

Ternopil'

Zhytomyr

Kyiv

Dnieper

Kharkiv

Lysychans'k

C A R P A T H I A N   M O U N T A I N S

OVAKIA

Košice

Uzhhorod

Miskolc

Budapest

Tisza

Nyiregyháza

Debrecen

NGARY

Szeged

SERBIA

R O M A N I A

Dniester

Khmel'nyts'kyy

Ivano-Frankivs'k

Kam'yanets'-Podil's'kyy

Chernivtsi

Bălţi

MOLDOVA

Chisinau

Prut

Tiraspol

Danube

Bila Tserkva

U K R A I N E

Vinnytsya

Cherkasy

Oleksandriya

Kirovohrad

Dniprodzerzhyns'k

Kryvyy Rih

Dniester

TRANSNISTRIA

Since 1990, Transnistria, a self-proclaimed breakaway state in Moldova's predominantly Russian-speaking area east of the Dniester River, has remained unrecognized by any UN member state.

Poltava

Slov"yans'k
Kramators'k
Kostyantynivka

Kremenchuk

Dnipro

Horlivka

Donets'k

Zaporizhzhya

Nikopol'

Melitopol'

Kadiivka
Luhans'k
Alchevs'k
Krasnyy Luch
Yenakiyeve
Makiyivka

Mariupol'

Berdyans'k

Mykolayiv

Dnieper

Kherson

Odesa

Line of Russian control

SEA OF AZOV

Boundary claimed by Ukraine

CRIMEA

B L A C K   S E A

Map Key

⊛ Country capital
◎ Other capital
●●● City or town
····· Boundary
····· Claimed boundary
···· · Disputed or undefined boundary

UNDISTURBED FOREST

DENMARK
BALTIC SEA
LATVIA
LITHUANIA
Russia
GERMANY
POLAND
BELARUS
Old-growth forest

0 ____ 300 miles
0 ____ 300 kilometers

CZECHIA
SLOVAKIA
UKRAINE
SWITZ.
AUSTRIA
SLOVENIA
HUNGARY
MOLDOVA
RUSSIA
ITALY
CROATIA
BOSNIA & HERZEGOVINA
SERBIA
ROMANIA
CRIMEA
BLACK SEA

Old-growth forests have minimal signs of human interaction and are usually found in remote areas.

0 ____ 200 miles
0 ____ 200 kilometers

Azimuthal Equidistant Projection

THE BASICS

STATS

Largest country
Romania
92,043 sq mi (238,391 sq km)

Smallest country
Cyprus
3,572 sq mi (9,251 sq km)

Most populous country
Romania 21,457,000

Least populous country
Montenegro 614,000

Predominant languages
Romanian, Greek, Serbian, Croatian, Bulgarian, Albanian, Turkish, English

Predominant religions
Christianity, Islam

Highest GDP per capita
Cyprus $37,000

Lowest GDP per capita
Kosovo $10,500

Highest life expectancy
Greece 81 years

Lowest life expectancy
Bulgaria, Romania
75 years

GEO WHIZ

The Dalmatian, a popular breed of dog, is named for the region where it originated: Dalmatia, along the Adriatic coast of the Balkan Peninsula.

Dracula tours are popular in Romania, home of Vlad Dracula (Vlad the Impaler), who ruled the region between the Danube and the Transylvanian Alps in the 15th century.

The Balkans & Cyprus

The Balkans—named for a Bulgarian mountain range—make up a rugged land with a rough history. Ethnic and religious conflicts have long troubled the area. After 1991, seven new countries stretching from Slovenia to North Macedonia emerged as a result of the breakup of Yugoslavia. Kosovo is the most recent. The Danube River winds east across the Balkans, separating Bulgaria from Romania, the region's largest country. Rimmed by four seas—the Black, Aegean, Ionian, and Adriatic—the Balkans, particularly Greece, have a long maritime history. In 2004, Cyprus, which has been uneasily divided for three decades into Turkish and Greek sections, joined the European Union along with Greece.

RURAL LIFE. Villagers walk down a cobbled street in Gusinje, a rural town in northeastern Montenegro. A place of rugged mountains, Montenegro is one of the countries that emerged from the former Yugoslavia.

SEISMIC HISTORY. Blue-domed Greek Orthodox churches on the island of Thira (Santorini) cling to cliffs above the remains of a volcano that erupted more than 3,000 years ago.

COLORFUL BOUNTY. An open-air fruit market in Kotor, Montenegro, overflows with grapes, plums, apples, and other produce that grow in the moderate climate of the Mediterranean region. Warm, dry summers and cool, rainy winters provide ideal growing conditions for a variety of fruits, many of which had their origins in the region.

◗ **ANCIENT WARRIORS.** Soldiers and horsemen from Thrace, an ancient territory in present-day Bulgaria and Greece, wore battle masks, such as this one.

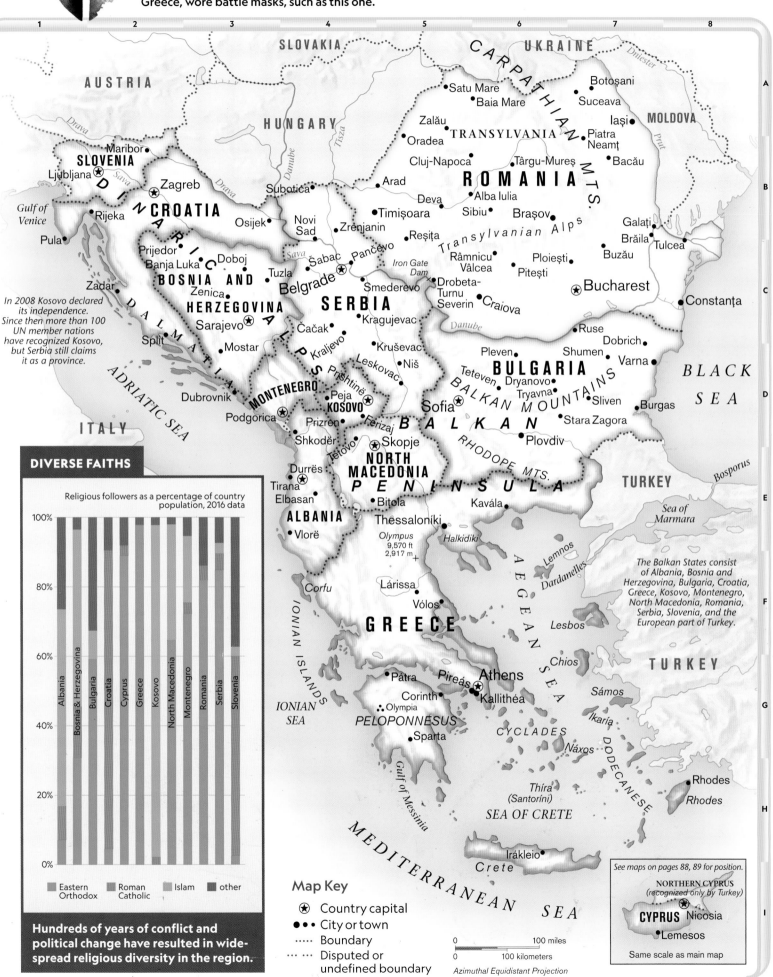

SLOVAKIA

UKRAINE

Dniester

AUSTRIA

HUNGARY

Drava

Tisza

Danube

Satu Mare
Baia Mare
Botoşani
Suceava
Iaşi
MOLDOVA
Prut

Zalău
Oradea

TRANSYLVANIA

Piatra Neamţ

Maribor
SLOVENIA
Ljubljana ✪
Zagreb
Sava
Drava

Cluj-Napoca
Târgu-Mureş
Bacău

Arad
ROMANIA

DINARIC

CROATIA

Subotica
Deva
Alba Iulia

Rijeka
Gulf of Venice

Osijek

Novi Sad

Timişoara

Sibiu
Braşov

Galaţi

Pula

Zrenjanin

Reşiţa

Transylvanian Alps

Brăila
Tulcea

Prijedor
Doboj

Sava

Buzău

Zadar
Banja Luka
Tuzla

BOSNIA AND

Šabac
Pančevo
Belgrade ✪

Iron Gate Dam

Râmnicu Vâlcea
Ploieşti
Piteşti

Bucharest ✪

Zenica

Smederevo

Drobeta-Turnu Severin

HERZEGOVINA
Sarajevo ✪

SERBIA

Craiova
Constanţa

In 2008 Kosovo declared its independence. Since then more than 100 UN member nations have recognized Kosovo, but Serbia still claims it as a province.

Split
DALMATIA

Mostar

Kragujevac

Danube

Ruse
Dobrich

Čačak
Kraljevo

Pleven
Shumen
Varna

Kruševac

BLACK SEA

ALPS

Leskovac
Niš

Teteven
Dryanovo
BULGARIA

ITALY

ADRIATIC SEA

Dubrovnik
MONTENEGRO
Prishtinë
Peja

Sofia ✪
Tryavna
Sliven

Podgorica ✪

KOSOVO

Stara Zagora
Burgas

Prizren
Ferizaj

BALKAN
Plovdiv
RHODOPE MTS.

Shkodër

DIVERSE FAITHS

Tetovo
Skopje ✪

NORTH
MACEDONIA

TURKEY

Bosporus

Durrës
Tirana ✪

PENINSULA

Sea of Marmara

Religious followers as a percentage of country population, 2016 data

Elbasan

Bitola

Kavála

ALBANIA

Thessaloníki

Vlorë

Olympus 9,570 ft 2,917 m

Halkidikí

Lemnos
Dardanelles

The Balkan States consist of Albania, Bosnia and Herzegovina, Bulgaria, Croatia, Greece, Kosovo, Montenegro, North Macedonia, Romania, Serbia, Slovenia, and the European part of Turkey.

Corfu

Lárissa

Lesbos

TURKEY

Vólos

GREECE

Chios

IONIAN ISLANDS

AEGEAN SEA

Pátra
Pireás
Athens ✪

IONIAN SEA

Corinth
Kallithéa

Sámos
Ikaría

Olympia
PELOPONNESUS

CYCLADES
Náxos

Sparta

DODECANESE

100% Albania
Bosnia & Herzegovina
Bulgaria
Croatia
Cyprus
Greece
Kosovo
North Macedonia
Montenegro
Romania
Serbia
Slovenia

80%

60%

40%

Thíra (Santoríni)
Rhodes
Rhodes

Gulf of Messinia

SEA OF CRETE

20%

0%

Irákleio
Crete

MEDITERRANEAN SEA

☐ Eastern Orthodox
☐ Roman Catholic
☐ Islam
☐ other

Map Key

✪ Country capital

●●● City or town

····· Boundary

····· Disputed or undefined boundary

See maps on pages 88, 89 for position.

NORTHERN CYPRUS
(recognized only by Turkey)

CYPRUS ✪ Nicosia

Lemesos

Same scale as main map

Hundreds of years of conflict and political change have resulted in widespread religious diversity in the region.

0 ——— 100 miles
0 ——— 100 kilometers
Azimuthal Equidistant Projection

THE CONTINENT:
EUROPE

European Russia

CHECKMATE! Bystanders watch intently as one player prepares to make his move in this chess game in a park in St. Petersburg. In Russia, chess is a national pastime, popular with people from all walks of life.

Home to four-fifths of Russia's 144 million people, European Russia contains most of the country's agriculture and industry. Prior to 1991, Russia was the largest of the former republics of the Soviet Union. Here also is Moscow, its capital and Europe's largest city. Far to the north, Murmansk provides a year-round seaport—a gift of the warming currents of the North Atlantic Drift. This European region of Russia, spanning 994 miles (1,600 km), is home to the Volga, Europe's longest river, and Mount El'brus, its highest peak. The Caucasus and Urals form a natural boundary between Europe and Asia. Although parts of Azerbaijan, Georgia, and Kazakhstan span the continental boundary, only Russia is counted as part of Europe.

EUROPE'S GREAT RIVERS

Volga	2,290 mi (3,685 km)
Danube	1,795 mi (2,888 km)
Dnieper	1,423 mi (2,290 km)
Rhine	820 mi (1,320 km)
Elbe	678 mi (1,091 km)
Vistula	651 mi (1,047 km)
Tagus	645 mi (1,038 km)
Loire	629 mi (1,012 km)
Rhône	497 mi (800 km)
Po	405 mi (652 km)

Europe's rivers, many linked by canals, form a transportation network that connects the continent's people and places to each other and the world beyond.

CATHEDRAL ON THE SQUARE. The onion-shaped domes atop the towers of St. Basil's are a key landmark on Red Square in Moscow. Built between 1555 and 1561 to commemorate military campaigns led by Ivan the Terrible, the building is rich in Christian symbolism.

RUSSIAN DELICACY. Caviar is the eggs (called roe) of sturgeon fish caught in the Caspian Sea. The eggs are aged in a salty brine, then packaged in cans (left) for export.

Map Key

- ★ Country capital
- ◎ Other capital
- ●●● City or town
- ····· Boundary
- ····· Claimed boundary
- ····· Disputed or undefined boundary

0 — 200 miles
0 — 200 kilometers
Azimuthal Equidistant Projection

See map on pages 112–113 for the Asian part of Russia.

ARCTIC OCEAN

NORWAY

NOVAYA ZEMLYA

KARA SEA

Yamal Peninsula

Gulf of Ob

BARENTS SEA

LAPLAND

Murmansk

Kolguyev I.

Kanin Peninsula

Vorkuta

ARCTIC CIRCLE

SWEDEN

Kola Peninsula

Usinsk

FINLAND

Pechora

WHITE SEA

Pechora

Gulf of Bothnia

Severodvinsk

Arkhangel'sk

Ukhta

Sosnogorsk

U R A L

Gulf of Finland

Petrozavodsk

Northern Dvina

Zheleznodorozhnyy

Syktyvkar

S I B E R I A

BALTIC SEA

St. Petersburg

Lake Ladoga

Lake Onega

Kotlas

Sukhona

Pechora

M O U N T A I N S

ESTONIA

Lake Peipus

Cherepovets

Vologda

Rybinsk Reservoir

Kirov

Berezniki

Perm'

EUROPE-ASIA BOUNDARY

LATVIA

Pskov

Velikiy Novgorod

Izhevsk

Kama

Velikiye Luki

Rybinsk

Kostroma

Ivanovo

Nizhniy Novgorod

Kazan'

Naberezhnyye Chelny

Ufa

Ural

Russia

LITHUANIA

Tver'

Volga

Yaroslavl'

Vladimir

Oka

Cheboksary

Volga

Magnitogorsk

POLAND

Moscow

Smolensk

Kaluga

Saransk

Ul'yanovsk

Tol'yatti

Sterlitamak

N O R T H E R N   E U R O P E A N   P L A I N

R U S S I A

BELARUS

Tula

Ryazan'

Syzran'

Samara

Belaya

Bryansk

Dnieper

C E N T R A L

Orel

Oka

Lipetsk

Tambov

Penza

Orenburg

Novotroitsk

Orsk

R U S S I A N

Kursk

Voronezh

Saratov

Balakovo

Belgorod

Engels

U P L A N D

Kamyshin

KAZAKHSTAN

Ural

UKRAINE

Don

Donets

MOLDOVA

Volgograd

Volzhskiy

Don

Russia invaded Crimea in 2014 and, after secession from Ukraine was approved in a disputed and boycotted referendum held in Crimea, the Russian parliament voted to annex Crimea into the Russian Federation. The United Nations General Assembly subsequently adopted a nonbinding resolution declaring the annexation invalid and affirming Ukraine's territorial jurisdiction. As of 2019, Russia administers and controls all aspects of the peninsula, while Ukraine continues to maintain that Crimea is its sovereign territory.

Shakhty

Volga

CASPIAN DEPRESSION

Dnieper

Don

Rostov na Donu

Line of Russian control

SEA OF AZOV

Taganrog

Boundary claimed by Ukraine

Astrakhan'

CASPIAN SEA

Yevpatoriya

CRIMEA

Kerch

Simferopol'

Novorossiysk

Krasnodar

Stavropol'

Sevastopol'

Maykop

Pyatigorsk

BLACK SEA

El'brus 18,510 ft 5,642 m

CHECHNYA

Sochi

Groznyy

Makhachkala

CAUCASUS MOUNTAINS

Vladikavkaz

GEORGIA

TURKEY

ARMENIA

AZERBAIJAN

THE CONTINENT:
ASIA

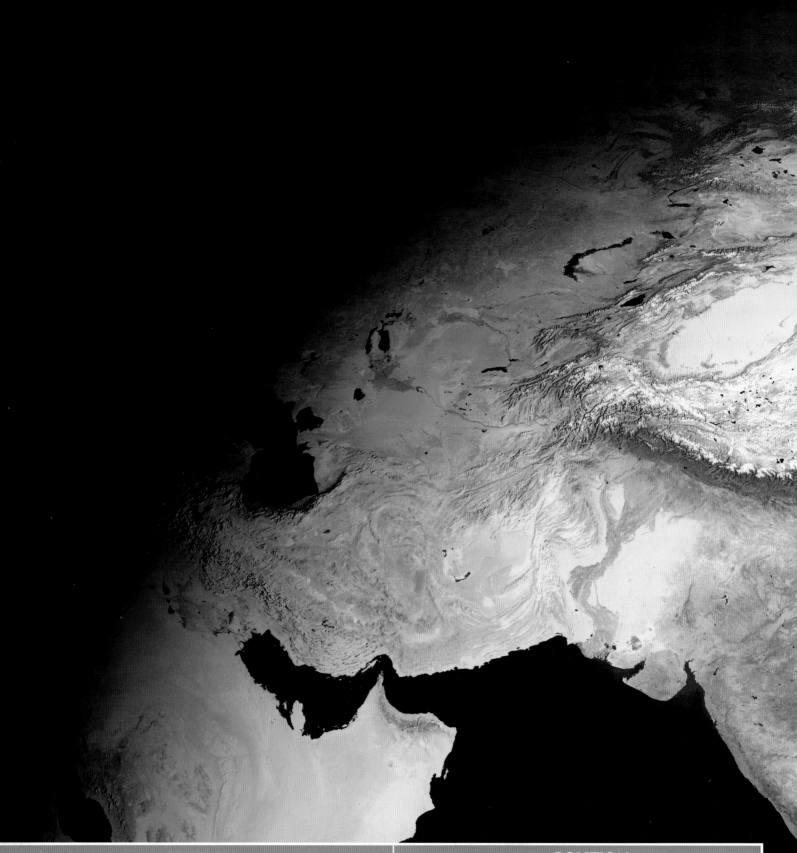

PHYSICAL			POLITICAL	
TOTAL AREA 17,208,000 sq mi (44,570,000 sq km)	**LOWEST POINT** Dead Sea, Israel-Jordan -1,424 ft (-434 m)	**LARGEST LAKE ENTIRELY IN ASIA** Lake Baikal 12,200 sq mi (31,500 sq km)	**POPULATION** 4,641,055,000	**LARGEST COUNTRY ENTIRELY IN ASIA** China 3,705,405 sq mi (9,596,960 sq km)
HIGHEST POINT Mount Everest, China-Nepal 29,035 ft (8,850 m)	**LONGEST RIVER** Yangtze (Chang), China 3,880 mi (6,244 km)		**LARGEST METROPOLITAN AREA** Tokyo, Japan Pop. 37,468,000	**MOST DENSELY POPULATED COUNTRY** Singapore 22,281 people per sq mi (8,603 per sq km)

ASIA

Asia

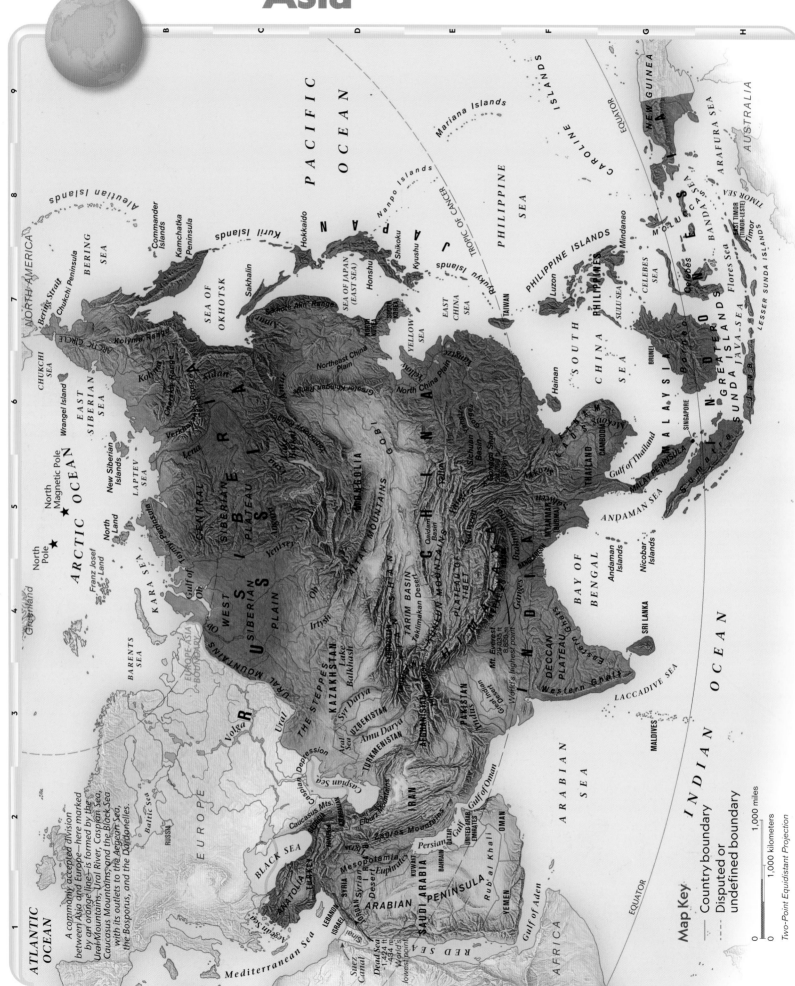

A commonly accepted division
between Asia and Europe—here marked
by an orange line—is formed by the
Ural Mountains, Ural River, Caspian Sea,
Caucasus Mountains, and the Black Sea
with its outlets to the Aegean Sea,
the Bosporus, and the Dardanelles.

ATLANTIC
OCEAN

Map Key:
— Country boundary
---- Disputed or
undefined boundary

0   1,000 miles
0   1,000 kilometers

Two-Point Equidistant Projection

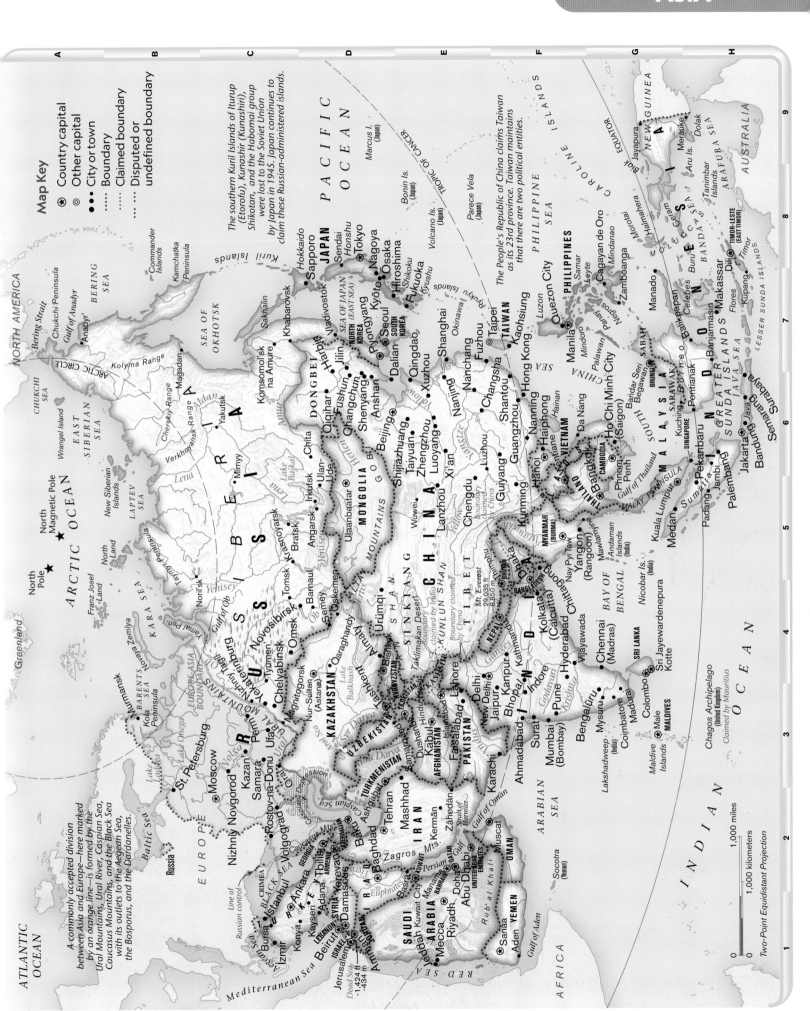

Map Key

⊛ Country capital
◎ Other capital
•• City or town
•••• Boundary
•••• Claimed boundary
•••• Disputed or undefined boundary

The southern Kuril Islands of Iturup (Etorofu), Kunashir (Kunashiri), Shikotan, and the Habomai group were lost to the Soviet Union by Japan in 1945. Japan continues to claim these Russian-administered islands.

The People's Republic of China claims Taiwan as its 23rd province. Taiwan maintains that there are two political entities.

A commonly accepted division between Asia and Europe—here marked by an orange line—is formed by the Ural Mountains, Ural River, Caspian Sea, Caucasus Mountains, and the Black Sea with its outlets to the Aegean Sea, the Bosporus, and the Dardanelles.

1,000 miles
1,000 kilometers
Two-Point Equidistant Projection

Asia
WORLD CHAMPION

○ **TASTY SNACK.** This giant panda, native to China, munches on a stalk of bamboo, the mainstay of its diet.

From Turkey to the eastern tip of Russia, Asia sprawls across nearly 180 degrees of longitude—almost half the globe! It boasts the highest (the Himalaya) and lowest (the Dead Sea) places on Earth's surface. Then there are Asia's people—more than four billion of them. More people live here than on all the other continents put together. Asia has both the most farmers and the most million-plus cities. The world's first civilization arose in Sumer, in what is now southern Iraq. Rich cultures also emerged along rivers in present-day India and China, strongly influencing the world ever since.

○ **CULTURE.** An Afghan woman wearing a traditional burka, a loose garment worn by women in some branches of Islam, sits with young girls in Kabul. In Afghanistan the burka is known as a chadri.

LUNAR NEW YEAR. Men carry a writhing paper dragon on poles in this Chinese New Year's parade in Singapore.

WINGED HUNTER. A Kazakh falconer sits astride his pony as he releases his golden eagle to pursue prey on the dry Asian steppe.

TOURISM. One of the world's most popular hot air ballooning destinations is in Cappadocia, Turkey. Riders soar through valleys and above volcanic formations in Göreme National Park.

THE CONTINENT:
ASIA

more about
Asia

◔ **EASTERN BELIEF.** From its origins in the foothills of the Himalaya, Buddhism has spread across much of eastern Asia. Statues of the Buddha, such as this one in Bangkok, Thailand, are an important part of the region's cultural landscape.

◔ **RECREATION.** Rich in oil and natural gas, Qatar has developed areas with grassy fields and trails for recreation. With the skyline of Doha behind her, this woman runs along the Corniche, a popular trail that follows the Persian Gulf coast.

◔ **FINAL TOUCH.** A silk kimono and makeup identify a maiko, or apprentice geisha, in Kyoto, Japan. Geishas are entertainers who perform traditional Japanese songs and dances.

STONE BARRIER. Built as a defense against invaders in the northeastern part of China, the Great Wall's construction started in 220 B.C.E.

WHERE THE PICTURES ARE

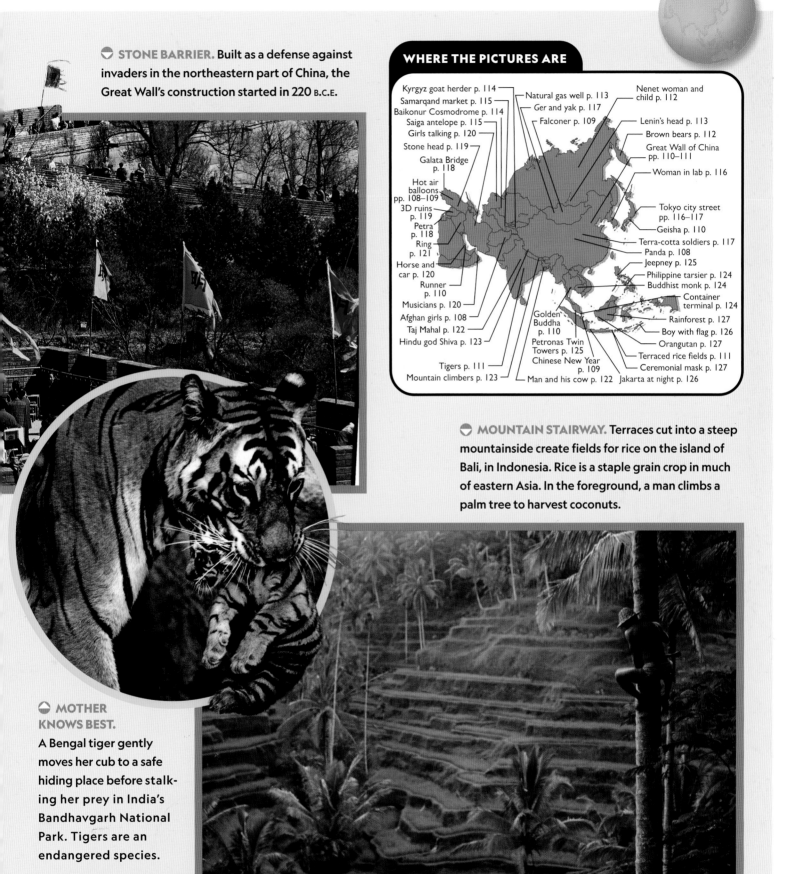

Kyrgyz goat herder p. 114
Samarqand market p. 115
Baikonur Cosmodrome p. 114
Saiga antelope p. 115
Girls talking p. 120
Stone head p. 119
Galata Bridge p. 118
Hot air balloons pp. 108–109
3D ruins p. 119
Petra p. 118
Ring p. 121
Horse and car p. 120
Runner p. 110
Musicians p. 120
Afghan girls p. 108
Taj Mahal p. 122
Hindu god Shiva p. 123
Tigers p. 111
Mountain climbers p. 123

Natural gas well p. 113
Ger and yak p. 117
Falconer p. 109

Nenet woman and child p. 112
Lenin's head p. 113
Brown bears p. 112
Great Wall of China pp. 110–111
Woman in lab p. 116
Tokyo city street pp. 116–117
Geisha p. 110
Terra-cotta soldiers p. 117
Panda p. 108
Jeepney p. 125
Philippine tarsier p. 124
Buddhist monk p. 124
Container terminal p. 124
Rainforest p. 127
Boy with flag p. 126
Orangutan p. 127
Terraced rice fields p. 111
Ceremonial mask p. 127

Golden Buddha p. 110
Petronas Twin Towers p. 125
Chinese New Year p. 109
Man and his cow p. 122
Jakarta at night p. 126

MOUNTAIN STAIRWAY. Terraces cut into a steep mountainside create fields for rice on the island of Bali, in Indonesia. Rice is a staple grain crop in much of eastern Asia. In the foreground, a man climbs a palm tree to harvest coconuts.

MOTHER KNOWS BEST.
A Bengal tiger gently moves her cub to a safe hiding place before stalking her prey in India's Bandhavgarh National Park. Tigers are an endangered species.

THE BASICS

STATS

Area
6,601,665 sq mi
(17,098,234 sq km)

Population
144,478,000

Predominant language
Russian (official)

Predominant religions
Christianity, Islam

GDP per capita
$27,800

Life expectancy
71 years

*Note: These figures are for all of Russia. For European Russia, see pages 102–103.

GEO WHIZ

The name Siberia comes from the Turkic language and means "sleeping land."

It takes at least six days to travel 6,000 miles (9,656 km) on the Trans-Siberian Railway from Moscow to the Pacific port of Vladivostok. The trip crosses eight time zones.

Lake Baikal, nicknamed Siberia's "blue eye," is home to 1,500 unique species of plants and animals, including the nerpa, the world's only freshwater seal.

The Chukchi, the largest group of indigenous people in Siberia, take their name from a word meaning "rich in reindeer." They share their name with their homeland, a peninsula bordered by the Arctic and Pacific Oceans.

A region of northern coniferous forest called taiga stretches across northern Russia as far as Norway.

Asian Russia

◉ **NOMADIC HERDERS.** A Nenet woman and her grandson prepare to follow the family reindeer herd to northern Siberia for spring and summer grazing.

Forming more than half of Russia, this region stretches from the Ural Mountains east to the Pacific, and from the Arctic Ocean south to mountains and deserts along borders with Central Asia, Mongolia, China, and North Korea. Siberia, as this region is commonly known, has limited croplands but bountiful forests (the taiga) and rich mineral resources such as oil, natural gas, and gold. The Trans-Siberian Railway, built between 1891 and 1905, opened up the region for settlement, but not too much. Fewer than 33 million people—23 percent of Russia's population—live in sprawling Siberia.

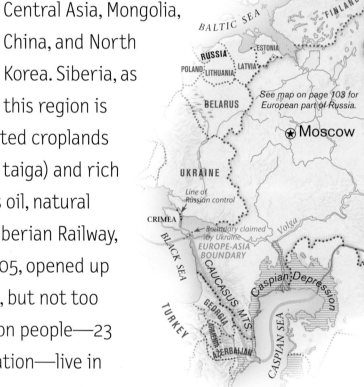

See map on page 103 for European part of Russia.

◗ **FISHING FOR A MEAL.**
A brown bear and her cubs hunt for fish in a river below the slopes of a volcano on Russia's Kamchatka Peninsula. Part of the Pacific Ring of Fire, this peninsula has 29 active volcanoes.

REVOLUTIONARY LEADER. Vladimir Ilyich Lenin, a founder of the Soviet Union, was honored with many statues. This one in Siberia is the largest still standing in Russia.

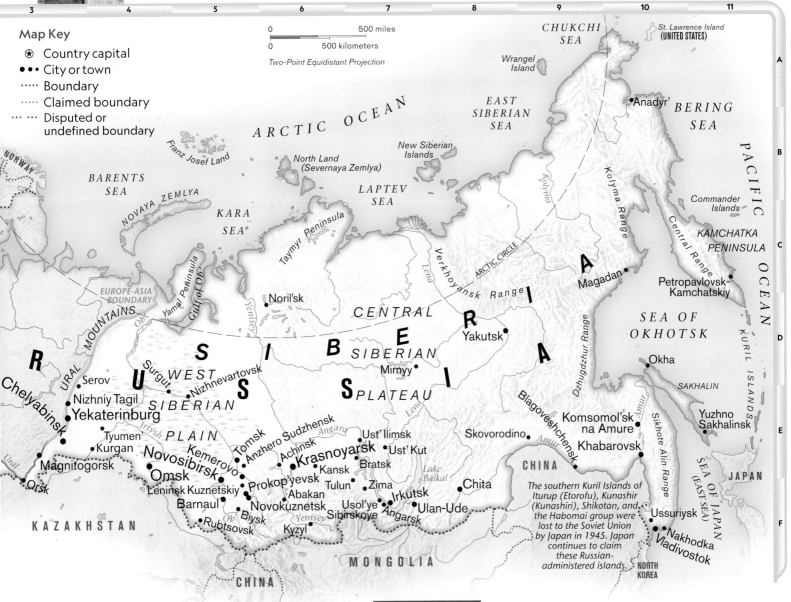

Map Key

- ⊛ Country capital
- ••• City or town
- ····· Boundary
- ····· Claimed boundary
- ····· Disputed or undefined boundary

0 — 500 miles
0 — 500 kilometers
Two-Point Equidistant Projection

NORWAY

ARCTIC OCEAN

BARENTS SEA

NOVAYA ZEMLYA

Franz Josef Land

North Land (Severnaya Zemlya)

New Siberian Islands

LAPTEV SEA

KARA SEA

EAST SIBERIAN SEA

Wrangel Island

CHUKCHI SEA

St. Lawrence Island (UNITED STATES)

•Anadyr'

BERING SEA

Commander Islands

KAMCHATKA PENINSULA

PACIFIC OCEAN

Yamal Peninsula

Gulf of Ob

Taymyr Peninsula

EUROPE-ASIA BOUNDARY

Ob

Yenisey

•Noril'sk

CENTRAL

Lena

Verkhoyansk Range

ARCTIC CIRCLE

Kolyma

Kolyma Range

Central Range

Magadan•

Petropavlovsk-Kamchatskiy•

URAL MOUNTAINS

•Serov

Surgut

SIBERIAN

BEGIN

•Nizhnevartovsk

WEST

SIBERIAN

Yakutsk•

SIBERIAN

Mirnyy•

PLATEAU

Dzhugdzhur Range

SEA OF OKHOTSK

•Okha

SAKHALIN

KURIL ISLANDS

Chelyabinsk

•Nizhniy Tagil

Yekaterinburg

Tyumen•

•Kurgan

Irtysh

PLAIN

Tomsk•

Anzhero Sudzhensk•

Achinsk•

Ust'Ilimsk•

Angara

Ust' Kut•

Skovorodino•

Blagoveshchensk•

Amur

Komsomol'sk na Amure•

Khabarovsk•

Sikhote Alin Range

Yuzhno Sakhalinsk

Magnitogorsk•

Novosibirsk

Kemerovo•

Krasnoyarsk

Bratsk•

Lake Baikal

CHINA

Amur

JAPAN

Orsk•

Omsk

•Kansk

Lena

SEA OF JAPAN (EAST SEA)

Ural

•Leninsk Kuznetskiy

Prokop'yevsk•

Tulun•

Zima•

Irkutsk•

Chita•

Ussuriysk•

Barnaul

Abakan•

Usol'ye•

Angarsk•

Ulan-Ude•

Nakhodka•

KAZAKHSTAN

Novokuznetsk•

Biysk•

Ob

Sibirskoye•

Yenisey

The southern Kuril Islands of Iturup (Etorofu), Kunashir (Kunashiri), Shikotan, and the Habomai group were lost to the Soviet Union by Japan in 1945. Japan continues to claim these Russian-administered islands.

Vladivostok•

•Rubtsovsk

Kyzyl•

MONGOLIA

CHINA

NORTH KOREA

DEEPEST LAKE

Lake Baikal	Lake Tanganyika	Caspian Sea	Lake Malawi	Ysyk-Köl	Great Slave Lake	Crater Lake
5,369 ft (1,637 m)	4,708 ft (1,435 m)	3,104 ft (946 m)	2,316 ft (706 m)	2,297 ft (700 m)	2,015 ft (614 m)	1,943 ft (592 m)

Most of Earth's freshwater surface water is stored in lakes. The deepest of all is Lake Baikal, which contains about 20 percent of Earth's total surface freshwater.

COLD POWER. A liquefied natural gas well on the Yamal Peninsula in northwestern Siberia taps into Russia's largest gas reserves. Bitterly cold Arctic winters are a major challenge to this project.

THE CONTINENT:
ASIA

Central Asia

Located along the historic Silk Road, Central Asia is made up of five former republics of the Soviet Union, often referred to as the stans, or "homelands." This region's population includes Kazakhs, Turkmen, Uzbeks, Tajiks, Kyrgyz, and Russians. The population is largely Muslim. Kazakhstan's short-grass steppes give way to deserts, arid plateaus, and rugged mountains to the south. The Amu Darya and the Syr Darya provide water for irrigating wheat, rice, cotton, and fruit crops. Although this landlocked region lies far from any ocean, it includes several large bodies of water, including the Caspian Sea, which is actually a saltwater lake.

⬤ **BEST FRIENDS.** A boy carries his goat in mountainous Kyrgyzstan, where almost half the land is used for pasture and hay to support herds of goats and sheep.

THE BASICS

STATS

Largest country
Kazakhstan 1,052,089 sq mi
(2,724,900 sq km)

Smallest country
Tajikistan 55,637 sq mi
(144,100 sq km)

Most populous country
Uzbekistan 30,024,000

Least populous country
Turkmenistan 5,411,000

Predominant languages
Russian, Kazakh, Uzbek,
Kyrgyz, Tajik, Turkmen

Predominant religions
Islam, Christianity

Highest GDP per capita
Kazakhstan $26,300

Lowest GDP per capita
Tajikistan $3,200

Highest life expectancy
Uzbekistan 74 years

Lowest life expectancy
Tajikistan 68 years

GEO WHIZ

The main musical instrument of the steppes in Kazakhstan is the dombra, a long-necked lute with two strings.

Uzbekistan, one of the world's top gold-producing countries, has the world's deepest open-pit gold mine. Muruntau Mine is said to hold more gold reserves than any other mine in the world.

Mountains, including the ranges Pamir and Tian Shan, cover more than 90 percent of Tajikistan.

◖ **INTO SPACE.**
Baikonur Cosmodrome, located east of the Aral Sea in Kazakhstan, has been the launch site for Russian space missions since Sputnik 1 in 1957. U.S. astronauts have taken off from here to the International Space Station.

◖ **CRITICALLY ENDANGERED.** Loss of habitat, illegal hunting, and disease have put the saiga antelope, found mainly in Kazakhstan, at risk.

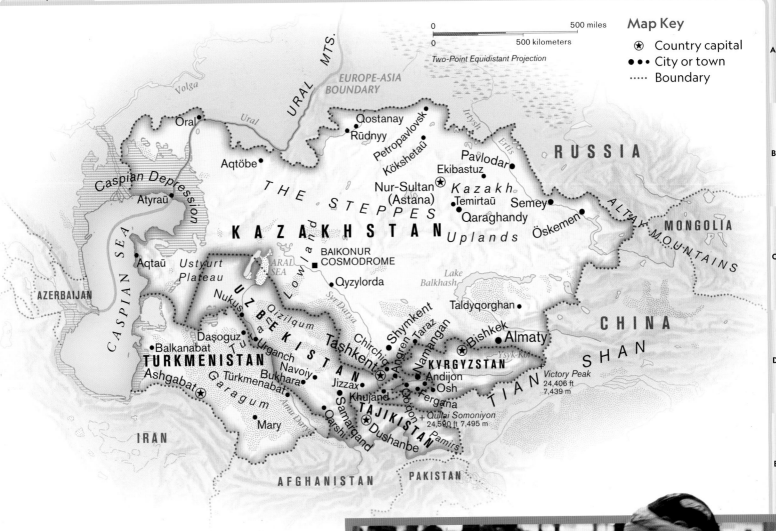

Map Key

⊛ Country capital
••• City or town
······ Boundary

500 miles
500 kilometers
Two-Point Equidistant Projection

◖ **WHERE BARGAINING IS AN ART.** Two men bargain over the price of cherries in a bazaar in Samarqand, Uzbekistan. Located on the fabled Silk Road, the country relies on agriculture, especially cotton production, to support its economy.

VANISHING SEA

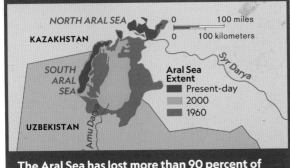

NORTH ARAL SEA
KAZAKHSTAN
SOUTH ARAL SEA
UZBEKISTAN

Syr Darya
Amu Darya

0   100 miles
0   100 kilometers

Aral Sea Extent
■ Present-day
■ 2000
■ 1960

The Aral Sea has lost more than 90 percent of its area because water from feeder rivers is being used to irrigate millions of acres of cotton and rice.

**THE CONTINENT:
ASIA**

THE BASICS

STATS

Largest country
China 3,705,405 sq mi
(9,596,960 sq km)

Smallest country
South Korea
38,502 sq mi (99,720 sq km)

Most populous country
China 1,384,689,000

Least populous country
Mongolia 3,103,000

Predominant languages
Standard Chinese (Mandarin),
Japanese, Korean, Mongol

Predominant religions
Daoism, Buddhism, Shintoism,
Christianity, Confucianism

Highest GDP per capita
Japan $42,800

Lowest GDP per capita
North Korea $1,700

Highest life expectancy
Japan 85 years

Lowest life expectancy
Mongolia
70 years

GEO WHIZ

The only surviving breed of
wild horse, the Przewalski, is
named for the count who
"discovered" it in Mongolia in
the 1880s. Careful breeding
has saved it from extinction.
About 2,000 remain.

Each year on October 9, people
in South Korea celebrate their
alphabet, which was created
in 1446 to increase literacy.

Eastern Asia

China, Mongolia, the Koreas, and Japan make up eastern Asia. Rich river valleys have supported Chinese civilization for more than four millennia. The Tibetan Plateau, dry basins, and the towering Himalaya border China to the west. Mongolia, the land of Genghis Khan, lies to China's north. Japan and South Korea have used technology and manufacturing to become economic powerhouses. While China has opened to global markets, North Korea has remained a communist government that leans toward isolation. North Korea's isolation creates a lack of economic opportunity, and its people remain poor.

HIGH TECH. This South Korean woman works in a laboratory that makes microcircuits in a semi-conductor plant in Seoul.

NIGHTLIGHTS. Tokyo's Shinjuku is both a shopping center and a theater district, as well as the city's busiest train station. It averages more than 3.6 million passengers daily.

AUTO GIANTS

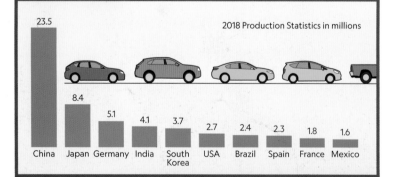

2018 Production Statistics in millions

China	Japan	Germany	India	South Korea	USA	Brazil	Spain	France	Mexico
23.5	8.4	5.1	4.1	3.7	2.7	2.4	2.3	1.8	1.6

Once the leader in car production, the United States now ranks sixth. Holding first place, China's production is almost triple that of second-ranked Japan.

THE CONTINENT:
ASIA

◖ **HOME ON THE STEPPE.** A *ger* is the traditional Mongolian dwelling. The cowlike yak works as a pack animal and is a source of milk.

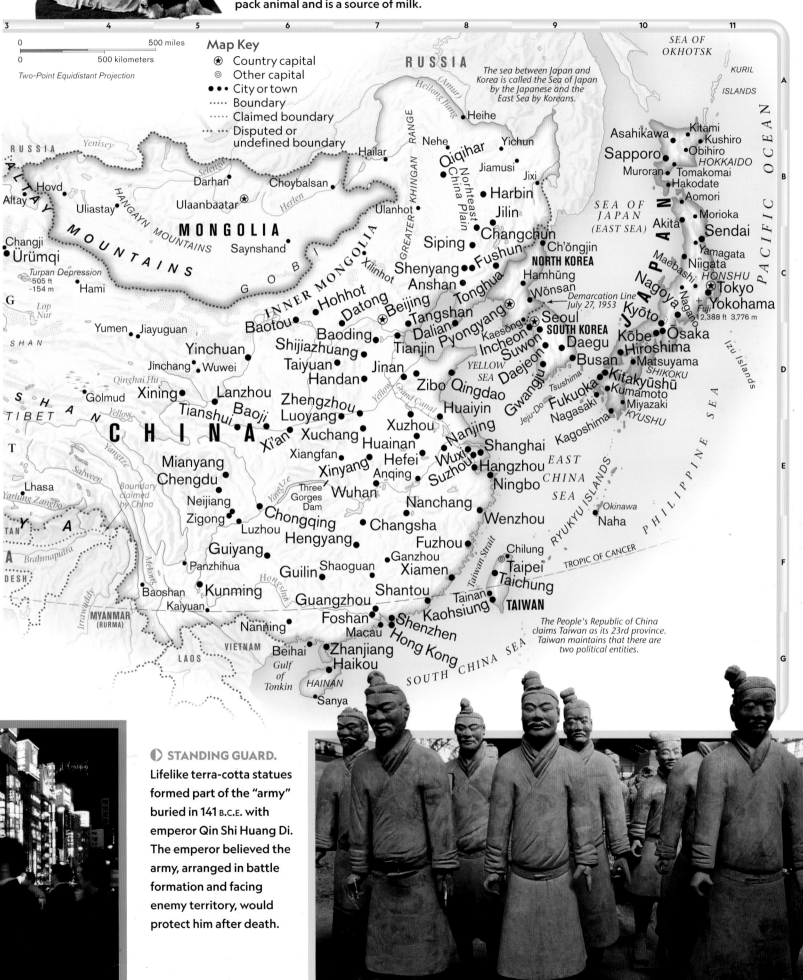

0   500 miles
0   500 kilometers
Two-Point Equidistant Projection

Map Key
★ Country capital
◎ Other capital
• • • City or town
····· Boundary
––––· Claimed boundary
–··–· Disputed or undefined boundary

The sea between Japan and Korea is called the Sea of Japan by the Japanese and the East Sea by Koreans.

The People's Republic of China claims Taiwan as its 23rd province. Taiwan maintains that there are two political entities.

RUSSIA

SEA OF OKHOTSK

KURIL ISLANDS

PACIFIC OCEAN

Heilong Jiang (Amur)

ALTAY
Hovd
Altay
Yenisey
RUSSIA
Uliastay
Darhan
Choybalsan
Ulaanbaatar
Hangayn Mountains
Selenga
Herlen
MONGOLIA
Saynshand
GOBI
GREATER KHINGAN RANGE
Hailar
Nehe
Qiqihar
Heihe
Yichun
Jiamusi
Jixi
Northeast China Plain
Harbin
Jilin
Ulanhot
Changchun
Siping
Fushun
Shenyang
Anshan
Tonghua
Hamhŭng
Ch'ŏngjin
NORTH KOREA
Wŏnsan
Demarcation Line July 27, 1953
Pyongyang
Kaesŏng
Seoul
Incheon
SOUTH KOREA
Suwon
Daejeon
Daegu
Gwangju
Jeju-Do
Tsushima

Changji
Ürümqi
Turpan Depression –505 ft –154 m
Hami
G
SHAN
Lop Nur
Yumen
Jiayuguan
Hohhot
Baotou
Datong
Beijing
Tangshan
Baoding
Dalian
Tianjin
INNER MONGOLIA
Xilinhot
Yinchuan
Jinchang
Wuwei
Shijiazhuang
Taiyuan
Handan
Jinan
Zibo
Qingdao
YELLOW SEA
Golmud
Qinghai Hu
Xining
Lanzhou
Zhengzhou
Luoyang
Grand Canal
Yellow
Huaiyin
TIBET
Tianshui
Baoji
CHINA
Xi'an
Xuchang
Xuzhou
SHAN
Yangtze
Lhasa
Yarlung Zangbo
Mianyang
Chengdu
Xiangfan
Xinyang
Huainan
Hefei
Nanjing
Wuxi
Shanghai
Suzhou
Hangzhou
Ningbo
HIMALAYA
Boundary claimed by China
TAN
Brahmaputra
DESH
Neijiang
Zigong
Three Gorges Dam
Wuhan
Nanchang
Wenzhou
EAST CHINA SEA
Chongqing
Luzhou
Changsha
Hengyang
Mekong
Fuzhou
Hongshui
Guiyang
Panzhihua
Guilin
Shaoguan
Ganzhou
Xiamen
Chilung
Taipei
Taichung
RYUKYU ISLANDS
Okinawa
Naha
TROPIC OF CANCER
Baoshan
Kunming
Kaiyuan
Guangzhou
Shantou
Tainan
Kaohsiung
TAIWAN
Taiwan Strait
MYANMAR (BURMA)
Irrawaddy
Nanning
Foshan
Shenzhen
Macau
Hong Kong
SOUTH CHINA SEA
VIETNAM
LAOS
Beihai
Zhanjiang
Haikou
Gulf of Tonkin
HAINAN
Sanya

JAPAN
Asahikawa
Kitami
Kushiro
Sapporo
Obihiro
HOKKAIDO
Muroran
Tomakomai
Hakodate
Aomori
SEA OF JAPAN (EAST SEA)
Akita
Morioka
Yamagata
Sendai
Maebashi
Niigata
HONSHU
Nagoya
Nagano
Tokyo
Kyōto
Yokohama
Fuji 12,388 ft 3,776 m
Kōbe
Ōsaka
Hiroshima
Matsuyama
Busan
SHIKOKU
Fukuoka
Kitakyūshū
Kumamoto
Nagasaki
Miyazaki
KYUSHU
Kagoshima
Izu Islands
PHILIPPINE SEA

◖ **STANDING GUARD.**
Lifelike terra-cotta statues formed part of the "army" buried in 141 B.C.E. with emperor Qin Shi Huang Di. The emperor believed the army, arranged in battle formation and facing enemy territory, would protect him after death.

THE CONTINENT:
ASIA

Eastern Mediterranean

1

THE BASICS

STATS

Largest country
Turkey
302,535 sq mi (783,562 sq km)

Smallest country
Lebanon
4,015 sq mi (10,400 sq km)

Most populous country
Turkey 81,257,000

Least populous country
Armenia 3,038,000

Predominant languages
Turkish, Arabic, Azerbaijani, Hebrew, Georgian, Armenian, English, French, Kurdish

Predominant religions
Islam, Judaism, Christianity

Highest GDP per capita
Israel $36,300

Lowest GDP per capita
Syria $2,900

Highest life expectancy
Israel 82 years

Lowest life expectancy
Azerbaijan 73 years

GEO WHIZ

Some English and Spanish words have origins in Arabic, such as algebra, coffee, and hasta (until).

Israelis capture runoff from seasonal rains to support crops in the Negev, a desert region that extends across more than half their country.

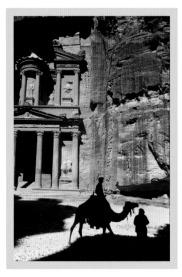

⬤ **ANCIENT MYSTERY.**
A camel walks past Al-Khazneh in Petra, a World Heritage site in Jordan. Carved out of a mountainside more than 2,500 years ago, Petra was the capital of the Nabateans.

This region forms a bridge between Europe and Asia, from the Caucasus Mountains to the desert lands of Jordan. Turkey, framed by the Black, Aegean, and Mediterranean Seas, leads the region in population and area. The historic and life-giving Tigris and Euphrates Rivers begin in Turkey and flow southeast through arid Syria and Iraq. Israel, Lebanon, Syria, and Turkey share the Mediterranean shore. While Islam claims the majority of followers across these lands, Judaism, Christianity, and other faiths are present. Many of the holiest sites for Christians, Jews, and Muslims are found in this region.

BULGARIA
Edirne
GREECE
Tekirdağ
Dardanelles
AEGEAN SEA
İzmir
Aydın
DODECANESE

BELOW SEA LEVEL

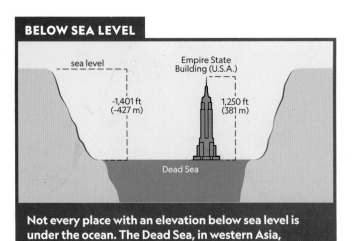

sea level

Empire State Building (U.S.A.)

-1,401 ft
(-427 m)

1,250 ft
(381 m)

Dead Sea

Not every place with an elevation below sea level is under the ocean. The Dead Sea, in western Asia, plunges to -1,401 feet (-427 m) below sea level. That's deeper than the Empire State Building is tall.

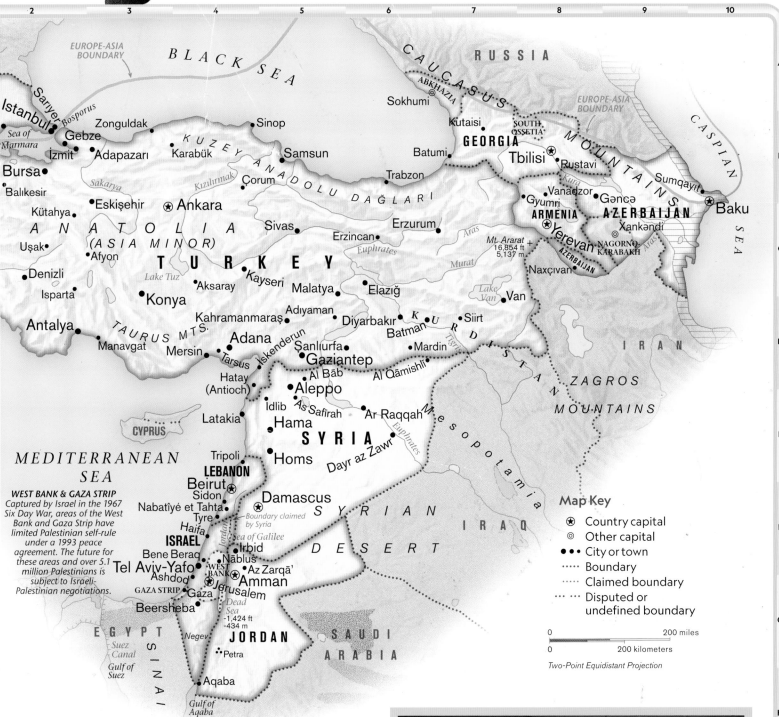

◗ **WATCHERS FROM THE PAST.** Giant stone heads, representing Greek gods, guard the first-century B.C.E. burial site of King Antiochus I in southeastern Turkey.

EUROPE-ASIA BOUNDARY

BLACK SEA

CAUCASUS

RUSSIA

EUROPE-ASIA BOUNDARY

Sariyer
Istanbul
Bosporus
Sea of Marmara
Gebze
İzmit
Bursa
Balıkesir
Zonguldak
Adapazarı
Karabük
Sinop
Samsun
Çorum
Sokhumi
ABKHAZIA
Kutaisi
Batumi
SOUTH OSSETIA
GEORGIA
Trabzon
Tbilisi
Rustavi
Sumqayıt
CASPIAN SEA

Sakarya
Kızılırmak
KUZEY ANADOLU DAĞLARI

Kütahya
Eskişehir
Ankara
Sivas
Erzincan
Erzurum
Vanadzor
Gyumri
Gəncə
ARMENIA
AZERBAIJAN
Baku
Xankəndi

Uşak
ANATOLIA
(ASIA MINOR)
TURKEY
Aras
Mt. Ararat
16,854 ft
5,137 m
Yerevan
NAGORNO-
KARABAKH
AZERBAIJAN

Afyon
Lake Tuz
Aksaray
Kayseri
Malatya
Elazığ
Murat
Lake Van
Van
Naxçıvan

Denizli
Isparta
Konya
Adıyaman
Kahramanmaraş
Diyarbakır
Siirt
IRAN

Antalya
Manavgat
TAURUS MTS.
Adana
İskenderun
Şanlıurfa
Batman
Mardin
K U R D I S T A N
ZAGROS MOUNTAINS

Mersin
Tarsus
Gaziantep
Al Qāmishli
Tigris

Hatay
(Antioch)
Al Bāb
Aleppo

Latakia
CYPRUS
Idlib
As Safirah
Ar Raqqah
Mesopotamia

MEDITERRANEAN SEA
Hama
SYRIA
Euphrates

Tripoli
Homs
Dayr az Zawr

WEST BANK & GAZA STRIP
Captured by Israel in the 1967 Six Day War, areas of the West Bank and Gaza Strip have limited Palestinian self-rule under a 1993 peace agreement. The future for these areas and over 5.1 million Palestinians is subject to Israeli-Palestinian negotiations.

LEBANON
Beirut
Sidon
Nabatîyé et Tahta
Tyre
Haifa
Damascus
SYRIAN DESERT
IRAQ

Boundary claimed by Syria
Sea of Galilee
ISRAEL
Bene Beraq
Irbid
Nāblus
Tel Aviv-Yafo
WEST BANK
Az Zarqā'
Ashdod
Jerusalem
Amman
GAZA STRIP
Gaza
Beersheba
Dead Sea
-1,424 ft
-434 m

EGYPT
Negev
JORDAN
SAUDI ARABIA
Suez Canal
Gulf of Suez
Petra
SINAI
Aqaba
Gulf of Aqaba

Map Key

✴ Country capital
◎ Other capital
••• City or town
····· Boundary
····· Claimed boundary
···· Disputed or undefined boundary

0 ——— 200 miles
0 ——— 200 kilometers

Two-Point Equidistant Projection

◗ **BETWEEN TWO WORLDS.** The Galata Bridge crosses the Golden Horn, connecting the Asian part of Istanbul, Turkey (foreground), to the Galata area in the city's European part.

◗ **AN INSIDE LOOK.** Visitors to the Bonn Bundeskunsthalle in Bonn, Germany, can experience 3D views of the ruins of Mosul, Iraq, and the Syrian cities Aleppo and Palmyra. The three cities sustained significant destruction during the Syrian civil war that began in March 2011.

Southwestern Asia

THE BASICS

STATS

Largest country
Saudi Arabia 830,000 sq mi
(2,149,690 sq km)

Smallest country
Bahrain 293 sq mi (760 sq km)

Most populous country
Iran 83,025,000

Least populous country
Bahrain 1,443,000

Predominant languages
Arabic, Persian (Farsi),
Kurdish

Predominant religion
Islam

Highest GDP per capita
Qatar $124,500

Lowest GDP per capita
Yemen $1,300

Highest life expectancy
Bahrain, Qatar 79 years

Lowest life expectancy
Yemen 66 years

GEO WHIZ

The Rub' al Khali, or Empty
Quarter, is the world's largest
sand desert. It covers an area
larger than France.

More than 4,000 years ago, the
Sumerians built the world's first
cities on the plain between the
Tigris and Euphrates Rivers in
what is now Iraq.

The ancient Romans called
Yemen "Arabia Felix," meaning
"Happy Land," as it was the
most fertile part of the region.

⬤ **GIRL TALK.** Young
Iranian girls get together
at a film festival in Tehran.
They are wearing hijabs,
a head covering worn by
many Muslim women.

This region, made up largely of deserts and mountains, includes the countries of the Arabian Peninsula and those that border the Persian Gulf. Islam is the dominant religion, and the two holiest places for Muslims—Mecca and Medina—are here. Arabic is the main language everywhere but Iran, where most people speak Persian (Farsi). While water has been the most important natural resource here for millennia, global attention has focused in recent decades on the region's extensive oil reserves. Ongoing conflict and political tensions also have kept this region in headlines around the world.

⬤ **THEY'VE GOT THE BEAT.**
Omani musicians play for a tribal
dance in Muscat, Oman, preserv-
ing their heritage through music.

WORLD OIL RESERVES

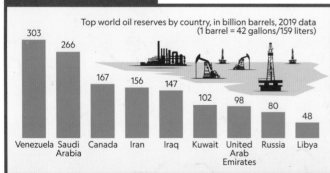

Top world oil reserves by country, in billion barrels, 2019 data
(1 barrel = 42 gallons/159 liters)

Venezuela	Saudi Arabia	Canada	Iran	Iraq	Kuwait	United Arab Emirates	Russia	Libya
303	266	167	156	147	102	98	80	48

Saudi Arabia, second in oil reserves, and four other
southwestern Asia countries account for almost
46 percent of all oil production.

⬤ **MERGING WORLDS.** This roadside meeting in Qatar highlights
the transportation options and heritage of southwestern Asia. The oil
industry and horse breeding support economic growth in the region.

◑ **LOST AND FOUND.** Ancient treasures were destroyed, lost, or stolen during the 2003 invasion of Iraq. This ring is among the few items recovered.

1 2 3 4 5 6 7 8

BLACK SEA

GEORGIA

TURKEY

ARMENIA

AZERBAIJAN

CASPIAN SEA

TURKMENISTAN

Orūmīyeh
Marand
Tabrīz
Ardabīl

KURDISTAN
Zakho
Miāndoāb
Urmia
Rasht
Gorgān
Bojnūrd
Gondad-e Kāvūs
Mashhad

Tall 'Afar
Dihok
Nineveh
Zanjān
Sārī
Semnān
Sabzevār

MEDITERRANEAN SEA

Mosul
Erbil
As
Qazvīn
Elburz Mts.
KHORĀSĀN

SYRIA
Kirkuk
Sulaymānīyah
Tehran ⊛
Kūh-e Damāvand 18,602 ft 5,670 m
Gonābad

LEBANON
Tikrīt
Sanandaj
Kermānshāh
Hamadān
Dasht-e Kavīr (Kavir Desert)

ISRAEL
Sāmarrā
Qom
Bīrjand

JORDAN
Turaybīl
Ar Ramādī
Baghdad
Arāk
IRAN

IRAQ
Al Fallūjah
Karbalā
Dezfūl
Isfahan
Qomsheh
Dasht-e Lūt
Zābol

SYRIAN DESERT
Al Hillah
Al 'Amārah
Ahvāz
Yazd
Noṣratābād

Al Qurayyāt
An Najaf
Nippur
Persepolis
Kermān
Zāhedān

'Ar'ar
Ur
An Nāṣirīyah
Al Baṣrah
Ābādān
Shīrāz
Marv Dasht
Sa'īdābād
Bam

EGYPT
Sakākā
Az Zubayr
KUWAIT
Būshehr
Jahrom
Fasā
Tārom
Īrānshahr

Al Jawf
Gulf of Aqaba
Tabūk
Kuwait City ⊛
Bandar 'Abbās
Strait of Hormuz
Angohrān
BALUCHISTAN

An Nafūd
Ḥā'il
Al Jubayl
Qeshm
Chāh Bāhar

AL HIJĀZ
Buraydah
Ad Dammām
BAHRAIN
Ra's al-Khaimah
OMAN

SAUDI ARABIA
Manama ⊛
Al Mubarraz
Sharjah
Suḥār

Medina
Riyadh ⊛
Al Hufūf
Doha ⊛
Dubai

RED SEA
Al Hillah
Abu Dhabi ⊛
Al Ain
Muscat ⊛
Qurayyāt

UNITED ARAB EMIRATES
'Ibrī
Nizwā
Sūr

Jeddah
Aṭ Ṭā'if
ARABIAN PENINSULA
Al Ḥadīdah (meteorite craters)
Khalūf
Masira

Mecca
Qal'at Bīshah
Jabal Ṭuwayq
Rub' al Khali (Empty Quarter)
Duqm

SUDAN
Al Qunfudhah
OMAN

Abā as Sa'ūd
ẒUFĀR
ARABIAN SEA

Jīzān
Mirbāṭ

ERITREA
Nishtūn
Ḥawf
Ṣalālah

Sanaa ⊛
YEMEN
Ḥaḍramawt

Al Hudaydah
Dhamār
Ridā
Ash Shiḥr

Ibb
Al Mukallā

ETHIOPIA
Ta'izz
Lahij
Socotra (Yemen)

DJIBOUTI
Aden
GULF OF ADEN

SOMALIA

Historically and most commonly known as the Persian Gulf, this body of water is referred to by some as the Arabian Gulf.

PERSIAN GULF

GULF OF OMAN

TROPIC OF CANCER

Map Key
⊛ Country capital
••• City or town
····· Boundary

0 ————— 300 miles
0 ————— 300 kilometers

Two-Point Equidistant Projection

THE CONTINENT:
ASIA

Southern Asia

THE BASICS

STATS

Largest country
India 1,269,219 sq mi
(3,287,263 sq km)

Smallest country
Maldives 115 sq mi (298 sq km)

Most populous country
India 1,296,834,000

Least populous country
Maldives 392,000

Predominant languages
Hindi, English, Punjabi,
Bangla, Dari, Burmese,
Pashto, Urdu, Sinhala,
Nepali, Dzongkha

Predominant religions
Hinduism, Islam, Buddhism

Highest GDP per capita
Maldives $19,100

Lowest GDP per capita
Afghanistan $2,000

Highest life expectancy
Sri Lanka 77 years

Lowest life expectancy
Afghanistan 52 years

GEO WHIZ

India's rail system transports
8.4 billion passengers each
year across nearly 41,890
miles (67,415 km) of track.

Bhutan, a Himalayan country
known as Land of the Thunder Dragon, is the world's
only Buddhist kingdom.

🔵 **TAJ MAHAL.** In 1631 in Agra, India,
the Mughal emperor Shah Jahan began
construction of this magnificent marble
memorial to his deceased wife.

This region is home to the world's highest peaks. Three of the world's famous rivers—the Indus, Ganges, and Brahmaputra—support the hundreds of millions of people who live here. India is at the center, greater in area than the other countries combined and more than double their population. Hinduism and Buddhism originated in India where Hinduism continues to be the main religion. There are large numbers of Buddhists in Bhutan, Nepal, Sri Lanka, and Myanmar, and Muslims form the majority in Afghanistan, Pakistan, and Bangladesh. Poverty and prosperity live side by side across the region, with streams of migrants flowing from rural areas to mushrooming cities.

🔵 **GOLDEN GRAIN.**
A man leads his cow
past a rice field
south of Rangpur,
Bangladesh. Rice
is the staple food
for 159 million
Bangladeshis
and provides
employment
for a lot of the
rural population.

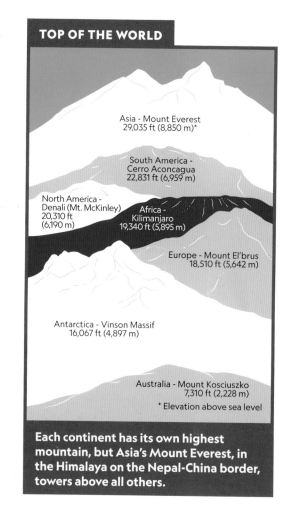

TOP OF THE WORLD

Asia - Mount Everest
29,035 ft (8,850 m)*

South America -
Cerro Aconcagua
22,831 ft (6,959 m)

North America -
Denali (Mt. McKinley)
20,310 ft
(6,190 m)

Africa -
Kilimanjaro
19,340 ft (5,895 m)

Europe - Mount El'brus
18,510 ft (5,642 m)

Antarctica - Vinson Massif
16,067 ft (4,897 m)

Australia - Mount Kosciuszko
7,310 ft (2,228 m)

* Elevation above sea level

Each continent has its own highest
mountain, but Asia's Mount Everest, in
the Himalaya on the Nepal-China border,
towers above all others.

◖ **EASTERN BELIEF.** The god Shiva (left) is part of the Hindu trinity, which also includes the gods Brahma and Vishnu. Hinduism is the world's third largest religion (after Christianity and Islam), with more than a billion followers.

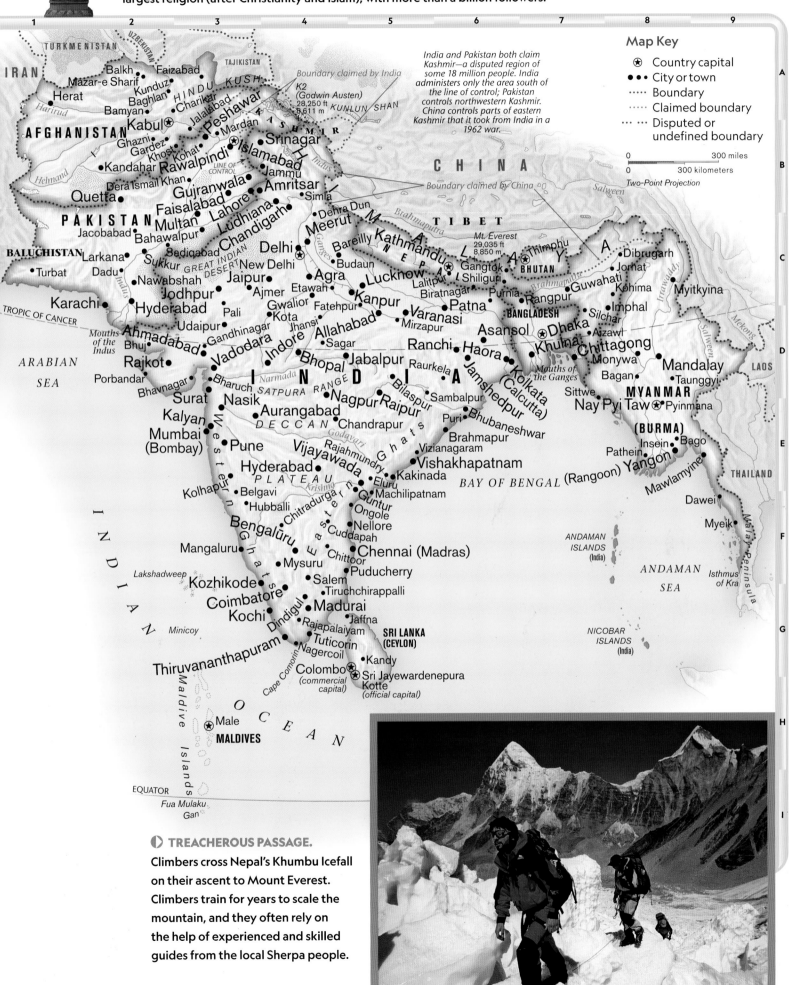

India and Pakistan both claim Kashmir—a disputed region of some 18 million people. India administers only the area south of the line of control; Pakistan controls northwestern Kashmir. China controls parts of eastern Kashmir that it took from India in a 1962 war.

Map Key

⬠ Country capital
••• City or town
····· Boundary
----- Claimed boundary
······ Disputed or undefined boundary

0 _____ 300 miles
0 _____ 300 kilometers
Two-Point Projection

TURKMENISTAN
UZBEKISTAN
IRAN
TAJIKISTAN
Balkh • Faizabad
Mazar-e Sharif • Kunduz
Herat • Baghlan • Charikar
Bamyan • HINDU KUSH
Kabul ⬠ • Jalalabad
Ghazni • Mardan • Peshawar
AFGHANISTAN
Gardez • Kohat • Rawalpindi • Islamabad
Kandahar • Khost • LINE OF CONTROL
Quetta • Dera Ismail Khan • Jammu
Gujranwala • Amritsar • Simla
PAKISTAN • Faisalabad • Lahore • Ludhiana
Multan • Chandigarh
Jacobabad • Bahawalpur
BALUCHISTAN • Larkana • Sadiqabad
Turbat • Dadu • Sukkur • Nawabshah
Karachi • Hyderabad
Mouths of the Indus
TROPIC OF CANCER
ARABIAN SEA
Porbandar • Bhavnagar
Rajkot • Bhuj
Ahmadabad • Gandhinagar
Surat • Bharuch
Kalyan • Nasik
Mumbai (Bombay) • Pune
Hyderabad
Kolhapur • Belgavi
Mangaluru • Hubballi
Bengaluru
Kozhikode
Lakshadweep
Coimbatore
Kochi
Thiruvananthapuram
Minicoy
INDIAN
Maldive Islands
Male ⬠
MALDIVES
EQUATOR
Fua Mulaku
Gan
OCEAN

K2 (Godwin Austen) 28,250 ft 8,611 m
Boundary claimed by India
KUNLUN SHAN
KASHMIR
Srinagar
KARAKORAM
Dehra Dun
Meerut
Delhi • Bareilly
New Delhi ⬠ • Budaun
Jaipur • Agra • Etawah
Ajmer • Gwalior • Fatehpur
Jodhpur • Kota • Jhansi
GREAT INDIAN DESERT
Udaipur • Pali
Indore • Sagar
Vadodara • Bhopal
Narmada
SATPURA RANGE
Jabalpur
Nagpur • Raipur
Aurangabad • Chandrapur
DECCAN • Godavari
PLATEAU
Vijayawada
Chitradurga • Guntur
Hubballi • Ongole
Mysuru • Chittoor • Nellore
Eastern Ghats
Salem • Cuddapah
Dindigul • Tiruchirappalli
Madurai • Jaffna
Rajapalaiyam
Tuticorin • Kandy
Nagercoil • SRI LANKA (CEYLON)
Cape Comorin
Colombo (commercial capital) ⬠ • Sri Jayewardenepura Kotte (official capital)

CHINA
Boundary claimed by China
TIBET
Brahmaputra
HIMALAYA
Mt. Everest 29,035 ft 8,850 m
Kathmandu ⬠ • Thimphu ⬠
NEPAL • Gangtok • BHUTAN
Lucknow • Shiliguri
Lalitpur • Biratnagar
Kanpur • Patna • Purnia
Varanasi • Rangpur
Allahabad • Mirzapur
Asansol • Dhaka ⬠
Ranchi • Haora • BANGLADESH
Jamshedpur • Khulna
Kolkata (Calcutta) • Chittagong
Bilaspur • Sambalpur
Raurkela • Mouths of the Ganges
Brahmapur • Bhubaneshwar
Puri • Sittwe
Vizianagaram
Vishakhapatnam
Kakinada
Machilipatnam
BAY OF BENGAL

Dibrugarh • Jorhat
Guwahati • Kohima
Silchar • Imphal
Aizawl
Monywa • Myitkyina
Bagan • Mandalay
Taunggyi
Nay Pyi Taw ⬠ • Pyinmana
(BURMA)
Insein • Bago
Pathein • Yangon (Rangoon)
MYANMAR
Mawlamyine
Dawei
Myeik
Salween
Irrawaddy
Mekong
LAOS
THAILAND
Malay Peninsula
Isthmus of Kra

ANDAMAN ISLANDS (India)
ANDAMAN SEA
NICOBAR ISLANDS (India)

◖ **TREACHEROUS PASSAGE.**
Climbers cross Nepal's Khumbu Icefall on their ascent to Mount Everest. Climbers train for years to scale the mountain, and they often rely on the help of experienced and skilled guides from the local Sherpa people.

THE CONTINENT:
ASIA

THE BASICS

STATS

Largest country
Thailand 198,117 sq mi
(513,120 sq km)

Smallest country
Singapore 269 sq mi
(697 sq km)

Most populous country
Philippines 105,893,000

Least populous country
Brunei 451,000

Predominant languages
Filipino (based on Tagalog),
English, Vietnamese, Thai,
Khmer, Lao, French, Malay,
Bahasa Melayu, Mandarin

Predominant religions
Christianity, Buddhism, Islam

Highest GDP per capita
Singapore $93,900

Lowest GDP per capita
Cambodia $4,000

Highest life expectancy
Singapore 85 years

Lowest life expectancy
Laos 64 years

GEO WHIZ

The Philippines has one of the world's highest rates of deforestation. Studies estimate that from 2001 to 2019, the country lost three million acres (1.23 million ha) of tree cover, a 6.6 percent decrease since 2000.

Thailand means "land of the free." It is the only country in southeastern Asia never ruled by a colonial power.

The Plain of Jars, in northern Laos, takes its name from hundreds of huge stone urns spread across the ground. Archaeologists believe Bronze Age people made the jars and used them to hold the cremated remains of their dead.

SHIPPING HUB.
Huge container terminals, such as this one at Tanjong Pagar, make Singapore the world's busiest transshipment center, connected to 600 ports in 123 countries around the world.

Southeastern Asia

The countries of southeastern Asia have long been influenced by neighboring giants India and China. The result is a mix of cultures, rich histories, violent conflicts, and future promise. Cambodia's spectacular 12th-century Angkor Wat provides a glimpse of former greatness. Colonial rule brought division and change, and struggles for independence took a heavy toll, as in Vietnam. Mainland countries are largely Buddhist, whereas peninsular Malaysia is mostly Muslim, and Christians dominate the Philippines. All but Laos have ocean access, with fisheries providing jobs and food for millions. Rivers like the Chao Phraya and the mighty Mekong provide transport and water-rich croplands dominated by rice growing. Tiny Singapore has gained global importance with its bustling port operations and high-tech focus.

SMILING BUDDHA.
A Buddhist monk admires a sculpture in Cambodia's Angkor temple complex. Built by the Khmer between 800 and 1200 C.E., the complex includes Buddhist and Hindu temples.

PRIMATES. Smaller than an adult human's hand, the Philippine tarsier is one of the world's smallest primates. Found on islands such as Bohol, the tarsier is active at night, hunting for insects.

FLASHY RIDE. Colorful Philippine taxis, called jeepneys because of their origin as rebuilt World War II jeeps, are a common sight on the streets of Manila.

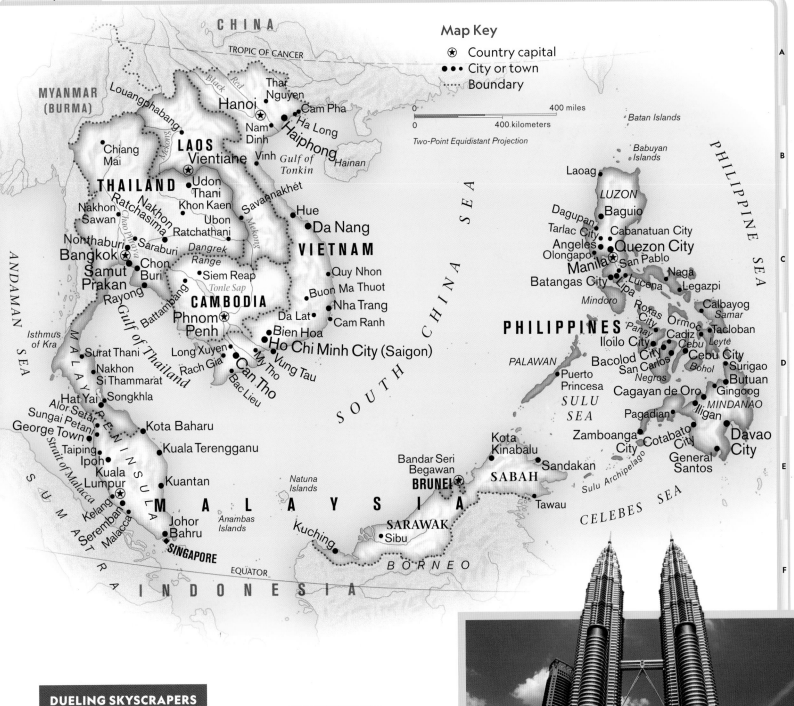

CHINA

TROPIC OF CANCER

MYANMAR (BURMA)

Map Key
⊛ Country capital
•••• City or town
···· Boundary

0 ——— 400 miles
0 ——— 400 kilometers
Two-Point Equidistant Projection

Louangphabang

Black · Red

Thai Nguyen

Hanoi ⊛

Cam Pha

Ha Long

Nam Dinh

Haiphong

Hainan

Gulf of Tonkin

LAOS

Vientiane ⊛

Vinh

Chiang Mai

THAILAND

Udon Thani

Khon Kaen

Savannakhét

Hue

Nakhon Sawan

Nakhon Ratchasima

Ubon Ratchathani

Da Nang

VIETNAM

Mekong

Nonthaburi

Saraburi

Dangrek Range

Bangkok ⊛

Chon Buri

Chao Phraya

Siem Reap

Quy Nhon

Samut Prakan

Tonle Sap

Buon Ma Thuot

Rayong

Battambang

CAMBODIA

Nha Trang

Phnom Penh ⊛

Da Lat

Cam Ranh

Bien Hoa

Long Xuyen

Ho Chi Minh City (Saigon)

Surat Thani

Rach Gia

My Tho

Vung Tau

Can Tho

Nakhon Si Thammarat

Bac Lieu

Hat Yai

Songkhla

SOUTH CHINA SEA

Alor Setar

Kota Baharu

Sungai Petani

George Town

Kuala Terengganu

Taiping

Ipoh

Kuala Lumpur

Kuantan

Natuna Islands

Kelang

Anambas Islands

Seremban

Malacca

Johor Bahru

Kuching

Sibu

SINGAPORE ◆

EQUATOR

SARAWAK

BORNEO

INDONESIA

SUMATRA

Strait of Malacca

MALAY PENINSULA

Gulf of Thailand

Isthmus of Kra

ANDAMAN SEA

MALAYSIA

BRUNEI

Bandar Seri Begawan ⊛

SABAH

Kota Kinabalu

Sandakan

Tawau

CELEBES SEA

SULU SEA

Batan Islands

Babuyan Islands

PHILIPPINE SEA

Laoag

LUZON

Dagupan

Baguio

Tarlac City

Cabanatuan City

Angeles

Quezon City ⊛

Olongapo

Manila ⊛

San Pablo

Naga

Batangas City

Lucena

Legazpi

Lipa

Mindoro

Roxas City

Calbayog

Samar

PHILIPPINES

Panay

Ormoc

Tacloban

PALAWAN

Iloilo City

Cadiz

Cebu

Leyte

Bacolod City

San Carlos

Cebu City

Surigao

Puerto Princesa

Negros

Bohol

Butuan

Gingoog

Cagayan de Oro

MINDANAO

SULU SEA

Pagadian

Iligan

Zamboanga City

Cotabato City

Davao City

Sulu Archipelago

General Santos

DUELING SKYSCRAPERS

2016 Data

2,717 ft (828 m)
Burj Khalifa (Dubai, United Arab Emirates)

2073 ft (632 m)
Shanghai Tower (Shanghai, China)

1,972 ft (601 m)
Makkah Clock Royal Tower (Makkah/Mecca, Saudi Arabia)

1,965 ft (599 m)
Ping An International Finance Center (Shenzhen, China)

The world's four tallest buildings are in Asia. The 2,717-foot (828-m) Burj Khalifa, in the United Arab Emirates, was completed in 2010.

STANDING TALL. The Petronas Twin Towers, the world's tallest twin towers, rise above Kuala Lumpur, Malaysia's capital.

THE CONTINENT:
ASIA

THE BASICS

STATS

Largest country
Indonesia 735,358 sq mi
(1,904,569 sq km)

Smallest country
Timor-Leste 5,743 sq mi
(14,874 sq km)

Most populous country
Indonesia 262,787,000

Least populous country
Timor-Leste 1,322,000

Predominant languages
Indonesian, English, Dutch,
Javanese, Tetum, Portuguese

Predominant religions
Islam, Christianity

Highest GDP per capita
Indonesia $12,400

Lowest GDP per capita
Timor-Leste $5,400

Highest life expectancy
Indonesia 73 years

Lowest life expectancy
Timor-Leste 68 years

GEO WHIZ

In 2006, two species of sharks
that use their fins to "walk"
on coral reefs were discovered
off the northwestern coast of
Indonesia's Papua province.

When seen from the air,
Timor Island resembles a croc-
odile. According to local leg-
end, a crocodile turned itself
into the island as a way of
saying thank-you to a boy
who saved its life.

Komodo dragons, the world's
heaviest lizard, live only on
Indonesia's Lesser Sunda
Islands. They eat all types
of prey.

Indonesia & Timor-Leste

Stretching more than 2,200 miles (3,520 km) from Sumatra to New Guinea, Indonesia is the world's largest island nation and the fourth most populous country. Most of its 262 million people live on the volcanically active island of Java. Indonesia shares rainforested Borneo with Malaysia and Brunei. Most Indonesians are of Malay ethnicity, though there are large numbers of Melanesians (see page 156), Chinese, and East Indians. Arab traders brought Islam to the islands in the 13th century, and today six out of seven Indonesians are Muslim. Timor-Leste gained independence from Indonesia in 2002. Timor-Leste and the Philippines are Asia's only mainly Catholic countries.

⬡ **PROUD CITIZEN.**
A boy smiles broadly as he waves the flag of Timor-Leste (also known as East Timor) in Díli, the capital city.

◑ **CITY ON THE MOVE.**
Skyscrapers and a busy freeway are just one face of Jakarta, Indonesia's national capital and center of trade and industry. In this city of more than 10 million people, the modern and traditional, the rich and poor, live side by side. Like the country, the city has a very diverse population.

◖ **SPIRIT WORLD.** Masks, such as this one from Bali, Indonesia, were probably created originally for dance and storytelling rituals.

THE CONTINENT:
ASIA

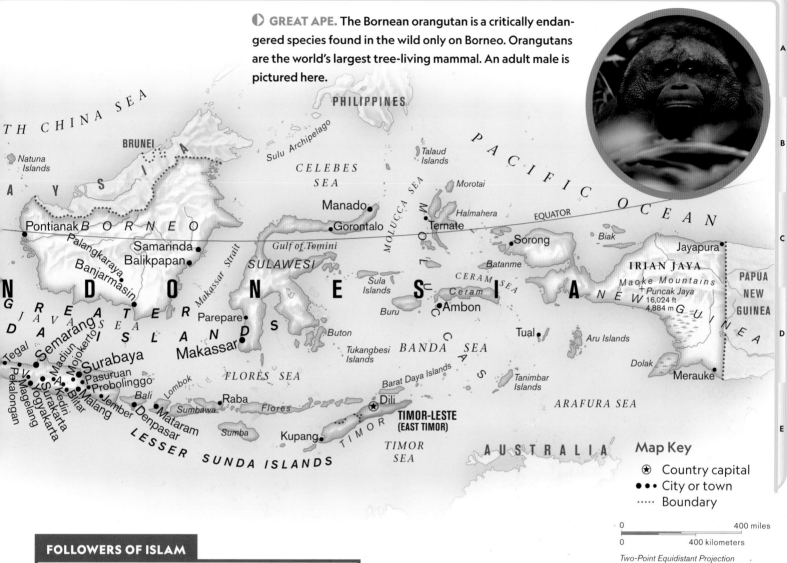

◖ **GREAT APE.** The Bornean orangutan is a critically endangered species found in the wild only on Borneo. Orangutans are the world's largest tree-living mammal. An adult male is pictured here.

Map Key
⊛ Country capital
••• City or town
····· Boundary

0 _____ 400 miles
0 _____ 400 kilometers
Two-Point Equidistant Projection

FOLLOWERS OF ISLAM

Country	Followers
Indonesia	204.8*
Pakistan	178.1
India	177.3
Bangladesh	148.6
Egypt	80.0
Nigeria	75.7
Iran	74.8
Turkey	74.7
Algeria	34.8
Morocco	32.4

*Figures are in millions, 2010 data

Islam's origins trace to southwestern Asia, but the religion has spread around the world. The country with the largest Muslim population is Indonesia.

◖ **GENETIC STOREHOUSE.** The rainforest in eastern Borneo's Kalimantan province is home to many rare species. Much of the forest has been lost as a result of activities such as logging and road building—a consequence of the spread of plantation agriculture, especially oil palm cultivation.

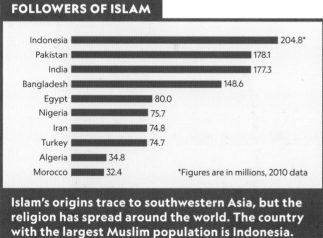

THE CONTINENT:
AFRICA

PHYSICAL			POLITICAL	
TOTAL AREA 11,608,000 sq mi (30,065,000 sq km)	**LOWEST POINT** Lake Assal, Djibouti -509 ft (-155 m)	**LARGEST LAKE** Lake Victoria 26,800 sq mi (69,500 sq km)	**POPULATION** 1,340,598,000	**LARGEST COUNTRY** Algeria 919,595 sq mi (2,381,741 sq km)
HIGHEST POINT Kilimanjaro, Tanzania 19,340 ft (5,895 m)	**LONGEST RIVER** Nile 4,160 mi (6,695 km)		**LARGEST METROPOLITAN AREA** Cairo, Egypt Pop. 20,901,000	**MOST DENSELY POPULATED COUNTRY** Mauritius 1,731 people per sq mi (669 per sq km)

AFRICA

THE CONTINENT:
AFRICA

Africa

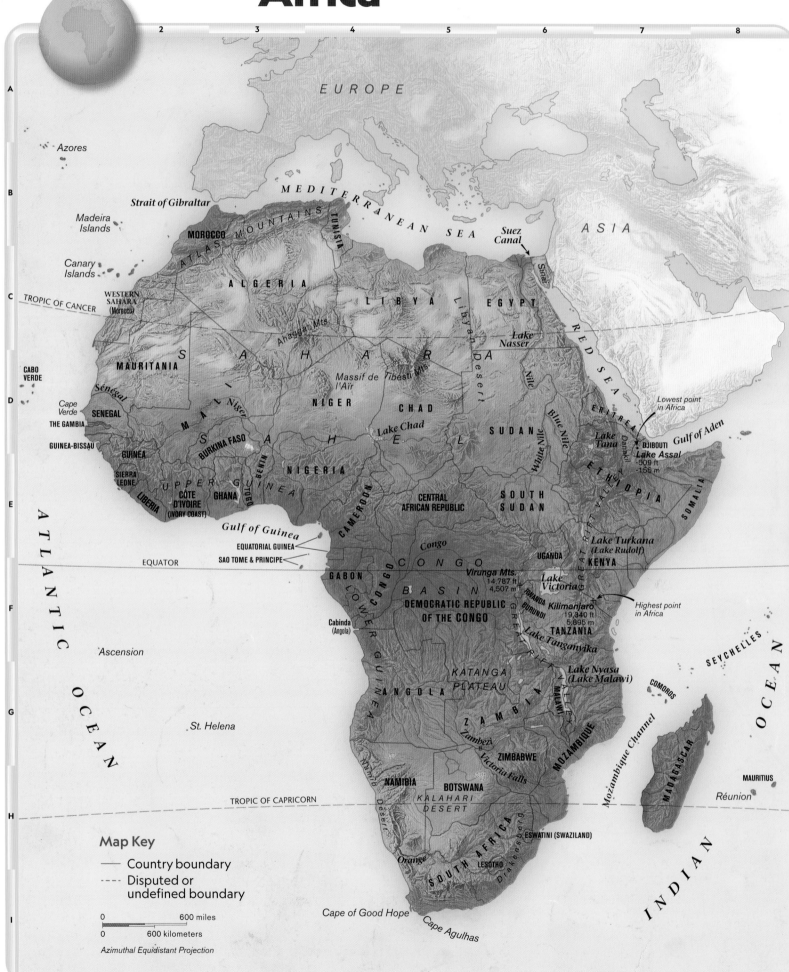

EUROPE

Azores

MEDITERRANEAN SEA

Strait of Gibraltar

Madeira
Islands

ASIA

Suez
Canal

Canary
Islands

TUNISIA

ATLAS MOUNTAINS

MOROCCO

Sinai

WESTERN
SAHARA
(Morocco)

TROPIC OF CANCER

ALGERIA

LIBYA

EGYPT

RED SEA

Libyan Desert

CABO
VERDE

MAURITANIA

S A H A R A

Ahaggar Mts.

Massif de
l'Aïr

Tibesti Mts.

Lake
Nasser

Lowest point
in Africa

Cape
Verde

SENEGAL

Sénégal

Niger

M A L I

NIGER

CHAD

Nile

ERITREA

Lake
Tana

Danakil

DJIBOUTI

Gulf of Aden

THE GAMBIA

GUINEA-BISSAU

GUINEA

BURKINA FASO

S A H E L

Lake Chad

SUDAN

White Nile

Blue Nile

Lake Assal
-509 ft
-155 m

ETHIOPIA

SIERRA
LEONE

LIBERIA

CÔTE
D'IVOIRE
(IVORY COAST)

GHANA

TOGO

BENIN

NIGERIA

UPPER GUINEA

CENTRAL
AFRICAN REPUBLIC

SOUTH
SUDAN

SOMALIA

Gulf of Guinea

EQUATORIAL GUINEA

SAO TOME & PRINCIPE

CAMEROON

Congo

CONGO

Lake Turkana
(Lake Rudolf)

EQUATOR

GABON

UGANDA

KENYA

A T L A N T I C   O C E A N

Cabinda
(Angola)

LOWER GUINEA

CONGO

B A S I N

Virunga Mts.
14,787 ft
4,507 m

Lake
Victoria

RWANDA

GREAT RIFT VALLEY

Kilimanjaro
19,340 ft
5,895 m

Highest point
in Africa

DEMOCRATIC REPUBLIC
OF THE CONGO

BURUNDI

TANZANIA

Ascension

Lake Tanganyika

SEYCHELLES

KATANGA
PLATEAU

Lake Nyasa
(Lake Malawi)

COMOROS

St. Helena

ANGOLA

MALAWI

GREAT RIFT VALLEY

ZAMBIA

Zambezi

MOZAMBIQUE

Mozambique Channel

MADAGASCAR

I N D I A N   O C E A N

Victoria Falls

ZIMBABWE

MAURITIUS

Réunion

Namib Desert

NAMIBIA

BOTSWANA

TROPIC OF CAPRICORN

KALAHARI
DESERT

ESWATINI (SWAZILAND)

Drakensberg

Orange

SOUTH AFRICA

LESOTHO

Map Key

—— Country boundary

---- Disputed or
     undefined boundary

Cape of Good Hope

Cape Agulhas

| 0 | 600 miles |

| 0 | 600 kilometers |

Azimuthal Equidistant Projection

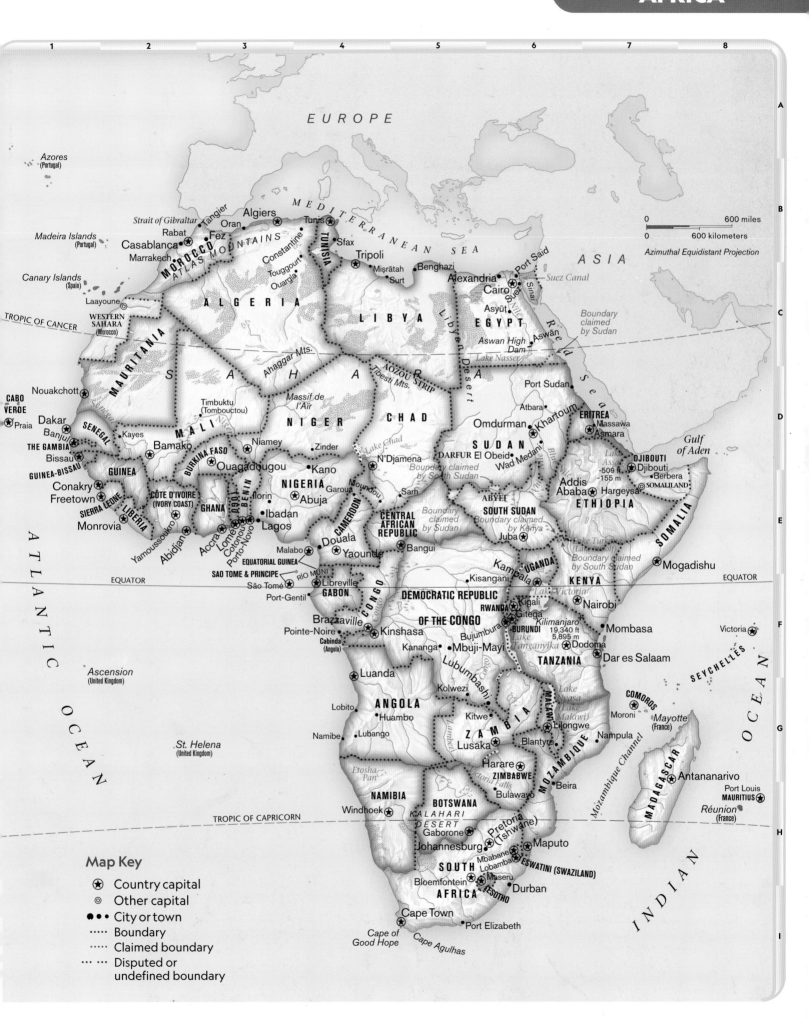

EUROPE

Azores
(Portugal)

Madeira Islands
(Portugal)

Canary Islands
(Spain)

Strait of Gibraltar
Tangier
Rabat
Fez
Casablanca
Marrakech

Algiers
Oran

Tunis
Sfax
Constantine
Touggourt
Ouargla

M E D I T E R R A N E A N   S E A

ASIA

TUNISIA
Tripoli
Mişrātah
Surt
Benghazi

Port Said
Suez Canal
Alexandria
Cairo
Suez
Sinai

**Boundary
claimed
by Sudan**

TROPIC OF CANCER

WESTERN
SAHARA
(Morocco)
Laayoune

MOROCCO
ATLAS MOUNTAINS

ALGERIA

LIBYA

EGYPT

Asyūṭ

Aswan High
Dam
Aswan
Lake Nasser

MAURITANIA

S A H A R A

Ahaggar Mts.

AOZOU STRIP
Tibesti Mts.

Libyan Desert

Port Sudan

CABO
VERDE
Praia

Nouakchott

Dakar
Banjul
THE GAMBIA
Bissau
GUINEA-BISSAU
Conakry
Freetown
SIERRA LEONE
Monrovia
LIBERIA

SENEGAL
Kayes

MALI
Timbuktu
(Tombouctou)

Bamako

GUINEA

Niger

BURKINA FASO
Ouagadougou

CÔTE D'IVOIRE
(IVORY COAST)
GHANA
Yamoussoukro
Abidjan
Accra
Lomé

NIGER
Niamey
Zinder

Massif de
l'Aïr

Lake Chad

N'Djamena

CHAD

Kano
NIGERIA
Garoua
Abuja
Ibadan
Lagos
Ilorin

TOGO
BENIN
Porto-Novo
Cotonou

CAMEROON
Moundou
Sarh

DARFUR

SUDAN

El Obeid
Wad Medani

Omdurman
Khartoum
Atbara

**Boundary claimed
by South Sudan**

ERITREA
Massawa
Asmara

DJIBOUTI
Djibouti
Berbera
SOMALILAND

Gulf
of Aden

Lake
Assal
-509 ft
-155 m

Hargeysa

Malabo
EQUATORIAL GUINEA
SAO TOME & PRINCIPE
São Tomé
RIO MUNI

Douala
Yaoundé

CENTRAL
AFRICAN
REPUBLIC
Bangui

ABYEI
SOUTH SUDAN
Juba

**Boundary
claimed
by Sudan**
**Boundary claimed
by Kenya**

Addis
Ababa

ETHIOPIA

SOMALIA
Mogadishu

EQUATOR

Libreville
Port-Gentil
GABON

Congo

Brazzaville
Pointe-Noire
Cabinda
(Angola)
Kinshasa
Kananga
Mbuji-Mayi

DEMOCRATIC REPUBLIC
OF THE CONGO

Kisangani

UGANDA
Kampala

Lake Victoria

RWANDA
Kigali
Gitega
BURUNDI
Bujumbura
Lake
Tanganyika

Kilimanjaro
19,340 ft
5,895 m
Dodoma

KENYA
Nairobi
Mombasa

Lake Turkana
(Lake Rudolf)

**Boundary claimed
by South Sudan**

EQUATOR

Victoria

SEYCHELLES

Luanda

Lubumbashi

Kolwezi

TANZANIA
Dar es Salaam

ANGOLA
Huambo
Lobito
Namibe
Lubango

Kitwe
ZAMBIA
Lusaka
Blantyre

MALAWI
Lilongwe
Nampula

Lake
Nyasa
(Lake
Malawi)

Moroni
COMOROS

Mayotte
(France)

MOZAMBIQUE
Beira

MADAGASCAR
Antananarivo

Port Louis
MAURITIUS
Réunion
(France)

St. Helena
(United Kingdom)

Ascension
(United Kingdom)

A T L A N T I C   O C E A N

Etosha
Pan
Victoria Falls
Harare
ZIMBABWE
Bulawayo

Zambezi

TROPIC OF CAPRICORN

NAMIBIA
Windhoek

BOTSWANA
Gaborone

K A L A H A R I
D E S E R T

Pretoria
(Tshwane)
Johannesburg
Mbabane
Lobamba
ESWATINI (SWAZILAND)
Maputo

Maseru
LESOTHO
Durban

SOUTH
AFRICA
Bloemfontein

Cape Town
Cape of
Good Hope
Cape Agulhas
Port Elizabeth

I N D I A N   O C E A N

Mozambique Channel

0   600 miles
0   600 kilometers
Azimuthal Equidistant Projection

Map Key

⊛ Country capital
◎ Other capital
●●● City or town
····· Boundary
····· Claimed boundary
····· Disputed or
      undefined boundary

Africa
A COMPLEX GIANT

Africa spans nearly as far west to east as it does north to south. The Sahara—the world's largest hot desert—covers Africa's northern third, while to the south lie bands of grassland, tropical rainforest, and more desert. The East African Rift system marks where shifting tectonic plates are splitting off the continent's edge. Africa has a wealth of cultures, speaking some 1,600 languages—more than on any other continent. Though the continent is mostly rural, Africans increasingly migrate to booming cities like Lagos, Cairo, and Johannesburg. Despite rich natural resources—from oil and coal to gemstones and precious metals—and partly as a result of them, many countries in Africa have endured colonization, corruption, and disease.

⬯ **COMMUNITY SERVICE.** Volunteer efforts by youth happen in countries around the world. In Saad Zaghloul Square, Egyptian teens take a break from painting and other cleanup efforts to beautify the area.

⬯ **CHARGE!** Sensing danger, an African elephant charges. The world's largest land mammal, African elephants are at risk due to poaching and loss of habitat.

⬯ **COLORFUL NEIGHBORHOOD.** South Africa's Bo-Kaap once was known as the Malay Quarter because of its early settlers from Malaysia. Dating to the 18th century, this multicultural suburb overlooks Cape Town's city center.

AFRICAN SAVANNA. Zebras graze on the tall grasses of the Serengeti Plain, in eastern Africa. Each year some 200,000 zebras migrate through the Serengeti, following the seasonal rains.

CRYSTAL WATERS. A snorkeler swims in the clear blue waters off the Seychelles, one of Africa's island countries. Made up of 115 granite and coral islands, it lies about 1,000 miles (1,600 km) east of Kenya.

FREE RIDE.
A woman in Kumasi, Ghana, goes about her day with her child wrapped snugly on her back in a Kente cloth carrier.

more about
Africa

◗ **WORSHIPPERS IN THE DESERT.** Muslim faithful gather before the Great Mosque in Mopti, Mali. An earthen structure typical of Muslim architecture in Africa's Sahel, the mosque was built between 1936 and 1943.

◗ **WINDOW ON THE PAST.** Traditional Egyptian sailing vessels called feluccas skim along the Nile River below the ruins at Qubbet al-Hawa. Tombs from ancient Egypt's sixth dynasty are carved into the hillside.

◗ **MODERN SKYLINE.** Established in 1899 as a railway supply depot, Nairobi, Kenya, is now one of Africa's most modern cities. In Maasai, an indigenous language, the name means "place of cold water."

◑ **POWER GRID.** In Uganda, about 40 percent of the rural population has access to the national electricity grid. In order to provide electricity to more rural residents, the country has supported renewable energy sources, such as solar, wind, and geothermal.

WHERE THE PICTURES ARE

Fort and freighter p. 136
Cooked snails p. 137
Muslims praying p. 134
Leptis Magna p. 137
Saad Zaghloul Square p. 132
Pyramids p. 137
Feluccas on the Nile pp. 134–135
Desert caravan p. 142
Sand dunes p. 136
Ngbaba players p. 143
Mountain gorilla p. 141
Shipping terminal p. 141
Coffee berries p. 140
Dishes p. 138
Mother and child p. 133
Solar panels p. 135
Nairobi skyline p. 134
Fody bird p. 135
Cocoa beans p. 138
Bronze head from Benin p. 139
Snorkeler p. 133
Whale sharks p. 140
Peanuts for export p. 138
Gold miners p. 135
Chokwe mask p. 143
Elephant p. 132
Active volcano p. 142
Zebras p. 133
Ring-tailed lemur p. 144
Cheetah p. 140
Bo-Kaap p. 132
Early man skull p. 145
Cape Town skyline p. 145
Victoria Falls p. 144

◒ **DIGGING FOR GOLD.** Miners dig a pit mine near the edge of the rainforest in Gabon. Oil and mineral extraction is an important part of the country's economy, but the practice exposes the fragile soil to erosion.

◒ **TROPICAL JEWEL.** A ruby red fody perches on a forest branch on Mahé Island in the Seychelles. Native to neighboring Madagascar, the fody eats seeds and insects.

THE BASICS

STATS

Largest country
Algeria 919,595 sq mi
(2,381,741 sq km)

Smallest country
Tunisia 63,170 sq mi
(163,610 sq km)

Most populous country
Egypt 99,413,000

Least populous country
Libya 6,755,000

Predominant languages
Arabic, French,
indigenous languages

Predominant religions
Islam, indigenous beliefs

Highest GDP per capita
Algeria $15,200

Lowest GDP capita
Morocco $8,600

Highest life expectancy
Algeria, Libya, Morocco 77 years

Lowest life expectancy
Egypt 73 years

GEO WHIZ

Ibn Battuta, who was born in Tangier, Morocco, in 1304, set off on a pilgrimage to Mecca that turned into a 29-year, 75,000-mile (120,700-km) journey that took him from the Middle East to India, China, the East Indies, and back home.

Egypt's Aswan High Dam, which forms Lake Nasser, produces up to 10 billion kilowatt hours of electricity every year and provides water for farms along the Nile in years of drought.

Kairouan, Tunisia, is considered to be Islam's fourth holiest city after Mecca, Medina, and Jerusalem.

Northern Africa

This region, which is made up of five countries, stretches from the Atlantic Ocean in the west to the Red Sea in the east. To the north the region is bounded by the Mediterranean Sea, while to the south lies the vast dry expanse of the Sahara. The world's longest river—the Nile—winds northward through Egypt, but most of the region is arid—meaning there is too little moisture to support trees or extensive vegetation. Most of the region's population lives in coastal areas or in the fertile valley of the Nile River. In recent years, the region has experienced widespread instability as a result of tensions between conservative Islamic groups and more liberal groups seeking modernization and democratic rule.

PORTUGAL

0   400 miles
0   400 kilometers
Albers Equal-Area Projection

(Spain) Ceuta
Strait of Gibraltar
Tangier
Rabat · Fez
Madeira Islands (Portugal)
Casablanca ·
ATLANTIC
OCEAN
Safi · Meknès
MOROCCO
Marrakech · 13,665 ft
+4,165 m
Canary Islands (Spain)
Agadir ·
ATLAS
Jebel Toubkal

Western Sahara's sovereign status is in dispute. It has been administered by Morocco since 1979. Fighting between Morocco and a Western Sahara independence movement called the Polisario Front ended with a UN-brokered cease-fire in 1991, but no agreement on the area's status has been reached.

Guelmim ·
· Tarfaya
Tindouf ·
Laayoune ·
Al Farciya
Ad Dakhla ·
WESTERN SAHARA (Morocco)
Iguid
Erg
· Cap Barbas
· Techla
Cap Blanc ·
MAURITANIA
SA
M

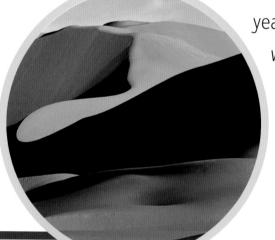

⬢ **SEA OF SAND.** Towering dunes as well as barren, rocky expanses define Earth's largest hot desert—the Sahara, which separates northern Africa from the rest of the continent.

◖ **TRADING HARBOR.** In Algeria, historic meets modern with an ancient fort and a modern freighter. Over time, historic harbors have adapted to host larger shipping vessels to exchange more supplies and increase cash flow.

◑ MONUMENTAL ACHIEVEMENT.
Pharaoh Khufu's Great Pyramid is the largest in Giza and towers some 481 feet (147 m). Its estimated 2.3 million stone blocks each weigh 2.5 to 15 tons (2.2 to 13 t).

THE CONTINENT: AFRICA

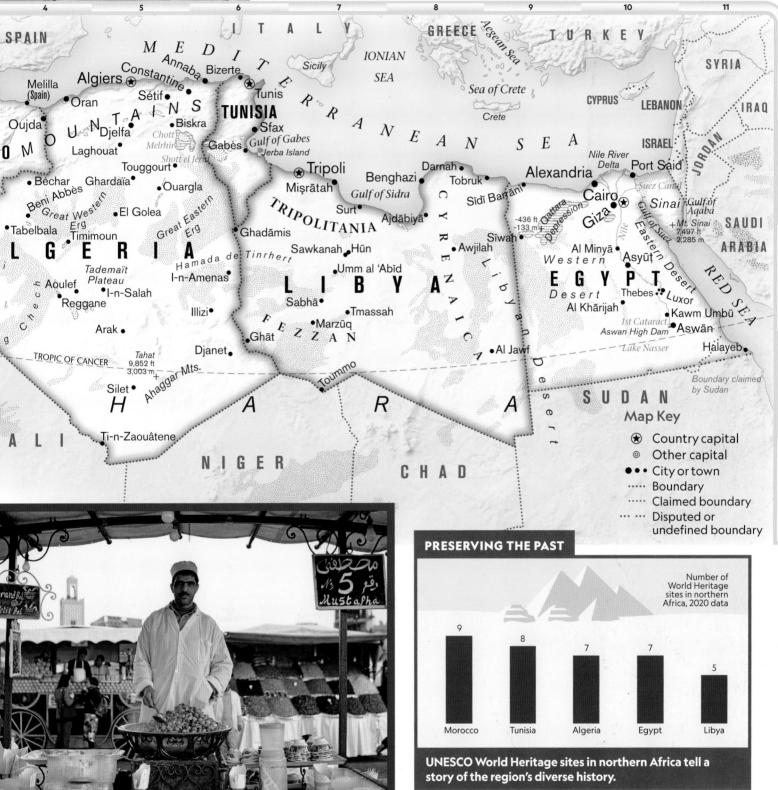

Map labels:

SPAIN · ITALY · GREECE · TURKEY · SYRIA
Melilla (Spain) · Algiers · Constantine · Annaba · Bizerte · Tunis
Oran · Sétif · TUNISIA · Sfax
Oujda · Djelfa · Biskra · Gabès · Gulf of Gabes · Jerba Island
Laghouat · Chott Melrhir · Shott el Jerid
Béchar · Ghardaïa · Ouargla · Touggourt · TRIPOLITANIA · Tripoli · Mişrātah · Benghazi · Darnah · Alexandria · Port Said
Beni Abbès · El Golea · Surt · Gulf of Sidra · Tobruk · Sīdī Barrānī · Cairo · Giza · Sinai · Gulf of Aqaba
Great Western Erg · Great Eastern Erg · Ghadāmis · Ajdābiyā · Qattara Depression −436 ft −133 m · Mt. Sinai 7,497 ft 2,285 m
Tabelbala · Timimoun · Hamada de Tinrhert · Sawkanah · Hūn · Awjilah · Sīwah · Al Minyā · Asyūṭ
ALGERIA · Tademaït Plateau · I-n-Amenas · Umm al 'Abīd · LIBYA · CYRENAICA · Western Desert · EGYPT
Aoulef · I-n-Salah · Sabhā · Tmassah · Thebes · Luxor · Al Khārijah
Reggane · Illizi · FEZZAN · Marzūq · 1st Cataract · Kawm Umbū
Arak · Ghāt · Aswan High Dam · Aswān
Tahat 9,852 ft 3,003 m · Djanet · Al Jawf · Lake Nasser · Halayeb
Silet · Ahaggar Mts. · SAHARA · SUDAN
Ti-n-Zaouâtene · Toummo · Boundary claimed by Sudan
MALI · NIGER · CHAD

MEDITERRANEAN SEA · Sicily · IONIAN SEA · Aegean Sea · Sea of Crete · Crete · CYPRUS · LEBANON · ISRAEL · JORDAN · IRAQ · SAUDI ARABIA · RED SEA
Nile River Delta · Suez Canal · Gulf of Suez · Eastern Desert · Nile
ATLAS MOUNTAINS · TROPIC OF CANCER · Oued Chech

Map Key
- ★ Country capital
- ◎ Other capital
- •●• City or town
- ····· Boundary
- ····· Claimed boundary
- ·-·-· Disputed or undefined boundary

PRESERVING THE PAST

Number of World Heritage sites in northern Africa, 2020 data

Morocco	Tunisia	Algeria	Egypt	Libya
9	8	7	7	5

UNESCO World Heritage sites in northern Africa tell a story of the region's diverse history.

◒ TASTY TREAT. Snails are a common snack served at roadside stalls, or souks, in Marrakech, Morocco. The seller above entices tourists and locals in Djemaa El Fna Square.

◑ COMPLEX CULTURE. Leptis Magna, a World Heritage site in Libya, was founded in the seventh century B.C.E. and became a major trade center. Following Roman and later Arab conquests, it fell into ruin.

**THE CONTINENT:
AFRICA**

THE BASICS

STATS

**Largest country
Niger 489,191 sq miles
(1,267,000 sq km)**

**Smallest country
Cabo Verde 1,557 sq miles
(4,033 sq km)**

**Most populous country
Nigeria 203,453,000**

**Least populous country
Cabo Verde 568,000**

**Predominant languages
French, English, Portuguese,
Arabic, Spanish, indigenous
languages**

**Predominant religions
Islam, Christianity,
indigenous beliefs**

**Highest GDP per capita
Cabo Verde $6,900**

**Lowest GDP per capita
Liberia $1,400**

**Highest life expectancy
Cabo Verde 72 years**

**Lowest life expectancy
Guinea-Bisseau 51 years**

GEO WHIZ

For more than 300 years,
the House of Slaves on
Senegal's Gorée Island served
as a holding pen for enslaved
people before they were
sent to the Americas and
elsewhere. Today, it is a
museum and a memorial.

Nigeria is a major producer
and exporter of oil. Port
Harcourt, in the Niger River
Delta, is the center of the
country's oil industry.

Western Africa

Stretching from Cabo Verde in the west (inset, opposite), Mauritania in the northwest, and the barren Sahara in the north, to Nigeria in the southeast, 16 countries make up western Africa. Three countries—Burkina Faso, Mali, and Niger—are landlocked, meaning they have no direct access to ocean trade. The remaining 13 have coastlines along the Atlantic Ocean or the Gulf of Guinea. Early kingdoms thrived in Mali, Ghana, and Benin, but European colonization disrupted traditional societies and economies, and left a legacy of political turmoil. Today, the countries are independent, but widespread use of French and English reflects the region's colonial past. Reliance on agriculture and falling global oil prices have left the region with a struggling economy.

◔ **PREPARING DESSERT.** In Côte d'Ivoire a man holds roasted cacao beans in a bowl. The beans are processed to create chocolate. About 70 percent of the world's cacao comes from African countries.

◔ **FULL OF COLOR.** Artistic ceramic plates brighten an outdoor marketplace in Kumasi, Ghana. This country has a long and rich cultural tradition of creating pottery for cooking and for serving food and water.

◔ **WAITING FOR SHIPMENT.** Sacks of peanuts create an artificial mountain in Kano, Nigeria, where they wait for transport to Lagos and then export to world markets. Nigeria produces more than half of the region's peanut crop.

MASTER ARTISANS. The ancient African kingdom of Benin produced outstanding bronze work. Each piece was created to honor the king.

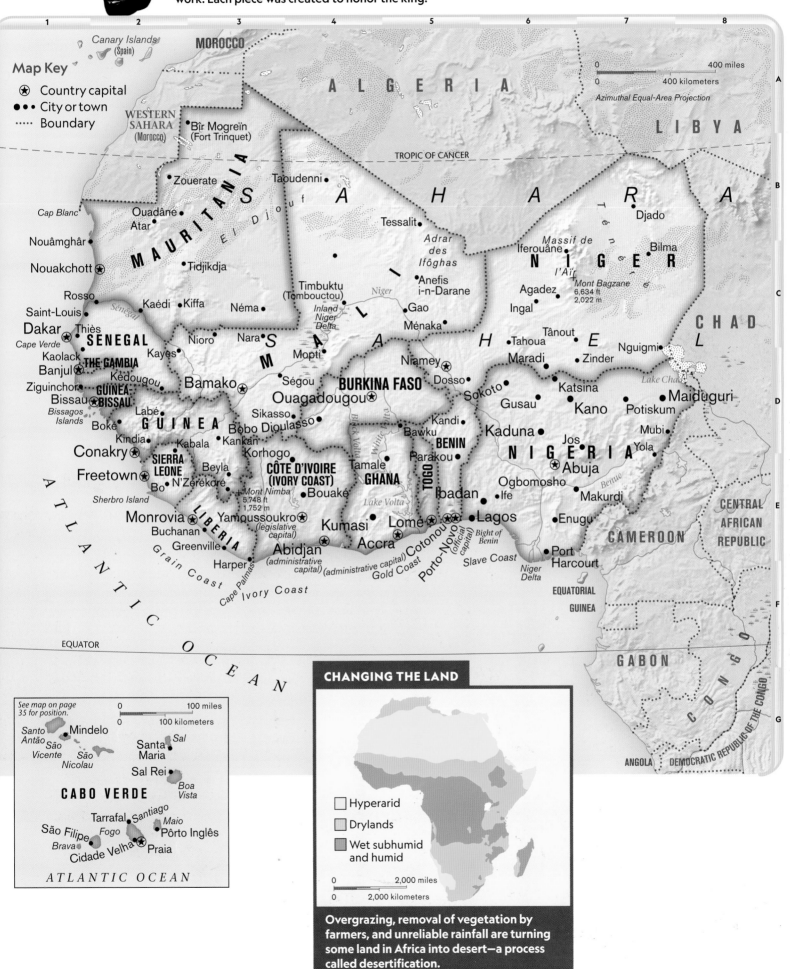

Map Key
★ Country capital
•• City or town
⋯ Boundary

0 ———— 400 miles
0 ———— 400 kilometers
Azimuthal Equal-Area Projection

MOROCCO

WESTERN SAHARA (Morocco)

CANARY ISLANDS (Spain)

Cap Blanc

ALGERIA

LIBYA

TROPIC OF CANCER

Bîr Mogreïn (Fort Trinquet)

Zouerate

Taoudenni

Djado

Ouadâne
Atar

MAURITANIA

El Djouf

SAHARA

Tessalit

Iferouâne
Massif de l'Aïr
Bilma

Nouâmghâr

Nouakchott ★

Tidjikdja

Adrar des Ifôghas

Anefis i-n-Darane

Agadez

NIGER

Ténéré

Mont Bagzane 6,634 ft 2,022 m

Rosso
Kaédi Kiffa

Néma

Timbuktu (Tombouctou)

Niger

Gao

Ingal

CHAD

Saint-Louis

Sénégal

Nioro
Nara

Inland Niger Delta

Ménaka

Tânout

SAHEL

Dakar
Thiès
Cape Verde

SENEGAL

Kayes

Mopti
Ségou

MALI

Niamey ★

Tahoua

Maradi

Zinder

Nguigmi

Lake Chad

Kaolack
Banjul ★
THE GAMBIA

Kédougou

Bamako ★

Dosso

Sokoto

Katsina

Kano

Potiskum

Maiduguri

Ziguinchor
Bissau ★
GUINEA-BISSAU

Labé

Sikasso

Ouagadougou ★

BURKINA FASO

Bawku
Kandi

Gusau

Kaduna

Mubi

Bissagos Islands

Boké

GUINEA

Bobo Dioulasso

Black Volta

Parakou

BENIN

Jos

Yola

Kindia
Kabala
Kankan

Korhogo

Tamale

TOGO

White Volta

NIGERIA

Abuja ★

Conakry ★

SIERRA LEONE

Beyla

CÔTE D'IVOIRE (IVORY COAST)

Bouaké

GHANA

Ibadan

Ogbomosho

Freetown ★

Bo
N'Zérékoré

Sherbro Island

Mont Nimba 5,748 ft 1,752 m

Lake Volta

Ife

Makurdi

Benue

CENTRAL AFRICAN REPUBLIC

Monrovia ★
Buchanan

LIBERIA

Yamoussoukro (legislative capital)

Kumasi

Lomé ★

Lagos

Enugu

CAMEROON

Greenville

Abidjan (administrative capital)

Accra ★ (administrative capital)

Cotonou
Porto-Novo ★ (official capital)

Port Harcourt

Harper
Cape Palmas

Grain Coast

Gold Coast

Bight of Benin

Slave Coast

Niger Delta

EQUATORIAL GUINEA

ATLANTIC OCEAN

Ivory Coast

EQUATOR

GABON

CONGO

DEMOCRATIC REPUBLIC OF THE CONGO

ANGOLA

Cabo Verde inset

See map on page 35 for position.

0 ———— 100 miles
0 ———— 100 kilometers

Santo Antão
Mindelo
São Vicente
São Nicolau

Santa Maria
Sal

Sal Rei
Boa Vista

CABO VERDE

Tarrafal
Santiago
Maio
Pôrto Inglês

São Filipe
Fogo
Brava
Cidade Velha ★ Praia

ATLANTIC OCEAN

CHANGING THE LAND

☐ Hyperarid
☐ Drylands
☐ Wet subhumid and humid

0 ———— 2,000 miles
0 ———— 2,000 kilometers

Overgrazing, removal of vegetation by farmers, and unreliable rainfall are turning some land in Africa into desert—a process called desertification.

THE BASICS

STATS

Largest country
Tanzania 365,754 sq miles
(947,300 sq km)

Smallest country
Djibouti 8,958 sq miles
(23,200 sq km)

Most populous country
Ethiopia 108,386,000

Least populous country
Djibouti 884,000

Predominant languages
French, Arabic, English,
Kiswahili, indigenous
languages

Predominant religions
Christianity, Islam,
indigenous beliefs

Highest GDP per capita
Djibouti, Kenya $3,500

Lowest GDP per capita
Somalia

Highest life expectancy
Djibouti 63 years

Lowest life expectancy
Somalia 52 years

GEO WHIZ

Mount Kilimanjaro is the
world's highest freestanding
mountain. It has three volcanic cones, two of which are
extinct while one is dormant.

In 2006, the 3.3-million-year-
old fossilized remains of a
child were found in northern
Ethiopia.

Eastern Africa

Eastern Africa's southern countries attract tourists to see big game—lions, elephants, giraffes, cape buffalo, zebras, wildebeests—that live on tropical grasslands called savannas. Some also come to the region to climb its towering volcanic mountains, such as Kilimanjaro and Mount Kenya. Along the western border lie Africa's Great Lakes, a part of the Rift Valley where tectonic forces are gradually separating eastern Africa from the rest of the continent. Religious and ethnic conflicts have plagued the region's northern countries for many years, leading to the political separation of Eritrea from Ethiopia. Civil unrest combined with drought has led to widespread famine, especially in Somalia.

⬤ **SAFARI.** With 23 national parks and 28 national reserves, ecotourism is a growing business in Kenya. In the Masai Mara National Reserve, visitors can observe cheetahs on the Serengeti.

◖ **FROM FIELD TO CUP.** A worker on a coffee estate in Kenya holds freshly harvested coffee berries, which will soon be on their way to world markets. Coffee production was introduced to Kenya in 1900. Today, it directly or indirectly employs more than five million workers.

⬤ **WHALE SHARKS.** Off the coast of Tanzania near Mafia Island, tourists get up-close views of whale sharks. About the size of a school bus, whale sharks are the world's largest fish. They feed mostly on plankton.

SOURCE OF THE NILE

Lake Victoria is Africa's largest lake. It is also the second largest freshwater lake in the world and a primary source of the Nile River. Pollution and overfishing are endangering the lake's environment.

THE CONTINENT:
AFRICA

◖ **CRITICALLY ENDANGERED.** About half of Earth's roughly 1,000 wild mountain gorillas live in forests on the slopes of the Virunga Mountains. Poaching, habitat loss, and civil conflict threaten their survival.

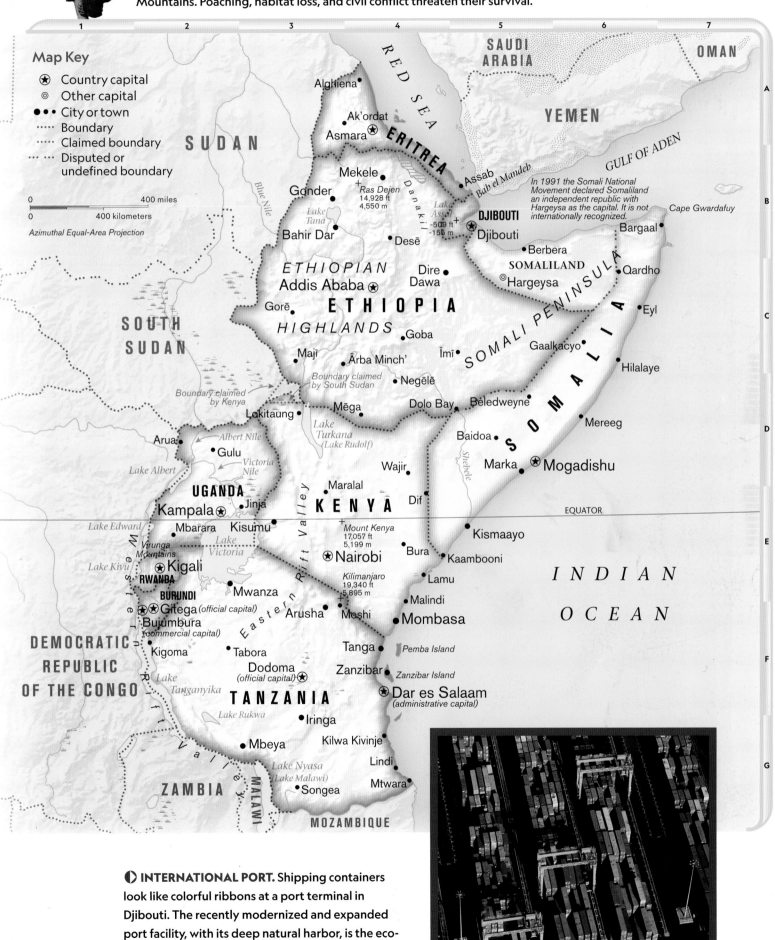

Map Key

★ Country capital
◎ Other capital
••• City or town
······ Boundary
······ Claimed boundary
······ Disputed or undefined boundary

0 ———— 400 miles
0 ———— 400 kilometers
Azimuthal Equal-Area Projection

SAUDI ARABIA
OMAN
RED SEA
YEMEN
Alghiena
Ak'ordat
Asmara ★ ERITREA
Assab
Bab el Mandeb
GULF OF ADEN
Cape Gwardafuy
SUDAN
Mekele
Gonder
+ Ras Dejen 14,928 ft 4,550 m
Danakil
Lake Assal -509 ft -155 m
DJIBOUTI ★ Djibouti
Bargaal
Lake Tana
Bahir Dar
Desē
Berbera
SOMALILAND
Qardho

In 1991 the Somali National Movement declared Somaliland an independent republic with Hargeysa as the capital. It is not internationally recognized.

ETHIOPIAN
Addis Ababa ★
Dire Dawa
◎ Hargeysa
SOUTH SUDAN
Gorē
ETHIOPIA
Goba
Eyl
HIGHLANDS
Majī
Ārba Minch'
Īmī
Gaalkacyo
Hilalaye
Boundary claimed by South Sudan
Negēlē
SOMALI PENINSULA
Boundary claimed by Kenya
Lokitaung
Mēga
Dolo Bay
Beledweyne
SOMALIA
Mereeg
Albert Nile
Lake Turkana (Lake Rudolf)
Baidoa
Arua
Gulu
Victoria Nile
Wajir
Marka ★ Mogadishu
Shebele
Lake Albert
Maralal
Dif
UGANDA
KENYA
EQUATOR
Kampala ★
Jinja
Kisumu
Lake Edward
Mbarara
Mount Kenya 17,057 ft 5,199 m
Kismaayo
Virunga Mountains
Lake Victoria
Bura
Kaambooni
Lake Kivu
Nairobi ★
Kilimanjaro 19,340 ft 5,895 m
Lamu
INDIAN OCEAN
★ Kigali
Mwanza
Malindi
RWANDA
BURUNDI
Arusha
Moshi
Mombasa
★ ◎ Gitega (official capital)
Tanga
Bujumbura (commercial capital)
Tabora
Pemba Island
DEMOCRATIC REPUBLIC OF THE CONGO
Kigoma
Dodoma (official capital) ★
Zanzibar
Zanzibar Island
Eastern Rift Valley
TANZANIA
★ Dar es Salaam (administrative capital)
Lake Tanganyika
Lake Rukwa
Iringa
Mbeya
Lake Nyasa (Lake Malawi)
Kilwa Kivinje
Lindi
ZAMBIA
MALAWI
Songea
Mtwara
MOZAMBIQUE

◖ **INTERNATIONAL PORT.** Shipping containers look like colorful ribbons at a port terminal in Djibouti. The recently modernized and expanded port facility, with its deep natural harbor, is the economic mainstay of this small country in eastern Africa.

THE BASICS

STATS

Largest country
Democratic Republic
of the Congo (DRC)
905,354 sq mi (2,344,858 sq km)

Smallest country
Sao Tome and Principe
372 sq mi (964 sq m)

Most populous country
Democratic Republic
of the Congo
85,281,000

Least populous country
Sao Tome and Principe 204,000

Predominant languages
English, French, Arabic,
Portuguese, indigenous
languages

Predominant religions
Christianity, Islam,
indigenous beliefs

Highest GDP per capita
Equatorial Guinea $36,000

Lowest GDP per capita
Central African Republic
$700

Highest life expectancy
Sao Tome and Principe 65 years

Lowest life expectancy
Chad 51 years

GEO WHIZ

The region is home to the
western lowland gorilla, which
relies on the tropical rainforest
habitats for food and habitat.

The two main tributaries of
the Nile join at Khartoum, in
Sudan. Farmers rely on the
world's longest river to water
their crops.

Central Africa

The Congo, a major commercial waterway of central Africa, flows through rainforests being cut for timber and palm oil plantations. This places a large area of Earth's biodiversity at risk. To the north, Lake Chad, a large, but shallow lake, fluctuates greatly in size due to high rates of evaporation, unreliable rainfall, and overuse by the 20 million people who live near its shores. Diamonds, copper, and chromium are mined in the Democratic Republic of the Congo (DRC) and the Central African Republic. Coffee is grown in the eastern highlands of the region, and livestock and cotton contribute to the economy of Chad. Religious and ethnic conflicts led to the separation of South Sudan from Sudan in 2011. Ongoing civil unrest and drought have led to widespread famine in South Sudan.

◐ **ACTIVE VOLCANO.**
Mount Nyiragongo, in the
Virunga Mountains of the
DRC, contains one of the
world's largest lava lakes.

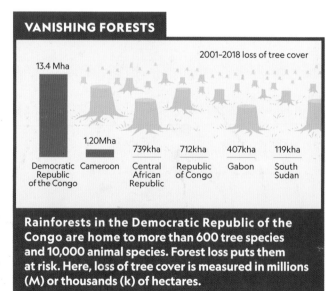

VANISHING FORESTS

2001–2018 loss of tree cover

13.4 Mha — Democratic Republic of the Congo

1.20 Mha — Cameroon

739 kha — Central African Republic

712 kha — Republic of Congo

407 kha — Gabon

119 kha — South Sudan

**Rainforests in the Democratic Republic of the
Congo are home to more than 600 tree species
and 10,000 animal species. Forest loss puts them
at risk. Here, loss of tree cover is measured in millions
(M) or thousands (k) of hectares.**

◑ **DESERT CARAVAN.** Tuareg tribesmen lead
their camels across the desert in northern Chad.
The camels, loaded with trade goods such as salt,
are destined for distant market towns.

CELEBRATING A KING. The Chokwe people of central Africa used masks such as this one to celebrate the inauguration of a new king.

1 2 3 4 5 6 7 8

ALGERIA

LIBYA
EGYPT
TROPIC OF CANCER
Boundary claimed by Sudan

SAUDI ARABIA

MALI

NIGER

SAHARA

AOZOU STRIP
Aozou
Aozi
Tibesti Mts.
Emi Koussi
11,302 ft
3,445 m
Ounianga
Kébir
Faya
Fada
Ennedi
Koro Toro
Biltine
Mao
Lake Chad
Ati
Abéché
Jabal
Marrah
9,980 ft
3,042 m
DARFUR
Nyala

CHAD

SAHEL

N'Djamena
Maroua
Am Timan
Chari
Birao
Dar Rounga
Kafia Kingi

Lake Nubia
2nd Cataract
Wadi Halfa
Nubian
Desert
3rd Cataract
Dongola
4th Cataract
5th Cataract
Merowe
Atbara
6th Cataract
Omdurman
Khartoum
North
Khartoum
El Fasher
El Obeid
Kosti
En Nahud
Kadugli
Renk
Melut

Port Sudan
Tokar

RED SEA

ERITREA
YEMEN

DJIBOUTI

SUDAN

Blue Nile
Atbara

NIGERIA

Garoua
Moundou
Sarh
Mbé
Ngaoundéré
Bamenda
Garoua Boulaï
Bouar
Bossangoa

Ndélé
Gabras
Boundary claimed by Sudan
ABYEI
Raga
Wau
Rumbek
Dobane
Obo
Maridi
Juba
Boundary claimed by Kenya
Boundary claimed by South Sudan

SOUTH SUDAN

Leer
Malakal
Bor
Towot
Mountain Nile

ETHIOPIA

CENTRAL AFRICAN REPUBLIC

Bambari
Bangassou
Bondo

Berbérati
Bangui
Nola
Gemena
Bumba
Isiro
(Paulis)
Arua
Albert Nile
Lake Albert
Bunia

SOMALIA

CAMEROON
Douala
Malabo
Bioko
EQUATORIAL GUINEA
Ebolowa
Bata
RÍO MUNI
Oyem
Quéssso
Makokou
Yaoundé
Sanaga
Ubangi
Uele
Congo
Basankusu

DEMOCRATIC

Kisangani
Boyoma Falls

UGANDA
KENYA
EQUATOR

GULF OF GUINEA
Príncipe
SAO TOME AND PRINCIPE
São Tomé
São Tomé
Cap Lopez
Libreville
Port-Gentil
Iguéla
Setté Cama
Mayumba

GABON

Mossaka
Franceville
Inongo
Bandundu

Mbandaka

REPUBLIC

OF THE CONGO

Kindu
Bukavu
Lake Edward
Virunga Mountains
Lake Victoria
RWANDA
Lake Kivu
BURUNDI
Western Rift

ATLANTIC OCEAN

Pointe-Noire
Tchibanga
Kasai
Kwango
CONGO

Kinshasa
Boma
Brazzaville
ANGOLA

Mweka
Kananga
Mbuji-Mayi
Kahemba

Kasongo
Kalemie
Lake Tanganyika

TANZANIA

INDIAN OCEAN

ANGOLA
Kamina
Sandoa
KATANGA PLATEAU
Kolwezi
Likasi
Lubumbashi
ZAMBIA

Pweto
Lake Mweru
Congo
Rift Valley
Lake
MALAWI
MOZAMBIQUE
COMOROS

Map Key
- ⊛ Country capital
- ••• City or town
- ····· Boundary
- ····· Claimed boundary
- ····· Disputed or undefined boundary

0 ___ 400 miles
0 ___ 400 kilometers
Azimuthal Equal-Area Projection

BACK IN THE GAME. Ngbaba (pronounced "g'baba") players use a long stick to hit a puck into the other team's pitch. A traditional Central African sport, ngbaba is returning after a pause due to regional conflict in the early 2000s.

Southern Africa

THE BASICS

STATS

Largest country
Angola 481,353 sq mi
(1,246,700 sq km)

Smallest country
Seychelles 176 sq mi
(455 sq km)

Most populous country
South Africa 55,380,000

Least populous country
Seychelles 95,000

Predominant languages
English, French, Portuguese,
indigenous languages

Predominant religions
Christianity, Islam,
indigenous beliefs

Highest GDP per capita
Seychelles $28,900

Lowest GDP per capita
Malawi $1,200

Highest life expectancy
Mauritius 76 years

Lowest life expectancy
Eswatini 52 years

GEO WHIZ

South Africa's Kruger National
Park, one of the largest in
Africa, covers about the same
area as the country of Israel.

Great Zimbabwe National
Monument has the largest
ancient stone ruins in Africa
south of the Sahara.

Treacherous crosscurrents
off the northwest coast of
Namibia have caused
countless ships to wreck,
earning the area the
nickname Skeleton Coast.

⊙ **NATURAL WONDER.**
Victoria Falls, third
largest waterfall in the
world, is 5,500 feet
(1,676 m) wide and
355 feet (108 m) high.

Ringed by uplands, the region's central basin holds the seasonally lush Okavango Delta and scorching Kalahari Desert. The mighty Zambezi thunders over Victoria Falls on its way to the Indian Ocean, where Madagascar is home to plants and animals found nowhere else in the world. Bantu and San are among the indigenous people who saw their hold on the land give way to Portuguese, Dutch, and British traders and colonists. The region offers a range of mineral resources and a variety of climates and soils that in some places yield bumper crops of grains, grapes, and citrus. Rich deposits of coal, diamonds, and gold have helped make South Africa the continent's economic powerhouse.

◖ **STARING EYES.**
This ring-tailed lemur rests
in the crook of a forest tree
branch. The ring-tail, found
only in Madagascar, spends
time both on the ground
and in trees. It eats fruits,
leaves, insects, small birds,
and even lizards.

GLITTERING GEMS

African gem diamond production in thousands of carats
2016 data

15,000 — Botswana
8,100 — Angola
2,800 — Democratic Republic of the Congo
2,800 — South Africa
2,050 — Namibia
400 — Sierra Leone
350 — Zimbabwe

Diamonds are prized both for jewelry and for industrial uses. More than
half of the world's diamond production comes from mines in Africa.

THE CONTINENT:
AFRICA

EARLY MAN. Dating back perhaps 70,000 years, this skull of "Broken Hill Man" was found in Zimbabwe.

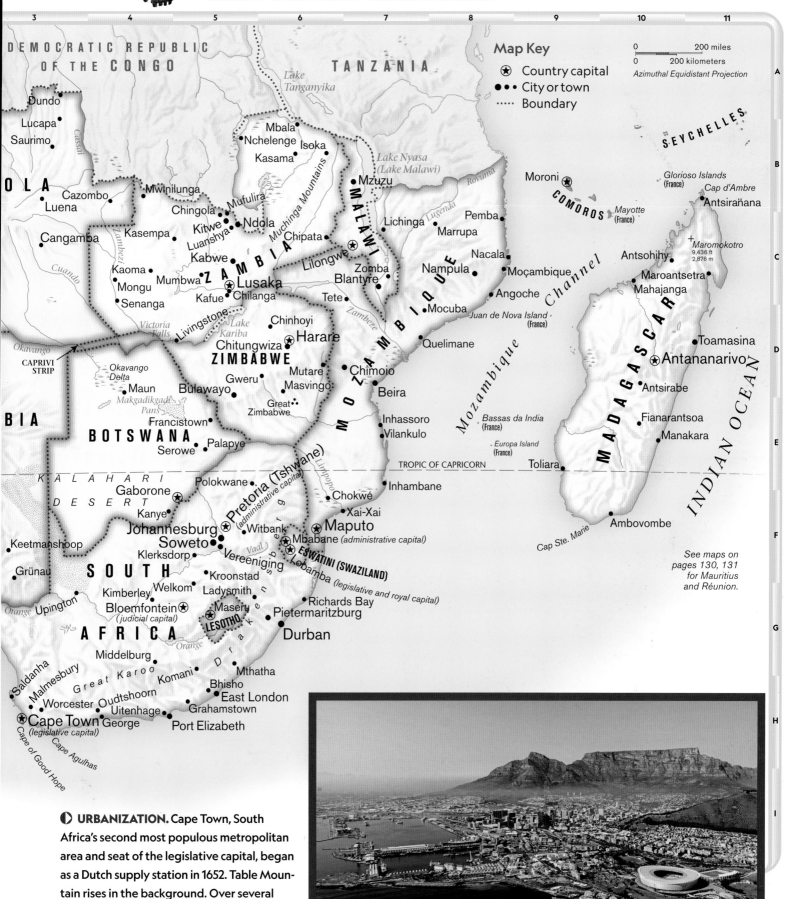

Map Key

⬢ Country capital
••• City or town
···· Boundary

0 ———— 200 miles
0 ———— 200 kilometers
Azimuthal Equidistant Projection

DEMOCRATIC REPUBLIC OF THE CONGO

TANZANIA

Lake Tanganyika

SEYCHELLES

Glorioso Islands (France)
Cap d'Ambre

COMOROS
Moroni ⬢
Mayotte (France)

Antsiranana

Dundo
Lucapa
Saurimo

Mbala
Nchelenge
Isoka
Kasama

Lake Nyasa (Lake Malawi)
Rovuma

Mzuzu

Lichinga
Lugenda

Pemba
Marrupa

Nacala

Antsohihy

+ Maromokotro
9,436 ft
2,876 m

Maroantsetra
Mahajanga

OLA
Cazombo
Luena
Cangamba

Mwinilunga
Chingola
Mufulira
Kitwe
Ndola
Luanshya
Kabwe

Muchinga Mountains

MALAWI

Chipata
Lilongwe

Zomba
Blantyre

Nampula

Moçambique

Angoche

MOZAMBIQUE CHANNEL

MADAGASCAR

Kasempa

Zambezi

ZAMBIA

Mocuba

Juan de Nova Island (France)

Toamasina

Kaoma
Mumbwa
Mongu
Senanga

⬢ Lusaka
Kafue
Chilanga

Tete

Zambeze

Quelimane

Antananarivo ⬢

Antsirabe

Cuando

Victoria Falls
Livingstone
Lake Kariba

Chinhoyi

Harare ⬢
Chitungwiza

Chimoio

Beira

Bassas da India (France)

Fianarantsoa

Manakara

Okavango
CAPRIVI STRIP

Okavango Delta

Maun

ZIMBABWE

Mutare
Gweru
Masvingo

Europa Island (France)

INDIAN OCEAN

BIA

Makgadikgadi Pans

Bulawayo

Great Zimbabwe

Inhassoro
Vilankulo

TROPIC OF CAPRICORN

Toliara

KALAHARI DESERT

Francistown

BOTSWANA
Serowe
Palapye

Polokwane

Inhambane

Cap Ste. Marie

Ambovombe

Gaborone ⬢
Kanye

Pretoria (Tshwane) (administrative capital)

Chokwé
Xai-Xai

Limpopo

See maps on pages 130, 131 for Mauritius and Réunion.

Keetmanshoop

Johannesburg ⬢
Soweto
Witbank

Maputo ⬢
Mbabane (administrative capital)

Grünau

Klerksdorp
Vereeniging
Vaal

ESWATINI (SWAZILAND)
Lobamba (legislative and royal capital)

SOUTH

Kroonstad

Orange
Upington

Welkom
Kimberley

Ladysmith

Richards Bay

Bloemfontein ⬢
(judicial capital)

Maseru
LESOTHO

Pietermaritzburg

AFRICA

Orange

Durban

Middelburg

Drakensberg

Saldanha
Malmesbury
Great Karoo
Komani

Mthatha

Worcester
Oudtshoorn
Uitenhage

Bhisho
East London
Grahamstown

⬢ Cape Town
(legislative capital)
George
Port Elizabeth

Cape of Good Hope
Cape Agulhas

URBANIZATION. Cape Town, South Africa's second most populous metropolitan area and seat of the legislative capital, began as a Dutch supply station in 1652. Table Mountain rises in the background. Over several years, starting in 2015, dry winters created a water shortage that required residents and visitors to reduce consumption.

PHYSICAL

Area and population totals are for the independent countries in the region only.

HIGHEST POINT
Mount Wilhelm,
Papua New Guinea
14,793 ft (4,509 m)

LOWEST POINT
Lake Eyre, Australia
-49 ft (-15 m)

LAND AREA
3,297,000 sq mi
(8,538,000 sq km)

LONGEST RIVER
Murray-Darling, Australia
2,282 mi (3,672 km)

LARGEST LAKE
Lake Eyre, Australia
3,741 sq mi (9,690 sq km)

POLITICAL

POPULATION
37,557,000

LARGEST METROPOLITAN AREA
Melbourne, Australia
Pop. 4,968,000

LARGEST COUNTRY
Australia
2,988,901 sq mi (7,741,220 sq km)

MOST DENSELY POPULATED COUNTRY
Nauru
1,250 people per sq mi (476 per sq km)

AUSTRALIA, NEW ZEALAND & OCEANIA

Australia, New Zealand & Oceania

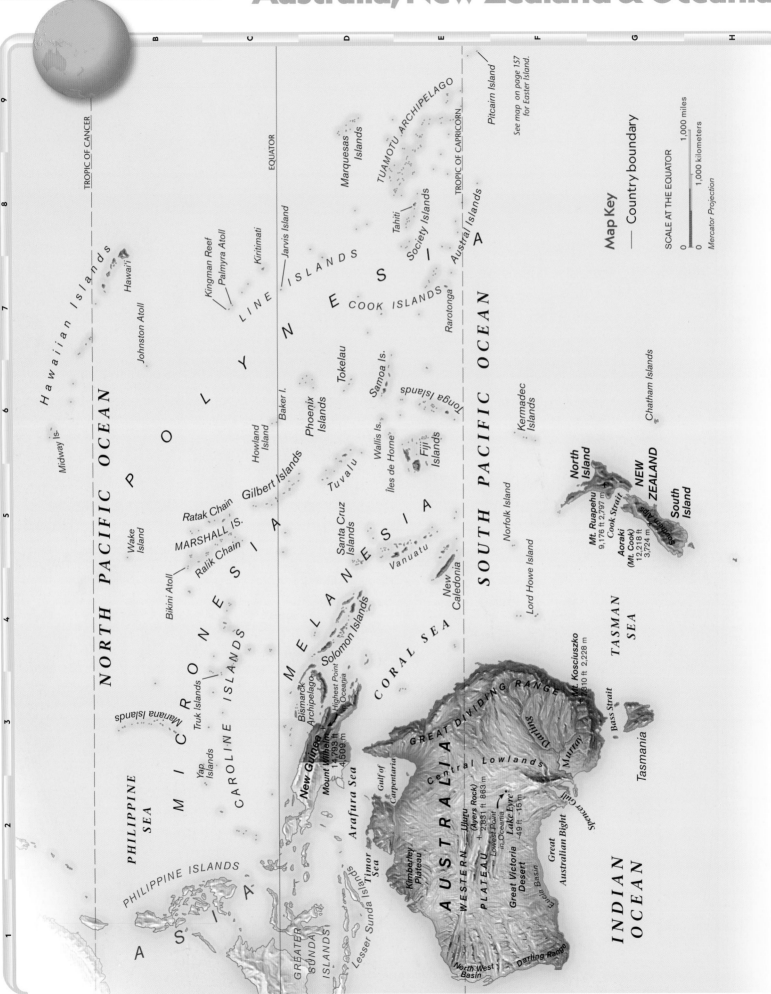

B   C   D   E   F   G   H

Map Key
— Country boundary

SCALE AT THE EQUATOR
0 — 1,000 miles
0 — 1,000 kilometers
Mercator Projection

See map on page 157
for Easter Island.

TROPIC OF CANCER

EQUATOR

TROPIC OF CAPRICORN

Pitcairn Island

Hawaiian Islands

Hawai'i

Johnston Atoll

Kingman Reef
Palmyra Atoll
Kiritimati

Jarvis Island

Marquesas
Islands

TUAMOTU ARCHIPELAGO

Tahiti
Society Islands

Austral Islands

LINE ISLANDS

COOK ISLANDS

Rarotonga

NORTH PACIFIC OCEAN

P O L Y N E S I A

Midway Is.

Wake
Island

Ratak Chain
MARSHALL IS.
Ralik Chain

Bikini Atoll

Gilbert Islands

Howland
Island
Baker I.

Phoenix
Islands

Tokelau

Samoa Is.

Tonga Islands

Wallis Is.
Îles de Horne
Fiji
Islands

Tuvalu

Kermadec
Islands

Chatham Islands

SOUTH PACIFIC OCEAN

**NEW
ZEALAND**

North
Island

Mt. Ruapehu
9,176 ft 2,797 m
Cook Strait
Aoraki
(Mt. Cook)
12,218 ft
3,724 m

Southern Alps

South
Island

M I C R O N E S I A

Mariana Islands

Yap
Islands

Truk Islands

CAROLINE ISLANDS

Santa Cruz
Islands

Vanuatu

M E L A N E S I A

New
Caledonia

Norfolk Island

Lord Howe Island

**PHILIPPINE
SEA**

Bismarck
Archipelago

Mount Wilhelm +
14,793 ft
4,509 m

Highest Point
in Oceania

New Guinea

Solomon Islands

CORAL SEA

**TASMAN
SEA**

Bass Strait

Tasmania

Darling

GREAT DIVIDING RANGE

Mt. Kosciuszko
7,310 ft 2,228 m

Murray

Darling

A S I A

**GREATER
SUNDA
ISLANDS**

PHILIPPINE ISLANDS

Lesser Sunda Islands

Timor
Sea

Arafura Sea

Gulf of
Carpentaria

Kimberley
Plateau

A U S T R A L I A

WESTERN
PLATEAU

Great Victoria
Desert

Eucla Basin

Central Lowlands

Uluru
(Ayers Rock)
2,831 ft 863 m

Lake Eyre
-49 ft -15 m
Lowest Point
in Oceania

Great
Australian Bight

Spencer Gulf

**INDIAN
OCEAN**

North West
Basin

Darling Range

9

8

7

6

5

4

3

2

1

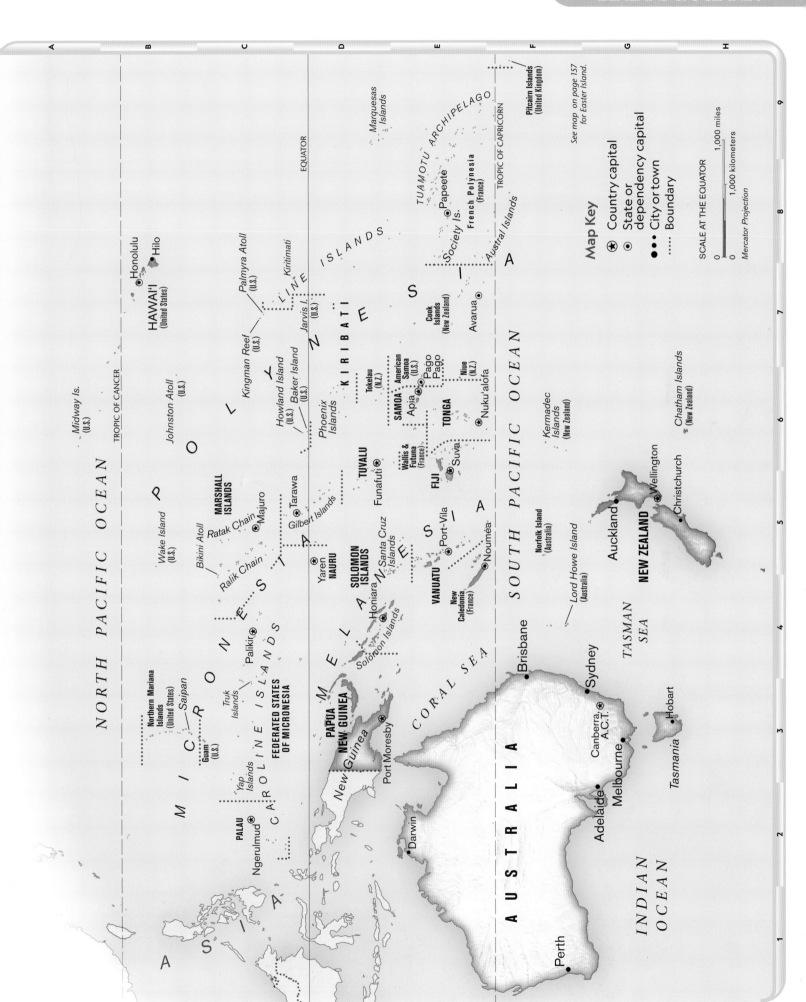

A B C D E F G H

9

8

Pitcairn Islands
(United Kingdom)

*See map on page 157
for Easter Island.*

Map Key

⍟ Country capital
◉ State or
  dependency capital
•••• City or town
····· Boundary

SCALE AT THE EQUATOR

1,000 miles

1,000 kilometers

Mercator Projection

*Marquesas
Islands*

EQUATOR

TUAMOTU ARCHIPELAGO

TROPIC OF CAPRICORN

Society Is. ◉ Papeete
*French Polynesia
(France)*

Austral Islands

*Midway Is.
(U.S.)*

TROPIC OF CANCER

Honolulu
⦿ ● Hilo
HAWAI'I
(United States)

*Palmyra Atoll
(U.S.)*

Kiritimati

L I N E   I S L A N D S

*Johnston Atoll
(U.S.)*

*Kingman Reef
(U.S.)*

*Jarvis I.
(U.S.)*

*Cook
Islands
(New Zealand)* ◉ Avarua

KIRIBATI

P O L Y N E S I A

N O R T H   P A C I F I C   O C E A N

*Wake Island
(U.S.)*

Bikini Atoll

**MARSHALL
ISLANDS**

*Howland Island
(U.S.)*
*Baker Island
(U.S.)*

*Phoenix
Islands*

Tokelau
(N.Z.)

American
Samoa
(U.S.)
Pago
Pago

Niue
(N.Z.)

Ratak Chain
⍟ Majuro

Tarawa

Gilbert Islands

SAMOA
Apia

TONGA
⍟ Nuku'alofa

TUVALU
⍟ Funafuti

Wallis &
Futuna
(France)

FIJI
Suva

M I C R O N E S I A

Ralik Chain

⍟ Yaren
NAURU

*Santa Cruz
Islands*

Port-Vila

*Kermadec
Islands
(New Zealand)*

*Chatham Islands
(New Zealand)*

*Northern Mariana
Islands
(United States)*
Saipan

*Truk
Islands*

Palikir ⍟

**FEDERATED STATES
OF MICRONESIA**

C A R O L I N E   I S L A N D S

M E L A N E S I A

**SOLOMON
ISLANDS**
Honiara ⍟

VANUATU

New
Caledonia
(France)
⦿ Nouméa

*Norfolk Island
(Australia)*

Auckland ●

NEW ZEALAND
⍟ Wellington
Christchurch

*Guam
(U.S.)*

*Yap
Islands*

PALAU
Ngerulmud ⍟

S O U T H   P A C I F I C   O C E A N

*Lord Howe Island
(Australia)*

*TASMAN
SEA*

A S I A

**PAPUA
NEW GUINEA**
⍟ Port Moresby

New Guinea

Solomon Islands

C O R A L   S E A

Brisbane ●

Sydney ●

Canberra,
A.C.T. ⍟

Melbourne ●
Adelaide ●

Hobart ●

Tasmania

● Darwin

A U S T R A L I A

I N D I A N
O C E A N

● Perth

1

2

3

4

5

6

7

Australia,
New Zealand
& Oceania
WORLDS APART

⬭ **AUSTRALIAN TEDDY BEAR.**
Koalas, which are not bears at all, are native to the eucalyptus forests of eastern Australia.

This vast region includes Australia—the world's smallest continent—New Zealand, and a fleet of mostly tiny island worlds scattered across the Pacific Ocean. Apart from Australia, New Zealand, and Papua New Guinea, Oceania's other 11 independent countries cover about 25,000 square miles (65,000 sq km), an area only slightly larger than half of New Zealand's North Island. Twenty-one other island groups are dependencies of the United States, France, Australia, New Zealand, or the United Kingdom. Long isolation has allowed the growth of diverse marine communities, such as Australia's Great Barrier Reef, and the evolution of platypuses, kangaroos, kiwis, and other land animals that live nowhere else on the planet.

⬭ **ANCIENT VOYAGERS.** The Maoris are believed to have sailed to New Zealand from islands far to the northeast. *Tā moko*, the unique Maori art of marking the skin, is a sacred tradition, symbolizing a person's connection to their family, tribe, and cultural identity.

PLACE OF LEGENDS. Once part of an ancient seabed, Uluṟu, also known as Ayers Rock, was exposed by erosion. This massive sandstone block is sacred to native Aboriginals. In 2017, the Uluṟu–Kata Tjuṯa National Park Board banned climbing on Uluṟu in an effort to promote respect for the sacred area.

TROPICAL HABITAT.
Brilliantly colored fish swim among branching corals in the warm waters of the Vatu-i-Ra Channel in the Fiji Islands. The waters around Fiji have some of the richest and most diverse fish populations in the world.

NATIVE COWBOYS.
Competition is fierce during a rodeo in Hope Vale, a community on Australia's Cape York Peninsula. Hope Vale is home to several Aboriginal clan groups.

THE REGION:
AUSTRALIA, NEW ZEALAND & OCEANIA

more about

Australia, New Zealand & Oceania

◒ **A WATER WORLD.** Located just seven degrees north of the Equator, the islands of the Republic of Palau were a United Nations Trust Territory until 1994, when they gained independence.

◒ **BIG JUMPER.** The red kangaroo, the largest living marsupial—an animal that carries its young in a pouch—is at home on the dry inland plains of Australia. It can cover 30 feet (9 m) in a single hop.

◖ **WOOLLY POPULATION.**
Sheep outnumber people in Australia and New Zealand. Wool production is an important part of the economies of these two countries.

◖ **STILT HOUSES.**
In Port Moresby, Papua New Guinea, people build stilt houses over the water in the Gulf of Papua. Stilt houses are used in this region to prevent homes from flooding and to keep out pests.

WHERE THE PICTURES ARE

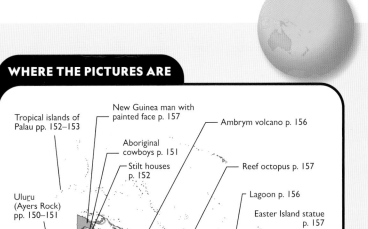

New Guinea man with painted face p. 157

Tropical islands of Palau pp. 152–153

Ambrym volcano p. 156

Aboriginal cowboys p. 151

Reef octopus p. 157

Stilt houses p. 152

Uluru (Ayers Rock) pp. 150–151

Lagoon p. 156

Easter Island statue p. 157

Coral reef with fish pp. 150–151

Red kangaroo p. 152

Auckland skyline pp. 152–153

Great white shark p. 154

Maori man p. 150

Koala p. 150

Sheep in pasture p. 152

Dingo p. 155

Aoraki (Mt. Cook) p. 153

Jet boat with tourists p. 153

Sydney Opera House p. 154

Mitre Peak p. 155

◗ **A WET RIDE.** Tourists go for a wild ride in a jet boat on the roaring waters of New Zealand's Shotover River.

◗ **MODERN METROPOLIS.**
Modern buildings rise against a twilight sky in Auckland, on New Zealand's North Island. It is home to almost one-third of the country's population.

◗ **SNOWY PEAK.** New Zealand's Aoraki (Mount Cook) rises above the clouds. Maori legend says that the peak is a frozen warrior surrounded by his brothers.

**THE REGION:
AUSTRALIA, NEW
ZEALAND & OCEANIA**

THE BASICS

STATS

Largest country
Australia 2,988,901 sq mi
(7,741,220 sq km)

Smallest country
New Zealand 103,799 sq mi
(268,838 sq km)

Most populous country
Australia 23,470,000

Least populous country
New Zealand 4,546,000

Predominant languages
English, Maori

Predominant religion
Christianity

Highest GDP per capita
Australia $50,300

Lowest GDP per capita
New Zealand $38,900

Highest life expectancy
Australia 82 years

Lowest life expectancy
New Zealand 81 years

GEO WHIZ

A tree trunk hollowed out
by termites is used by Australia's Aboriginals to make a
musical instrument called a
didgeridoo.

Wellington, in New Zealand,
is the southernmost national
capital city in the world.

Lake Eyre is Australia's largest
lake, but it is very shallow.
When filled to capacity, it is
not quite 20 feet (6 m) deep.

In September 2010, a magnitude 7.1 earthquake, followed
by a 6.3 aftershock in February 2011, caused widespread
destruction in Christchurch,
on New Zealand's South
Island.

Australia & New Zealand

Most people in Australia live along the coast, far from the country's dry interior, known as the Outback. The most populous cities and the best croplands are in the south-east. This "Land Down Under" is increasingly linked by trade to Asia and to 4.5 million "neigh-bors" in New Zealand. Lying 1,200 miles (1,930 km) across the Tasman Sea, New Zealand is cooler, wetter, and more mountainous than Australia. Geologically active, it has eco-systems ranging from subtropi-cal forests on North Island to snowy peaks on South Island. Both countries enjoy high standards of living and strong agricultural and mining outputs, including wool, wines, gold, coal, and iron ore.

SAILS AT SUNSET.
Reminiscent of a ship in
full sail, the Sydney
Opera House, in Sydney
Harbor, has become a
symbol of Australia that
is recognized worldwide.

OCEAN TRAVELER.
Great white sharks inhabit
the warm waters off the
coast of southern
Australia. These marine
predators can grow up to
20 feet (6 m) in length.

Map labels:
INDONESIA · TIMOR-LESTE (EAST TIMOR) · Timor Sea · Ashmore Islands · Joseph Bonaparte Gulf · Cartier I. · Cape Talbot · Admiralty Gulf · Collier Bay · King Sound · Cape Leveque · Wyndham · Cape Leveque · Derby · Ord · Dampier Land · Halls Creek · Broome · Fitzroy · Lagrange · Great Sandy Desert · Fitzroy Crossing · Port Hedland · Monte Bello Islands · Dampier · Barrow Island · Karratha · Marble Bar · North West Cape · Onslow · Gibson · Exmouth · TROPIC OF CAPRICORN · Desert · WESTERN · Carnarvon · AUS · Shark Bay · Meekatharra · Wiluna · Great Victoria · Cape Inscription · Denham · AUSTRALIA · Mount Magnet · Laverton · Nullarbor · Geraldton · Menzies · Dongara · Kalgoorlie · Haig · Perth · Northam · Norseman · Narrogin · Great · Geographe Bay · Bunbury · Cape Pasley · Cape Naturaliste · Busselton · Esperance · Augusta · Hopetoun · Cape Leeuwin · Albany · West Cape Howe · INDIAN OCEAN

0 | 400 miles
0 | 400 kilometers

Azimuthal Equidistant Projection

◑ **DOG OF THE OUTBACK.** The dingo is a wild dog found throughout Australia except Tasmania. Unlike most domestic dogs, the dingo does not bark, although it howls.

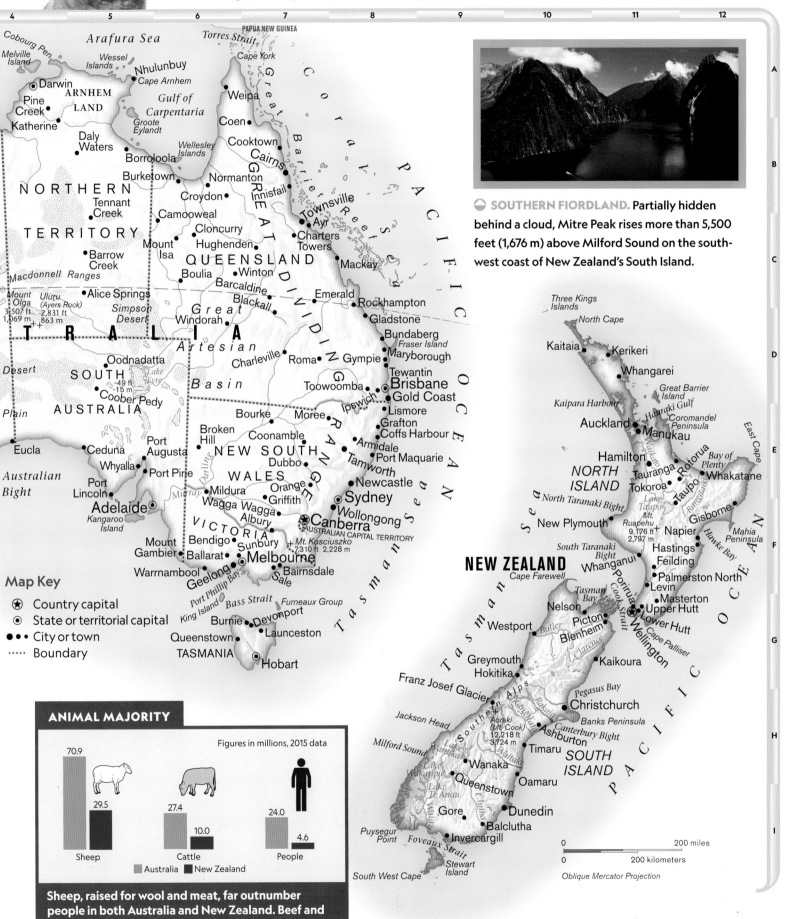

⬤ **SOUTHERN FIORDLAND. Partially hidden** behind a cloud, Mitre Peak rises more than 5,500 feet (1,676 m) above Milford Sound on the southwest coast of New Zealand's South Island.

Map Key

⊛ Country capital
◉ State or territorial capital
●●● City or town
····· Boundary

ANIMAL MAJORITY

Figures in millions, 2015 data

	Sheep	Cattle	People
Australia	70.9	27.4	24.0
New Zealand	29.5	10.0	4.6

■ Australia ■ New Zealand

Sheep, raised for wool and meat, far outnumber people in both Australia and New Zealand. Beef and dairy cattle also surpass the human population.

200 miles
200 kilometers

Oblique Mercator Projection

THE BASICS

STATS

Largest country
Papua New Guinea
178,703 sq mi (462,840 sq km)

Smallest country
Nauru 8 sq mi (21 sq km)

Most populous country
Papua New Guinea 7,027,000

Least populous country
Nauru 10,000

Predominant languages
English, indigenous languages

Predominant religions
Christianity, indigenous beliefs

Highest GDP per capita
Palau $16,200

Lowest GDP per capita
Kiribati $2,000

Highest life expectancy
Tonga 76 years

Lowest life expectancy
Kiribati 66 years

GEO WHIZ

Five uninhabited islands in the Solomon group have disappeared due to rising sea levels caused by climate change, and the inhabited island of Nuatambu has lost more than 50 percent of its land area.

Most of the islands of Pacific countries are atolls, which are coral reefs encircling a lagoon.

Palau, Micronesia, offers diving opportunities to view historic shipwrecks and marine life.

 **LIVING EARTH.**
Ambrym volcano, in Vanuatu, is one of the most active volcanoes in Oceania. Ambrym continues to erupt regularly, adding to the island's black sand beaches.

Oceania

Although in its broadest sense Oceania includes Australia and New Zealand, more commonly it refers to some 25,000 islands that make up three large cultural regions in the Pacific Ocean. Melanesia, which extends from Papua New Guinea to Fiji, is closest to Australia. Micronesia lies mostly north of the Equator and includes Palau and the Federated States of Micronesia. New Zealand, Hawai'i, and Rapa Nui (Easter Island) mark the western, northern, and eastern limits of Polynesia, with Tahiti, Samoa, and Tonga near its heart. Oceania's people often face problems of limited living space and freshwater. Plantation agriculture, fishing, tourism, or mining form the economic base for most of the islands in this region.

⬭ **TROPICAL PARADISE.**
A reef separates an area of seawater from the ocean, forming a quiet lagoon around the island of Bora Bora in the Society Islands of French Polynesia.

◐ **UNSOLVED MYSTERY.** Carved from volcanic rock, the giant stone heads, called *moai,* on Rapa Nui (Easter Island) remain a mystery.

◑ **PROBLEM-SOLVING.** Octopuses live on coral reefs in the tropical waters of the South Pacific Ocean. They are one of the few solitary animals with high levels of problem-solving skills.

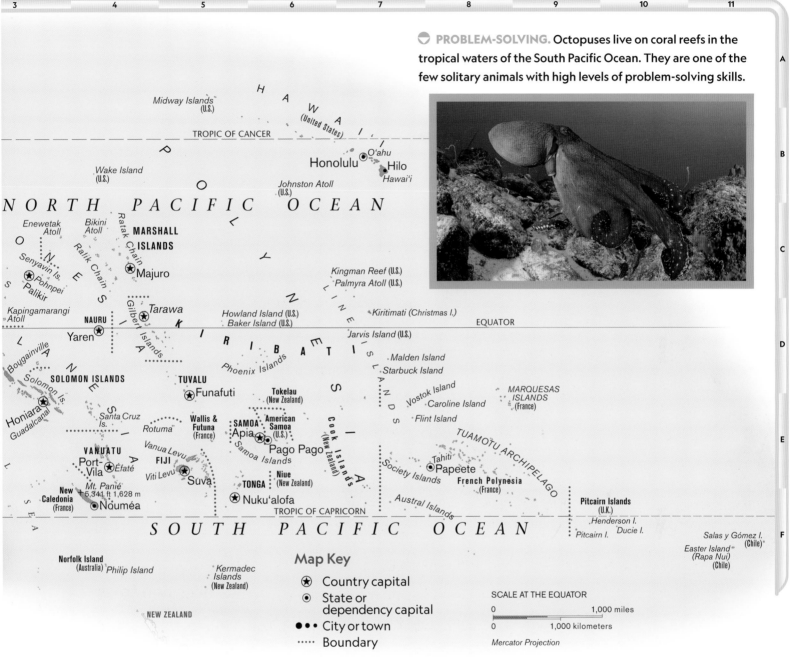

Midway Islands (U.S.)

HAWAII (United States)

TROPIC OF CANCER

Wake Island (U.S.)

Johnston Atoll (U.S.)

Honolulu   O'ahu
Hilo
Hawai'i

N O R T H   P A C I F I C   O C E A N

P O L Y N E S I A

Enewetak Atoll   Bikini Atoll
Ratak Chain
MARSHALL ISLANDS
Ralik Chain
Senyavin Is.
Pohnpei
Palikir
M I C R O N E S I A
Majuro

Kapingamarangi Atoll
NAURU
Gilbert Islands
Tarawa

Kingman Reef (U.S.)
Palmyra Atoll (U.S.)

Yaren
K I R I B A T I
L I N E   I S L A N D S

Howland Island (U.S.)
Baker Island (U.S.)
Kiritimati (Christmas I.)
EQUATOR

Jarvis Island (U.S.)

Bougainville
Solomon Is.
M E L A N E S I A
SOLOMON ISLANDS
Honiara
Guadalcanal
Santa Cruz Is.

TUVALU
Funafuti
Phoenix Islands

Malden Island
Starbuck Island
Vostok Island
Caroline Island
Flint Island

MARQUESAS ISLANDS (France)

Tokelau (New Zealand)

Rotuma
Wallis & Futuna (France)
SAMOA American Samoa (U.S.)
Apia
Samoa Islands
Pago Pago

Cook Islands (New Zealand)

Society Islands
Tahiti
Papeete

TUAMOTU ARCHIPELAGO

VANUATU
Vanua Levu
Port-Vila   Éfaté
FIJI
Viti Levu
Suva
Niue (New Zealand)
TONGA
Nuku'alofa

French Polynesia (France)
Austral Islands

Pitcairn Islands (U.K.)

New Caledonia (France)
Mt. Panié
+5,341 ft 1,628 m
Nouméa
TROPIC OF CAPRICORN

S O U T H   P A C I F I C   O C E A N

C O R A L   S E A

Henderson I.
Pitcairn I.   Ducie I.

Salas y Gómez I. (Chile)
Easter Island (Rapa Nui) (Chile)

Norfolk Island (Australia)   Philip Island
Kermadec Islands (New Zealand)

NEW ZEALAND

Map Key

⊛ Country capital
◉ State or dependency capital
●●● City or town
⋯⋯ Boundary

SCALE AT THE EQUATOR

0 ———————— 1,000 miles
0 ———————— 1,000 kilometers

Mercator Projection

◐ **MELANESIAN CUSTOM. In the** Huli culture of Papua New Guinea's Eastern Highlands, men adorn themselves with colorful paints, feathers, and grasses as they prepare to take part in festivals.

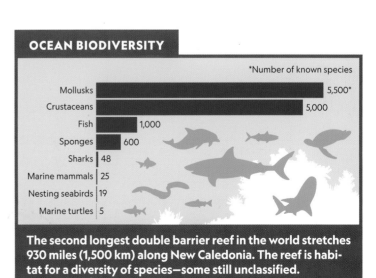

OCEAN BIODIVERSITY

*Number of known species

Mollusks	5,500*
Crustaceans	5,000
Fish	1,000
Sponges	600
Sharks	48
Marine mammals	25
Nesting seabirds	19
Marine turtles	5

The second longest double barrier reef in the world stretches 930 miles (1,500 km) along New Caledonia. The reef is habitat for a diversity of species—some still unclassified.

THE CONTINENT:
ANTARCTICA

PHYSICAL

LAND AREA 5,100,000 sq mi (13,209,000 sq km)	**LOWEST POINT** Byrd Glacier (depression) -9,416 ft (-2,870 m)	**AVERAGE PRECIPITATION ON THE POLAR PLATEAU** Less than 2 in (5 cm) per year	
HIGHEST POINT Vinson Massif 16,067 ft (4,897 m)	**COLDEST PLACE** Ridge A Annual average temperature -94°F (-70°C)		

POLITICAL

POPULATION There are no indigenous inhabitants, but there are scientists and other staff at both permanent and summer-only research stations.	**NUMBER OF INDEPENDENT COUNTRIES** 0	**NUMBER OF COUNTRIES OPERATING YEAR-ROUND RESEARCH STATIONS** 21
	NUMBER OF COUNTRIES CLAIMING LAND 7	**NUMBER OF YEAR-ROUND RESEARCH STATIONS** 40

ANTARCTICA

ANTARCTICA
THE FROZEN SOUTH

Antarctica is the coldest, windiest, and even driest continent. Though its immense ice sheet holds more than 60 percent of Earth's freshwater, its interior averages less than two inches (5 cm) of precipitation per year. Hidden beneath the ice is a continent of valleys, mountains, and lakes, but less than 2 percent of the land actually breaks through the ice cover. Like a finger pointing north toward South America, the Antarctic Peninsula is the most visited region of the continent, but scientists occupy a total of more than 70 permanent and seasonal research stations throughout the continent, from which they study this frozen land.

◯ **FORMAL DRESS.** Black-and-white gentoo penguins live in colonies year-round along the Antarctic Peninsula. These flightless birds dive to more than 300 feet (90 m) to catch fish and krill, their main food source.

DRIFTING RESEARCH. The U.S. Amundsen-Scott research station is located at the geographic South Pole. The station and the ice sheet on which it sits are drifting about 33 feet (10 m) each year.

WHERE THE PICTURES ARE

Researcher
p. 162

Leopard seal
p. 163

Tourists & whale
pp. 162–163

Iceberg
pp. 160–161

Gentoo
penguins
p. 160

Orcas
p. 163

Amundsen-
Scott
station p. 161

BLUE WONDER. An iceberg drifts in the Lemaire Channel near the Antarctic Peninsula. The dense, compressed ice reflects only short wavelengths, giving the ice a blue tint.

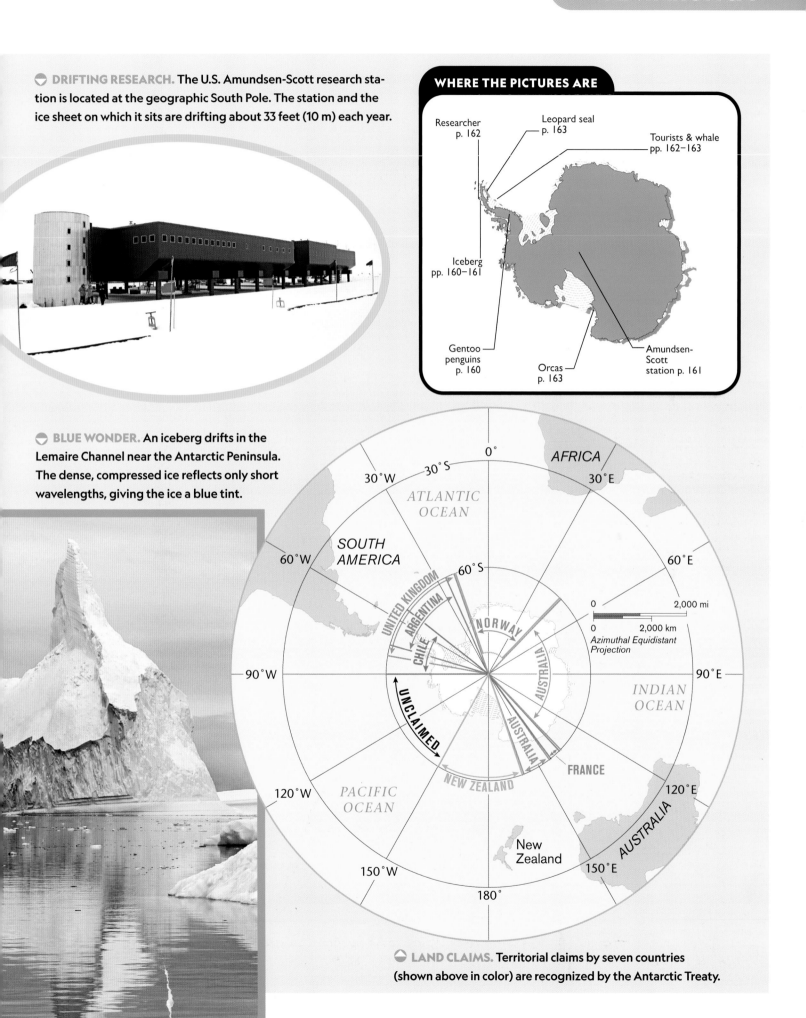

AFRICA

ATLANTIC
OCEAN

SOUTH
AMERICA

0°
30°S
30°W
30°E
60°W
60°S
60°E
90°W
90°E
120°W
120°E
150°W
150°E
180°

UNITED KINGDOM
ARGENTINA
CHILE
NORWAY
AUSTRALIA
UNCLAIMED
AUSTRALIA
NEW ZEALAND
FRANCE

INDIAN
OCEAN

PACIFIC
OCEAN

New
Zealand

AUSTRALIA

0   2,000 mi
0   2,000 km
Azimuthal Equidistant
Projection

LAND CLAIMS. Territorial claims by seven countries (shown above in color) are recognized by the Antarctic Treaty.

THE CONTINENT:
ANTARCTICA

Antarctica

THE BASICS

Antarctica is the only continent that has no political boundaries and no economy or permanent population. Seven countries claim portions of the landmass (map, page 161), but according to the Antarctic Treaty, which preserves the continent for peaceful use and scientific study, no country rules.

GEO WHIZ

The Antarctic Convergence, an area where the waters of Earth's four oceans meet the cold Antarctic Circumpolar Current, is one of the planet's richest marine ecosystems.

Krill, a tiny shrimplike creature that thrives in Antarctic waters, is important in the Antarctic food chain. Whales, seals, and penguins are among the creatures that depend on it for survival.

The tiny wingless midge—less than one-quarter inch (6 mm) long—is Antarctica's largest land animal. This insect is able to survive high levels of salt, freezing temperatures, and ultraviolet radiation in the continent's extreme climate.

Mount Erebus, named for a British explorer's ship, is the world's southernmost active volcano.

◯ **NATURE STUDY.**
A researcher at Palmer Station examines penguin eggs attacked by skuas, birds that feed on these eggs.

Under the terms of the Antarctic Treaty, the region beyond 60° south latitude is set aside for peaceful scientific study and research. Antarctica was first visited by Europeans in 1821, but there has never been a permanent human population. Today, more than 4,000 scientists live at research stations during the southern summer (October to March), studying climate history preserved in the ice sheets that cover the continent and observing the effects of current climate change on plant and animal life. During the cold, dark southern winter, the research population drops to only a little more than 1,000. In addition to scientists, almost 55,000 tourists visit Antarctica during the southern summer, mainly along the Antarctic Peninsula, where they view wildlife such as seals, whales, penguins, and other birds.

South Orkney Islands

South Shetland Islands

Joinville Island

Palmer Station (United States)

Antarc...

Bellingshausen Sea

1

DAY AND NIGHT

Average number of daylight hours per month, Palmer Station (64° 46'S; 64° 03'W), 2017 data

Month	Hours
JAN	19.42
FEB	15.78
MAR	12.51
APR	9.10
MAY	5.85
JUN	3.69
JUL	4.97
AUG	8.00
SEP	11.34
OCT	14.67
NOV	18.36
DEC	21.14

Because of its very high southern latitude, Antarctica experiences extreme fluctuations in the length of daylight hours. At the South Pole (90° S) there are months of total darkness.

STANDING GUARD. Leopard seals' preferred food is penguins, but they also eat other species of seals.

ATLANTIC OCEAN

Fimbul Ice Shelf

Cape Norvegia

Riiser-Larsen Ice Shelf

Riiser-Larsen Peninsula

Lützow-Holm Bay

INDIAN OCEAN

Q u e e n   M a u d   L a n d

Enderby Land

0   500 miles
0   500 kilometers
Azimuthal Equidistant Projection

ANTARCTIC CIRCLE

*W e d d e l l
S e a*

Larsen C iceberg
detached
July 12, 2017

Cape Darnley

*Larsen
Ice Shelf*

Mt. Jackson
10,446 ft 3,184 m

Coats Land

*Filchner
Ice Shelf*

*Amery
Ice Shelf*

Coldest place
in the world

Prydz Bay

tic Peninsula

**Alexander
Island**

**Berkner
Island**

*Ronne
Ice Shelf*

*Pensacola
Mountains*

R I D G E   A

*American
Highland*

*West
Ice Shelf*

P O L A R

E A S T

Ellsworth   Land

Vinson
Massif
16,067 ft
4,897 m

Highest point
in Antarctica

P L A T E A U

A N T A R C T I C A

**Thurston
Island**

Ellsworth Mts.

WEST

Vostok Station
(Russia)

Amundsen Sea

ANTARCTICA

Marie Byrd Land

★ South Pole
■ Amundsen-Scott Station
(United States)

T r a n s a n t a r c t i c   M o u n t a i n s

Getz Ice Shelf

*Ross
Ice Shelf*

Byrd
Glacier
-9,416 ft
-2,870 m

Lowest point
in Antarctica

Shackleton Ice Shelf

W i l k e s   L a n d

*Cape
Poinsett*

PACIFIC OCEAN

**Roosevelt
Island**

Mt. Erebus
12,448 ft
3,794 m

Ross I.

McMurdo Sound

Victoria   Land

*Ross
Sea*

Cape Crozier

Map Key
★ Pole
■ Research station

Mt. Minto
13,665 ft
4,165 m

Cape Adare

ANTARCTIC CIRCLE

★ South
Magnetic Pole

Porpoise Bay

SOUTHERN EXPLORATION. Adventurous tourists, riding in a Zodiac, get a close-up look at a humpback whale diving under the waters of the Weddell Sea. These motorized inflatable boats enable passengers to travel from their expedition ship, anchored in deep water, to the shores of the Antarctic Peninsula.

COLD SWIM. A mother orca and her calf come up for air in the icy waters of McMurdo Sound. Orcas live in social groups called pods and work together to catch meals of fish, seals, or sea lions.

THE OCEANS

TOTAL SURFACE AREA	LARGEST OCEAN	GREATEST OCEAN DEPTH	TALLEST MOUNTAIN	LARGEST CORAL
139,434,000 sq mi (361,132,000 sq km)	Pacific 69,000,000 sq mi (178,800,000 sq km)	Challenger Deep, Pacific Ocean -36,037 ft (-10,984 m)	**(SEAFLOOR TO SUMMIT)** Mauna Kea, Hawai'i, U.S.A. 32,696 ft (9,966 m)	REEF ECOSYSTEM Great Barrier Reef, Australia 134,000 sq mi (348,300 sq km)
PERCENTAGE OF EARTH'S SURFACE 71%	SMALLEST OCEAN Arctic 5,600,000 sq mi (14,700,000 sq km)	LONGEST MOUNTAIN RANGE Mid-Ocean Ridge 37,000 mi (60,000 km)	GREATEST TIDAL RANGE Bay of Fundy, Canada's Atlantic Coast 53 ft (16 m)	

THE OCEANS

THE OCEANS

Investigating the Oceans

The map at right shows that more than 70 percent of Earth's surface is underwater, mainly covered by four great oceans. There is growing support for recognizing a fifth ocean, called the Southern Ocean, in the area from Antarctica to 60° S latitude. The oceans are really inter-connected bodies of water that together form one global ocean.

The ocean floor is as varied as the surface of the continents, but mapping the oceans is challenging. Past explorers cut their way through jungles of the Amazon and conquered the icy heights of the Himalaya, but explorers could not march across the floor of the Pacific Ocean, which in places descends to more than 36,000 feet (10,970 m) below the surface of the water.

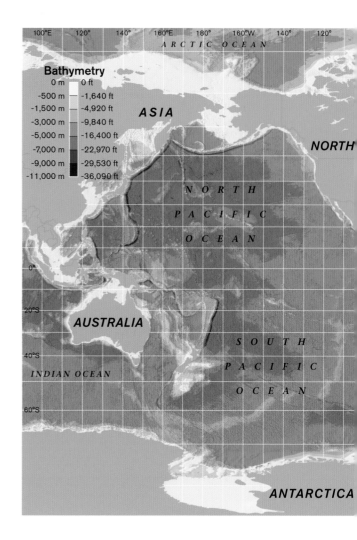

Bathymetry

0 m	0 ft
-500 m	-1,640 ft
-1,500 m	-4,920 ft
-3,000 m	-9,840 ft
-5,000 m	-16,400 ft
-7,000 m	-22,970 ft
-9,000 m	-29,530 ft
-11,000 m	-36,090 ft

ARCTIC OCEAN

ASIA

NORTH

NORTH PACIFIC OCEAN

AUSTRALIA

SOUTH PACIFIC OCEAN

INDIAN OCEAN

ANTARCTICA

🌐 **UNDERWATER LANDSCAPE.** The landscape of the ocean floor is varied and constantly changing. A continental edge that slopes gently beneath the water is called a continental shelf (1). Mountain ranges, called mid-ocean ridges (2), rise where ocean plates are spreading and magma flows out to create new land. Elsewhere, plates plunge into trenches (3) more than six miles (10 km) deep. In addition, magma, rising through vents called hot spots, pushes through ocean plates, creating seamounts (4) and volcanoes (5).

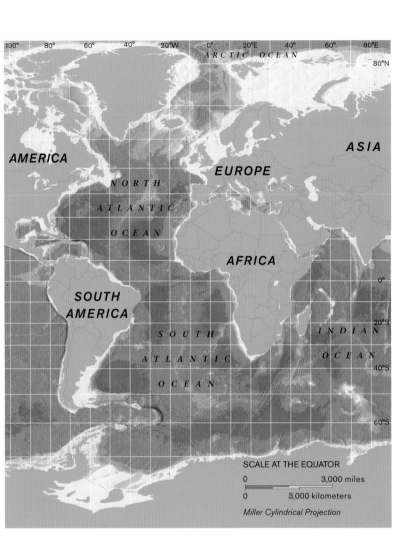

SCALE AT THE EQUATOR

0   3,000 miles

0   3,000 kilometers

Miller Cylindrical Projection

⬭ **FROM OCEAN TO SATELLITE.** In the 1990s, scientists developed the Argo Float to collect data from below the ocean surface. Argo Floats sink to a preset depth, often thousands of feet, where they gather data, such as temperature and salt content. At regular intervals, the floats rise to the surface (above) and transmit the data collected to a satellite. Then the cycle starts over again.

◗ **SEEING WITH YOUR EARS.** Special instruments, such as this acoustic buoy, use sound waves bounced off the ocean floor to record variations in water temperature. This technique, called Acoustic Thermometry of Ocean Climate (ATOC), may someday help monitor long-term climate changes.

◖ **EYE ON THE OCEAN.** Satellites orbiting high above Earth's surface record digital images of ocean colors, sea surface temperatures, and salinity levels. These can be used to identify and follow plant and animal activity as well as changes in the ocean environment.

Pacific Ocean

THE BASICS

STATS

Surface area
69,000,000 sq mi
(178,800,000 sq km)

Percentage of Earth's water area
49.5%

Greatest depth
Challenger Deep
(in the Mariana Trench)
-36,037 ft (-10,984 m)

Tides
Highest: 30 ft (9 m)
near Korean peninsula
Lowest: 1 ft (0.3 m)
near Midway Islands

GEO WHIZ

The Pacific Ocean has more islands—tens of thousands of them—than any other ocean.

The ocean's name comes from the Latin *Mare Pacificum,* meaning "peaceful sea," but earthquakes and volcanic activity along the Ring of Fire generate powerful waves called tsunamis, which cause death and destruction when they slam ashore.

With the greatest area of tropical waters, the Pacific is also home to the largest number of coral reefs, including Earth's longest: Australia's Great Barrier Reef.

Only about 1,000 Hawaiian monk seals remain in the wild. Most live in protected waters of the Hawaiian archipelago.

🔵 **IN THE MIDST OF DANGER.** A false-clown anemonefish swims among the tentacles of a sea anemone off the coast of the Philippines, in the western Pacific. This colorful fish is immune to the anemone's paralyzing sting.

The Pacific Ocean, largest of Earth's oceans, is more than 15 times larger than the United States and covers more than 30 percent of Earth's surface. The margins of the Pacific are often called the Ring of Fire because many active volcanoes and earthquakes occur where the ocean plate is moving under the edges of continental plates. The southwestern Pacific is dotted with many islands. Also in the western Pacific, Challenger Deep in the Mariana Trench plunges to 36,037 ft (10,984 m) below sea level. Most of the world's fish catch comes from the Pacific, and oil and gas reserves in the Pacific are an important energy source.

🔵 **CIRCLE OF LIFE.** Atolls, such as this one near Okinawa, Japan, are ocean landforms created by tiny marine animals called corals. These creatures live in warm tropical waters. The circular shapes of atolls often mark the coastlines of sunken volcanic islands.

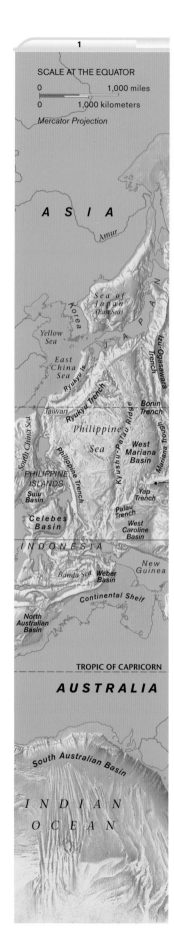

SCALE AT THE EQUATOR
0 — 1,000 miles
0 — 1,000 kilometers
Mercator Projection

ASIA

Amur

Sea of Japan (East Sea)

Korea

Yellow Sea

East China Sea

Taiwan

Ryukyu Is.

Ryukyu Trench

South China Sea

Philippine Sea

Philippine Trench

PHILIPPINE ISLANDS

Sulu Basin

Celebes Basin

INDONESIA

Banda Sea

Weber Basin

North Australian Basin

Izu-Ogasawara Trench

Bonin Trench

Kyushu-Palau Ridge

West Mariana Basin

Mariana Trench

Yap Trench

Palau Trench

West Caroline Basin

New Guinea

Continental Shelf

TROPIC OF CAPRICORN

AUSTRALIA

South Australian Basin

INDIAN OCEAN

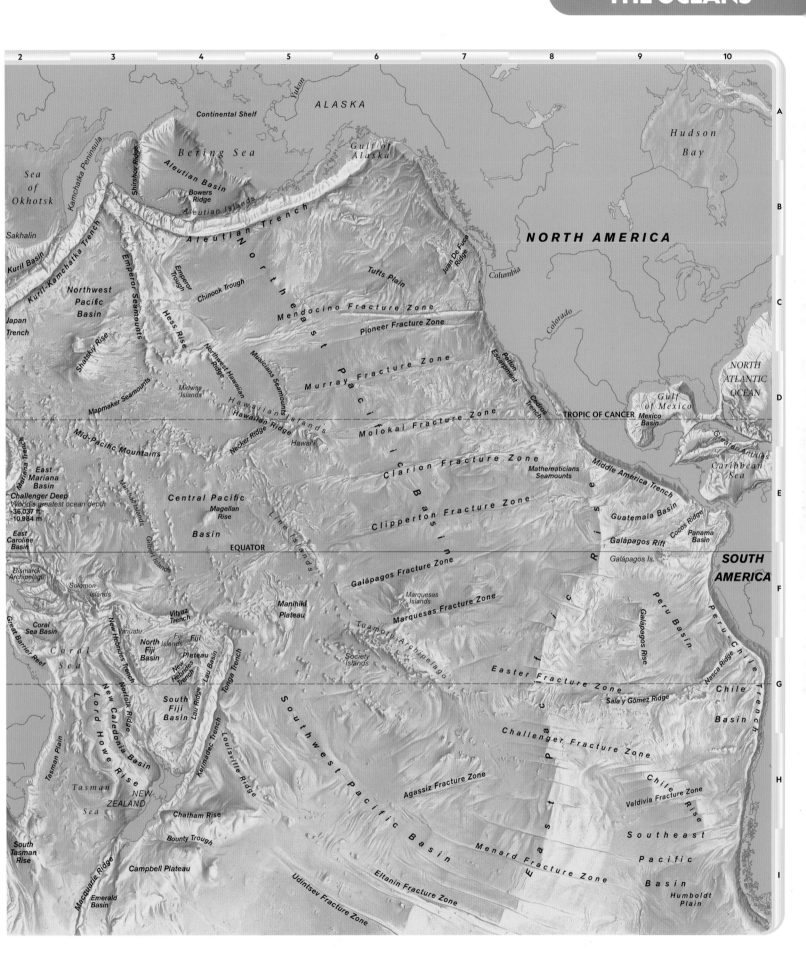

ALASKA

Continental Shelf

Hudson Bay

Bering Sea

Gulf of Alaska

Aleutian Basin

Bowers Ridge

NORTH AMERICA

Sea of Okhotsk

Sakhalin

Kamchatka Peninsula

Shirshov Ridge

Aleutian Islands

Aleutian Trench

Juan De Fuca Ridge

Columbia

Kuril Basin

Kuril-Kamchatka Trench

Emperor Seamounts

Emperor Trough

Chinook Trough

Tufts Plain

Northwest Pacific Basin

Hess Rise

Mendocino Fracture Zone

Pioneer Fracture Zone

Colorado

NORTH ATLANTIC OCEAN

Japan Trench

Shatskiy Rise

Northwest Hawaiian Ridge

Musicians Seamounts

Murray Fracture Zone

Patton Escarpment

Cedros Trench

Gulf of Mexico

Mapmaker Seamounts

Midway Islands

Hawaiian Islands

Molokai Fracture Zone

TROPIC OF CANCER

Mexico Basin

Mid-Pacific Mountains

Hawaiian Ridge

Necker Ridge

Hawai'i

Greater Antilles

Caribbean Sea

Mariana Trench

East Mariana Basin

Clarion Fracture Zone

Mathematicians Seamounts

Middle America Trench

Challenger Deep World's greatest ocean depth −36,037 ft −10,984 m

Marshall Islands

Central Pacific Magellan Rise Basin

Clipperton Fracture Zone

Guatemala Basin

Cocos Ridge

East Caroline Basin

Line Islands

Galápagos Rift

Panama Basin

EQUATOR

Gilbert Islands

Galápagos Is.

SOUTH AMERICA

Bismarck Archipelago

Solomon Islands

Galápagos Fracture Zone

Marquesas Islands

Peru Basin

Galápagos Rise

Coral Sea Basin

Vityaz Trench

Manihiki Plateau

Marquesas Fracture Zone

Nazca Ridge

New Hebrides Trench

Fiji Fiji Islands

Tuamotu Archipelago

Peru-Chile Trench

Great Barrier Reef

North Fiji Basin

New Plateau

Society Islands

Easter Fracture Zone

Chile Basin

Coral Sea

New Hebrides Trench

Lau Basin

Tonga Trench

Sala y Gómez Ridge

Vanuatu

Lau Ridge

South Fiji Basin

Norfolk Ridge

Challenger Fracture Zone

Chile Rise

Tasman Plain

New Caledonia Basin

Kermadec Trench

Louisville Ridge

Southwest Pacific Basin

Agassiz Fracture Zone

Valdivia Fracture Zone

Lord Howe Rise

Tasman Sea

NEW ZEALAND

Chatham Rise

Southeast Pacific Basin

South Tasman Rise

Bounty Trough

Menard Fracture Zone

Humboldt Plain

Macquarie Ridge

Campbell Plateau

Eltanin Fracture Zone

Emerald Basin

Udintsev Fracture Zone

THE OCEANS

THE BASICS

STATS

Surface area
35,400,000 sq mi
(91,700,000 sq km)

Percentage of Earth's water area
25.4%

Greatest depth
Puerto Rico Trench
-28,232 ft (-8,605 m)

Tides
Highest: 53 ft (16 m)
Bay of Fundy, Canada
Lowest: 1.5 ft (0.5 m)
Gulf of Mexico and
Mediterranean Sea

GEO WHIZ

The Atlantic Ocean gets its name from Greek mythology. "Atlantic" means "Sea of Atlas" in reference to the Greek god Atlas, who was forced to carry the weight of the heavens on his shoulders as a punishment.

The Atlantic Ocean is about half the size of the Pacific and is slowly growing. As molten rock from Earth's interior escapes where spreading occurs along the Mid-Atlantic Ridge, new ocean floor forms.

Each year, the amount of water that flows into the Atlantic Ocean from the Amazon River, in South America, is equal to 20 percent of Earth's available freshwater.

HIDDEN DANGER.
Icebergs (right) are huge blocks of ice that break away, or calve, from the edges of glaciers. They pose a danger to ships because only about 10 percent of their bulk is visible above the waterline. A tragic disaster associated with an iceberg was the 1912 sinking of the R.M.S. *Titanic,* whose ghostly ruins lie below the waters of the North Atlantic Ocean (far right).

Atlantic Ocean

CAMOUFLAGE ON ICE. A young harp seal, called a pup, rests on the ice in Canada's Gulf of St. Lawrence. Pups are cared for by their mothers for only 12 days. After that, they must survive on their own.

Among Earth's great oceans, the Atlantic is second only to the Pacific in size. The floor of the Atlantic is split by the Mid-Atlantic Ridge, which is part of the Mid-Ocean Ridge—the longest mountain chain on Earth. The Atlantic poses many hazards to human activity. Tropical storms called hurricanes form in the warm tropical waters off the west coast of Africa and move across the ocean to bombard the islands of the Caribbean and coastal areas of North and Central America with damaging winds, waves, and rain in the late summer and fall. In the cold waters of the North Atlantic, sea ice and icebergs pose risks to shipping, especially during winter and spring.

The Atlantic has rich deposits of oil and natural gas, but drilling has raised concerns about pollution. In addition, the Atlantic has important marine fisheries, but overfishing has put some species at risk. Sea lanes between Europe and the Americas are among the most heavily trafficked in the world.

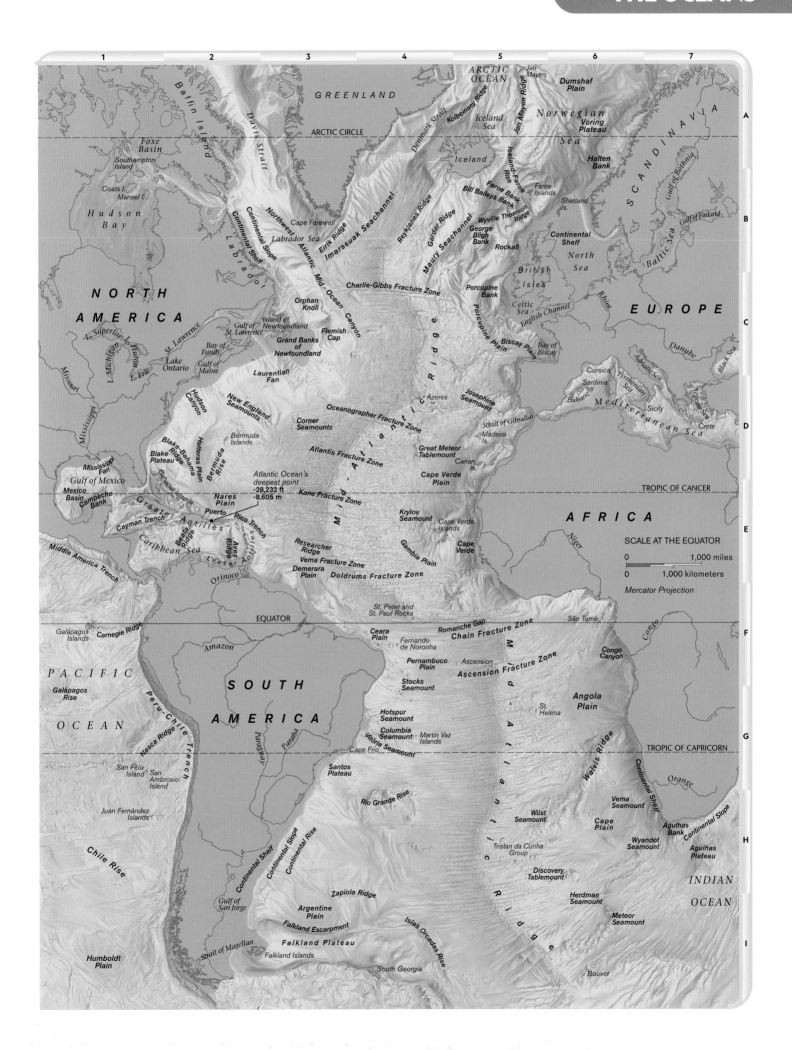

THE BASICS

STATS

Surface area
29,400,000 sq mi
(76,200,000 sq km)

Percentage of Earth's water area
21%

Greatest depth
Java Trench
-23,376 ft (-7,125 m)

Tides
Highest: 36 ft (11 m)
Lowest: 2 ft (0.6 m)
Both along Australia's west coast

GEO WHIZ

Some of the world's largest breeding grounds for humpback whales are in the Indian Ocean and the Arabian Sea, and off the east coast of Africa.

The Bay of Bengal is sometimes called Cyclone Alley because of the large number of tropical storms that occur there each year between May and November.

Sailors from what is now Indonesia used seasonal winds called monsoons to reach Africa's east coast. They arrived on the continent long before Europeans did.

A December 2004 earthquake caused a tsunami that killed more than 225,000 people in countries bordering the Indian Ocean. Waves reached as high as 49 feet (15 m).

Indian Ocean

The Indian Ocean stretches from Africa's east coast to the southern coast of Asia and the western coast of Australia. It is the third largest of Earth's great oceans. Changing air pressure systems over its warm waters trigger South Asia's famous monsoon climate—a weather pattern in which winds reverse directions seasonally. The Bay of Bengal, an arm of the Indian Ocean, experiences devastating tropical storms. (They are called cyclones in this region, another word for hurricanes.) Islands along the eastern edge of the Indian Ocean plate experience earthquakes that sometimes cause destructive ocean waves called tsunamis.

The Arabian Sea, Persian Gulf, and Red Sea, extensions of the Indian Ocean, are important sources of oil and natural gas and account for nearly half of Earth's offshore oil production. Sea routes of the Indian Ocean connect the Middle East to the rest of the world, carrying vital energy resources on huge tanker ships.

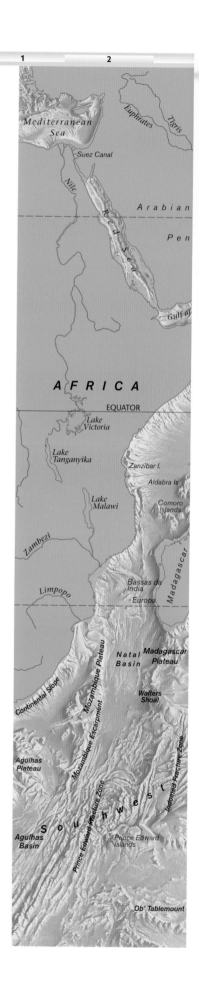

🌐 **LIVING FOSSIL.**
A coelacanth swims in the warm waters of the western Indian Ocean off the Comoro Islands. Once thought to have become extinct 66 million years ago along with the dinosaurs, a living coelacanth was discovered in 1938.

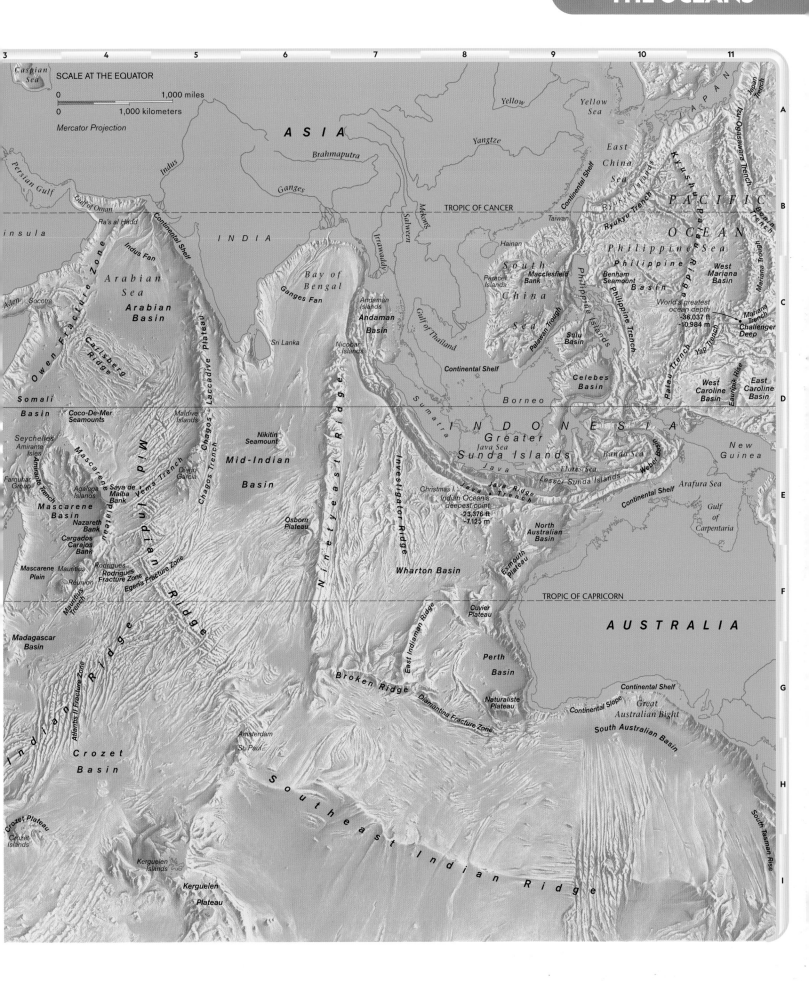

SCALE AT THE EQUATOR

0 _____ 1,000 miles

0 _____ 1,000 kilometers

Mercator Projection

ASIA

Caspian Sea

Persian Gulf

Gulf of Oman

Ra's al Hadd

Indus

Brahmaputra

Ganges

Yangtze

Yellow

Yellow Sea

East China Sea

JAPAN

Izu-Ogasawara Trench

Japan Trench

TROPIC OF CANCER

insula

Aden

Socotra

INDIA

Continental Shelf

Indus Fan

Arabian Sea

Arabian Basin

Carlsberg Ridge

Owen Fracture Zone

Bay of Bengal

Ganges Fan

Sri Lanka

Mekong

Salween

Irrawaddy

Andaman Islands

Andaman Basin

Nicobar Islands

Gulf of Thailand

Continental Shelf

Taiwan

Hainan

South China Sea

Paracel Islands

Macclesfield Bank

Palawan Trough

Sulu Basin

Celebes Basin

Borneo

Ryukyu Islands

Ryukyu Trench

PACIFIC OCEAN

Philippine Sea

Philippine Basin

Benham Seamount

Philippine Islands

Philippine Trench

Palau Trench

Yap Trench

West Mariana Basin

Mariana Trough

Mariana Trench

Challenger Deep

World's greatest ocean depth -36,037 ft -10,984 m

West Caroline Basin

East Caroline Basin

Eauripik Rise

Somali Basin

Coco-De-Mer Seamounts

Seychelles

Amirante Isles

Farquhar Group

Amirante Trench

Agalega Islands

Mascarene Plateau

Mascarene Basin

Nazareth Bank

Cargados Carajos Bank

Mascarene Plain

Mauritius

Réunion

Maldive Islands

Chagos-Laccadive Plateau

Chagos Trench

Diego Garcia

Mid Indian Ridge

Vema Trench

Nikitin Seamount

Mid-Indian Basin

Osborn Plateau

Ninetyeast Ridge

Investigator Ridge

Sumatra

INDONESIA

Greater Sunda Islands

Java Sea

Java

Christmas I. Indian Ocean's deepest point -23,376 ft -7,125 m

Java Trench

Java Ridge

Banda Sea

Flores Sea

Lesser Sunda Islands

Weber Basin

North Australian Basin

Exmouth Plateau

Continental Shelf

New Guinea

Arafura Sea

Gulf of Carpentaria

Rodrigues

Rodrigues Fracture Zone

Egeria Fracture Zone

Mauritius Trench

Wharton Basin

TROPIC OF CAPRICORN

Madagascar Basin

Indian Ridge

Atlantis II Fracture Zone

East Indiaman Ridge

Cuvier Plateau

Perth Basin

AUSTRALIA

Broken Ridge

Diamantina Fracture Zone

Naturaliste Plateau

Continental Slope

Continental Shelf

Great Australian Bight

South Australian Basin

Crozet Plateau

Crozet Islands

Crozet Basin

Amsterdam

St. Paul

Kerguelen Islands

Kerguelen Plateau

Southeast Indian Ridge

South Tasman Rise

THE OCEANS

Arctic Ocean

THE BASICS

STATS

Surface area
5,600,000 sq mi
(14,700,000 sq km)

Percentage of Earth's water area
4.1%

Greatest depth
Molloy Deep: -18,599 ft
(-5,669 m)

Tides
Less than a 1-ft (0.3-m) variation throughout the ocean

GEO WHIZ

Satellite monitoring of Arctic sea ice since the late 1970s shows that the extent of the sea ice is declining at a rate of 13 percent every 10 years—a result of climate change.

The geographic North Pole lies roughly in the middle of the Arctic Ocean under 13,000 feet (3,962 m) of water.

In 1958, a submarine named the U.S.S. *Nautilus* cruised beneath the frozen surface of the Arctic Ocean, proving that the enormous ice sheet rests on water, not land.

The Arctic Ocean lies mostly north of the Arctic Circle, bounded by North America, Europe, and Asia. Unlike the other oceans, the Arctic is subject to persistent cold throughout the year. Also, because of its very high latitude, the Arctic experiences winters of perpetual night and summers of continual daylight. Except for coastal margins, the Arctic Ocean is covered by permanent drifting pack ice that averages almost 10 feet (3 m) in thickness. Most scientists are concerned that the polar ice may be melting due to climate change, putting at risk the habitat of polar bears and other arctic animals.

◗ **ARCTIC RESEARCH.** Scientists wearing cold weather survival suits prepare to measure salt content, nutrients, and plant and animal life in ice and meltwater. They also record data related to climate change, such as the shrinking of polar sea ice.

◗ **FREE RIDE.** A baby polar bear catches a ride as its mother crosses the frozen landscape of Canada's Arctic. Polar bear populations are showing signs of stress as sea ice shrinks.

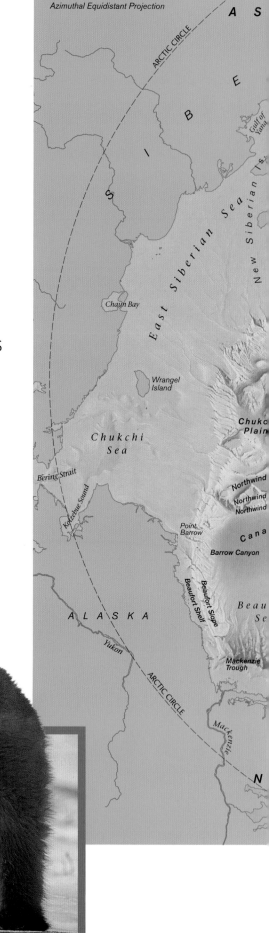

4 5 6 7 8 9 10 11

A I A A

R

EUROPE

Lena

Borkhaya Bay

Taymyr Peninsula

Yenisey Gulf

Gulf of Ob

Baydaratta Bay

Pechora Bay

Chesha Bay

White Sea

Continental Shelf

K a r a   S e a

East Novaya Zemlya Trough

Gusinaya Bank

ARCTIC CIRCLE

Laptev Sea

Cape Chelyuskin

N o v a y a   Z e m l y a

S C A N D I N A V I A

Gulf of Bothnia

Lyakhov Is.

Bol'shevik

North Land

October Revolution I.

Voronina Trough

Syataya Anna Trough

B a r e n t s

Murmansk Rise

Anjou Islands

Komsomolets I.

Franz Josef Land

S e a

North Cape

Zhokhov I.

Graham Bell I.

George Land

Syataya Anna Fan

Alexandra Land

Olga Basin

Spitsbergen Bank

Røst Bank

Henrietta I.

Jeannette I.

N a n s e n   B a s i n

North East Land

Bjørnøya

Halten Bank

N a n s e n   R i d g e

Svalbard

Continental Shelf

Pole Plain

Spitsbergen

N o r w e g i a n

Wrangel Plain

B a r e n t s

Voring Plateau

Continental Slope

Makarov

Fletcher Plain

L o m o n o s o v   R i d g e

Plain

Molloy Deep

Arctic Ocean's deepest point -18,599 ft -5,669 m

N o r w e g i a n   S e a

Continental Shelf

Continental Slope

Mendeleyev Ridge

Yermak Plateau

Mohns Ridge

Dumshaf Plain

B a s i n

Sargo Plateau

Mendeleyev Plain

Fram Basin

★ North Pole

Spitsbergen Fracture Zone

Boreas Plain

Greenland Fracture Zone

Jan Mayen

Aegir Ridge

hi

Chukchi Plateau

Morris Jesup Rise

Wandel Sea

Ob' Bank

G r e e n l a n d   S e a

Jan Mayen Fracture Zone

Jan Mayen Ridge

Plain

Marvin Spur

Oodaaq Island

Continental Shelf

Belgica Bank

Kolbeinsey Ridge

Iceland Plateau

I c e l a n d   S e a

Ridge

Alpha Cordillera

Escarpment

Lincoln Sea

Iceland

da Plain

C a n a d a   B a s i n

Denmark Strait

fort a

Continental Slope

Continental Shelf

Sverdrup Islands

Ellesmere Island

G R E E N L A N D

Reykjanes Ridge

Queen Elizabeth Islands

Parry Islands

M'Clure Strait

Banks Island

Parry

Devon Island

B a f f i n

Continental Slope

Viscount Melville Sound

Channel

B a y

Amundsen Gulf

Barrow Str.

Lancaster Sound

M'Clintock Channel

Somerset Island

ARCTIC CIRCLE

Victoria Island

Prince of Wales Island

Prince Regent Inlet

ATLANTIC OCEAN

ORTH AMERICA

Gulf of Boothia

B a f f i n   I s l a n d

Davis Strait

Great Bear Lake

FLAGS & FACTS

These flags and factoids represent the world's 195 independent countries—those with national governments that are recognized as having the highest legal authority over the land and people within their boundaries. Data are based on the CIA's 2020 *World Factbook*. The flags shown are national flags recognized by the United Nations. Area figures include land and inland water bodies. Languages are those most commonly spoken within a country or official languages, which are marked with an asterisk (*). Only the most commonly practiced religions are listed. All GDP per capita figures are in U.S. dollars and are adjusted to reflect purchasing power parity (PPP).

NORTH AMERICA

Antigua and Barbuda
Area: 171 sq mi
(443 sq km)
Population: 86,000
Percent urban: 24.6%
Capital: St. John's
Language: English*, Creole
Religion: Christianity
GDP per capita: $26,300
Life expectancy: 78 years

Bahamas, The
Area: 5,359 sq mi
(13,880 sq km)
Population: 333,000
Percent urban: 83%
Capital: Nassau
Language: English*, Creole
Religion: Christianity
GDP per capita: $31,200
Life expectancy: 73 years

Barbados
Area: 166 sq mi
(430 sq km)
Population: 293,000
Percent urban: 31.1%
Capital: Bridgetown
Language: English*, Bajan
Religion: Christianity
GDP per capita: $18,700
Life expectancy: 76 years

Belize
Area: 8,867 sq mi
(22,966 sq km)
Population: 386,000
Percent urban: 45.7%
Capital: Belmopan
Language: English*, Spanish,
Creole, Maya
Religion: Christianity
GDP per capita: $8,300
Life expectancy: 69 years

Canada
Area: 3,855,101 sq mi
(9,984,670 sq km)
Population: 35,882,000
Percent urban: 81.4%
Capital: Ottawa
Language: English*, French*
Religion: Christianity
GDP per capita: $48,300
Life expectancy: 82 years

Costa Rica
Area: 19,730 sq mi
(51,100 sq km)
Population: 4,987,000
Percent urban: 79.3%
Capital: San José
Language: Spanish*, English
Religion: Christianity
GDP per capita: $16,900
Life expectancy: 79 years

Cuba
Area: 42,803 sq mi
(110,860 sq km)
Population: 11,116,000
Percent urban: 77%
Capital: Havana
Language: Spanish*
Religion: Christianity
GDP per capita: $12,300
Life expectancy: 79 years

Dominica
Area: 290 sq mi
(751 sq km)
Population: 74,000
Percent urban: 70.5%
Capital: Roseau
Languages: English*, Creole
Religion: Christianity
GDP per capita: $11,100
Life expectancy: 77 years

Dominican Republic
Area: 18,792 sq mi
(48,670 sq km)
Population: 10,299,000
Percent urban: 81.1%
Capital: Santo Domingo
Language: Spanish*
Religion: Christianity
GDP per capita: $16,900
Life expectancy: 78 years

El Salvador
Area: 8,124 sq mi
(21,041 sq km)
Population: 6,187,000
Percent urban: 72%
Capital: San Salvador
Language: Spanish*
Religion: Christianity
GDP per capita: $8,900
Life expectancy: 75 years

Grenada
Area: 133 sq mi
(344 sq km)
Population: 112,000
Percent urban: 36.3%
Capital: St. George's
Language: English*, Creole
Religion: Christianity
GDP per capita: $14,900
Life expectancy: 75 years

Guatemala
Area: 42,042 sq mi
(108,889 sq km)
Population: 16,581,000
Percent urban: 51.1%
Capital: Guatemala City
Language: Spanish*, indigenous
languages
Religion: Christianity, indigenous
beliefs
GDP per capita: $8,100
Life expectancy: 73 years

Haiti
Area: 10,714 sq mi
(27,750 sq km)
Population: 10,788,000
Percent urban: 55.3%
Capital: Port-au-Prince
Language: French*, Creole*
Religion: Christianity, indigenous
beliefs
GDP per capita: $1,800
Life expectancy: 64 years

Honduras
Area: 43,278 sq mi
(112,090 sq km)
Population: 9,183,000
Percent urban: 57.1%
Capital: Tegucigalpa
Language: Spanish*, indigenous
languages
Religion: Christianity
GDP per capita: $5,600
Life expectancy: 71 years

Jamaica
Area: 4,244 sq mi
(10,991 sq km)
Population: 2,812,000
Percent urban: 55.7%
Capital: Kingston
Language: English, Creole
Religion: Christianity
GDP per capita: $9,200
Life expectancy: 74 years

Mexico
Area: 758,449 sq mi
(1,964,375 sq km)
Population: 125,959,000
Percent urban: 80.2%
Capital: Mexico City
Language: Spanish
Religion: Christianity
GDP per capita: $19,900
Life expectancy: 76 years

Nicaragua
Area: 50,336 sq mi
(130,370 sq km)
Population: 6,085,000
Percent urban: 58.5%
Capital: Managua
Language: Spanish*
Religion: Christianity
GDP per capita: $5,800
Life expectancy: 74 years

Panama
Area: 29,120 sq mi
(75,420 sq km)
Population: 3,801,000
Percent urban: 67.7%
Capital: Panama City
Language: Spanish*, English
Religion: Christianity
GDP per capita: $25,400
Life expectancy: 79 years

St. Kitts and Nevis
Area: 101 sq mi
(261 sq km)
Population: 53,000
Percent urban: 30.8%
Capital: Basseterre
Language: English*
Religion: Christianity
GDP per capita: $26,800
Life expectancy: 76 years

St. Lucia
Area: 238 sq mi
(616 sq km)
Population: 166,000
Percent urban: 18.7%
Capital: Castries
Language: English*, Creole
Religion: Christianity
GDP per capita: $14,400
Life expectancy: 78 years

St. Vincent and the Grenadines
Area: 150 sq mi
(389 sq km)
Population: 102,000
Percent urban: 52.2%
Capital: Kingstown
Language: English*, Creole
Religion: Christianity
GDP per capita: $11,500
Life expectancy: 76 years

Trinidad and Tobago
Area: 1,980 sq mi
(5,128 sq km)
Population: 1,218,000
Percent urban: 53.2%
Capital: Port of Spain
Language: English, Creole,
Caribbean Hindustani
Religion: Christianity, Hinduism
GDP per capita: $31,400
Life expectancy: 73 years

United States
Area: 3,796,741 sq mi
(9,833,517 sq km)
Population: 329,256,000
Percent urban: 82.3%
Capital: Washington, D.C.
Language: English, Spanish
Religion: Christianity
GDP per capita: $59,500
Life expectancy: 80 years

SOUTH AMERICA

Argentina
Area: 1,073,518 sq mi
(2,780,400 sq km)
Population: 44,694,000
Percent urban: 91.9%
Capital: Buenos Aires
Language: Spanish*, English, Italian,
German, French
Religion: Christianity
GDP per capita: $20,900
Life expectancy: 77 years

Bolivia
Area: 424,164 sq mi
(1,098,581 sq km)
Population: 11,306,000
Percent urban: 69.4%
Capital: La Paz (administrative),
Sucre (constitutional)
Language: Spanish*, Quechua*,
Aymara*
Religion: Christianity
GDP per capita: $7,500
Life expectancy: 70 years

Brazil
Area: 3,287,611 sq mi
(8,514,877 sq km)
Population: 208,847,000
Percent urban: 86.6%
Capital: Brasília
Language: Portuguese*
Religion: Christianity
GDP per capita: $15,600
Life expectancy: 74 years

Chile
Area: 291,932 sq mi
(756,102 sq km)
Population: 17,925,000
Percent urban: 87.6%
Capital: Santiago
Language: Spanish*, English
Religion: Christianity
GDP per capita: $24,500
Life expectancy: 79 years

Colombia
Area: 439,735 sq mi
(1,138,910 sq km)
Population: 48,169,000
Percent urban: 80.8%
Capital: Bogotá
Language: Spanish*
Religion: Christianity
GDP per capita: $14,500
Life expectancy: 76 years

Ecuador
Area: 109,483 sq mi
(283,561 sq km)
Population: 16,499,000
Percent urban: 63.8%
Capital: Quito
Language: Spanish*, indigenous
languages
Religion: Christianity
GDP per capita: $11,500
Life expectancy: 77 years

Guyana
Area: 83,000 sq mi
(214,969 sq km)
Population: 741,000
Percent urban: 26.6%
Capital: Georgetown
Language: English*, Creole,
Amerindian languages, Caribbean
Hindustani
Religion: Christianity, Hinduism
GDP per capita: $8,200
Life expectancy: 69 years

Paraguay
Area: 157,048 sq mi
(406,752 sq km)
Population: 7,026,000
Percent urban: 61.6%
Capital: Asunción
Language: Spanish*, Guaraní*
Religion: Christianity
GDP per capita: $9,800
Life expectancy: 77 years

Peru
Area: 496,224 sq mi
(1,285,216 sq km)
Population: 31,331,000
Percent urban: 77.9%
Capital: Lima
Language: Spanish*, Quechua*,
Aymara*
Religion: Christianity
GDP per capita: $13,300
Life expectancy: 74 years

Suriname
Area: 63,251 sq mi
(163,820 sq km)
Population: 598,000
Percent urban: 66.1%
Capital: Paramaribo
Language: Dutch*, English, Sranang
Tongo, Caribbean Hindustani,
Javanese
Religion: Christianity, Hinduism,
Islam
GDP per capita: $14,600
Life expectancy: 73 years

Uruguay
Area: 68,037 sq mi
(176,215 sq km)
Population: 3,369,000
Percent urban: 95.3%
Capital: Montevideo
Language: Spanish*
Religion: Christianity
GDP per capita: $22,400
Life expectancy: 77 years

Venezuela
Area: 352,144 sq mi
(912,050 sq km)
Population: 31,689,000
Percent urban: 88.2%
Capital: Caracas
Language: Spanish*, indigenous
languages
Religion: Christianity
GDP per capita: $12,100
Life expectancy: 76 years

EUROPE

Albania
Area: 11,100 sq mi
(28,748 sq km)
Population: 3,057,000
Percent urban: 60.3%
Capital: Tirana
Language: Albanian*
Religion: Islam, Christianity
GDP per capita: $12,500
Life expectancy: 79 years

Andorra
Area: 181 sq mi
(468 sq km)
Population: 86,000
Percent urban: 88.1%
Capital: Andorra la Vella
Language: Catalan*, French,
Spanish, Portuguese
Religion: Christianity
GDP per capita: $49,900
Life expectancy: 83 years

Austria
Area: 32,383 sq mi
(83,871 sq km)
Population: 8,793,000
Percent urban: 58.3%
Capital: Vienna
Language: German*
Religion: Christianity
GDP per capita: $49,900
Life expectancy: 82 years

FLAGS & FACTS

Belarus
Area: 80,155 sq mi
(207,600 sq km)
Population: 9,528,000
Percent urban: 78.6%
Capital: Minsk
Language: Russian*, Belarusian*
Religion: Christianity
GDP per capita: $18,900
Life expectancy: 73 years

Croatia
Area: 21,851 sq mi
(56,594 sq km)
Population: 4,270,000
Percent urban: 56.9%
Capital: Zagreb
Language: Croatian*
Religion: Christianity
GDP per capita: $24,400
Life expectancy: 76 years

Estonia
Area: 17,463 sq mi
(45,228 sq km)
Population: 1,244,000
Percent urban: 68.9%
Capital: Tallinn
Language: Estonian*, Russian
Religion: Christianity
GDP per capita: $31,800
Life expectancy: 77 years

Greece
Area: 50,949 sq mi
(131,957 sq km)
Population: 10,762,000
Percent urban: 79.1%
Capital: Athens
Language: Greek*
Religion: Christianity
GDP per capita: $27,700
Life expectancy: 81 years

Italy
Area: 116,348 sq mi
(301,340 sq km)
Population: 62,247,000
Percent urban: 70.4%
Capital: Rome
Language: Italian*
Religion: Christianity
GDP per capita: $38,100
Life expectancy: 82 years

Belgium
Area: 11,787 sq mi
(30,528 sq km)
Population: 11,571,000
Percent urban: 98%
Capital: Brussels
Language: Dutch*, French*, German*
Religion: Christianity
GDP per capita: $46,600
Life expectancy: 81 years

Cyprus
Area: 3,572 sq mi
(9,251 sq km)
Population: 1,237,000
Percent urban: 66.8%
Capital: Nicosia
Language: Greek*, Turkish*
Religion: Christianity, Islam
GDP per capita: $37,000
Life expectancy: 79 years

Finland
Area: 130,558 sq mi
(338,145 sq km)
Population: 5,537,000
Percent urban: 85.4%
Capital: Helsinki
Language: Finnish*, Swedish*
Religion: Christianity
GDP per capita: $44,300
Life expectancy: 81 years

Hungary
Area: 35,918 sq mi
(93,028 sq km)
Population: 9,826,000
Percent urban: 71.4%
Capital: Budapest
Language: Hungarian*, English,
German
Religion: Christianity
GDP per capita: $29,500
Life expectancy: 76 years

Kosovo
Area: 4,203 sq mi
(10,887 sq km)
Population: 1,908,000
Percent urban: 56.1%
Capital: Prishtinë
Language: Albanian*, Serbian*
Religion: Islam
GDP per capita: $10,500
Life expectancy: NA

Bosnia and Herzegovina
Area: 19,767 sq mi
(51,197 sq km)
Population: 3,850,000
Percent urban: 48.2%
Capital: Sarajevo
Language: Bosnian*, Serbian*,
Croatian*
Religion: Islam, Christianity
GDP per capita: $12,700
Life expectancy: 77 years

Czechia (Czech Republic)
Area: 30,451 sq mi
(78,867 sq km)
Population: 10,686,000
Percent urban: 73.8%
Capital: Prague
Language: Czech*
Religion: Christianity
GDP per capita: $35,500
Life expectancy: 79 years

France
Area: 248,573 sq mi
(643,801 sq km)
Population: 67,364,000
Percent urban: 80.4%
Capital: Paris
Language: French*
Religion: Christianity
GDP per capita: $43,800
Life expectancy: 82 years

Iceland
Area: 39,769 sq mi
(103,000 sq km)
Population: 344,000
Percent urban: 93.8%
Capital: Reykjavik
Language: Icelandic, English,
Nordic languages
Religion: Christianity
GDP per capita: $51,800
Life expectancy: 83 years

Latvia
Area: 24,938 sq mi
(64,589 sq km)
Population: 1,924,000
Percent urban: 68.1%
Capital: Riga
Language: Latvian*, Russian
Religion: Christianity
GDP per capita: $27,600
Life expectancy: 75 years

Bulgaria
Area: 42,811 sq mi
(110,879 sq km)
Population: 7,058,000
Percent urban: 75%
Capital: Sofia
Language: Bulgarian*
Religion: Christianity
GDP per capita: $21,700
Life expectancy: 75 years

Denmark
Area: 16,639 sq mi
(43,094 sq km)
Population: 5,810,000
Percent urban: 87.9%
Capital: Copenhagen
Language: Danish, English
Religion: Christianity
GDP per capita: $49,900
Life expectancy: 80 years

Germany
Area: 137,847 sq mi
(357,022 sq km)
Population: 80,458,000
Percent urban: 77.3%
Capital: Berlin
Language: German*
Religion: Christianity
GDP per capita: $50,400
Life expectancy: 81 years

Ireland (Éire)
Area: 27,133 sq mi
(70,273 sq km)
Population: 5,068,000
Percent urban: 63.2%
Capital: Dublin (Baile Átha Cliath)
Language: English*, Irish (Gaelic)*
Religion: Christianity
GDP per capita: $75,500
Life expectancy: 81 years

Liechtenstein
Area: 62 sq mi
(160 sq km)
Population: 39,000
Percent urban: 14.3%
Capital: Vaduz
Language: German*
Religion: Christianity
GDP per capita: $139,100
Life expectancy: 82 years

Lithuania
Area: 25,212 sq mi
(65,300 sq km)
Population: 2,793,000
Percent urban: 67.7%
Capital: Vilnius
Language: Lithuanian*
Religion: Christianity
GDP per capita: $32,300
Life expectancy: 75 years

Luxembourg
Area: 998 sq mi
(2,586 sq km)
Population: 606,000
Percent urban: 91%
Capital: Luxembourg
Language: Luxembourgish*, French*,
German*, Portuguese
Religion: Christianity
GDP per capita: $104,000
Life expectancy: 82 years

Malta
Area: 122 sq mi
(316 sq km)
Population: 449,000
Percent urban: 94.6%
Capital: Valletta
Language: Maltese*, English*
Religion: Christianity
GDP per capita: $42,000
Life expectancy: 81 years

Moldova
Area: 13,070 sq mi
(33,851 sq km)
Population: 3,438,000
Percent urban: 42.6%
Capital: Chisinau
Language: Moldovan*, Romanian*
Religion: Christianity
GDP per capita: $5,700
Life expectancy: 71 years

Monaco
Area: 1 sq mi
(2 sq km)
Population: 39,000
Percent urban: 100%
Capital: Monaco
Language: French*, English, Italian,
Monegasque
Religion: Christianity
GDP per capita: $115,700
Life expectancy: 89 years

Montenegro
Area: 5,333 sq mi
(13,812 sq km)
Population: 614,000
Percent urban: 66.8%
Capital: Podgorica
Language: Montenegrin*, Serbian
Religion: Christianity, Islam
GDP per capita: $17,700
Life expectancy: NA

Netherlands
Area: 16,040 sq mi
(41,543 sq km)
Population: 17,151,000
Percent urban: 91.5%
Capital: Amsterdam (official), The
Hague (administrative)
Language: Dutch*, Frisian
Religion: Christianity
GDP per capita: $53,600
Life expectancy: 81 years

North Macedonia
Area: 9,928 sq mi
(25,713 sq km)
Population: 2,119,000
Percent urban: 58%
Capital: Skopje
Language: Macedonian*, Albanian
Religion: Christianity, Islam
GDP per capita: $14,900
Life expectancy: 76 years

Norway
Area: 125,021 sq mi
(323,802 sq km)
Population: 5,372,000
Percent urban: 82.2%
Capital: Oslo
Language: Bokmal Norwegian*,
Nynorsk Norwegian*
Religion: Christianity
GDP per capita: $71,800
Life expectancy: 82 years

Poland
Area: 120,728 sq mi
(312,685 sq km)
Population: 38,421,000
Percent urban: 60.1%
Capital: Warsaw
Language: Polish*
Religion: Christianity
GDP per capita: $29,500
Life expectancy: 78 years

Portugal
Area: 35,556 sq mi
(92,090 sq km)
Population: 10,355,000
Percent urban: 65.2%
Capital: Lisbon
Language: Portuguese*,
Mirandese*
Religion: Christianity
GDP per capita: $30,400
Life expectancy: 79 years

Romania
Area: 92,043 sq mi
(238,391 sq km)
Population: 21,457,000
Percent urban: 54%
Capital: Bucharest
Language: Romanian*
Religion: Christianity
GDP per capita: $24,500
Life expectancy: 75 years

Russia
Area: 6,601,665 sq mi
(17,098,234 sq km)
Population: 144,478,000
Percent urban: 74.4%
Capital: Moscow
Language: Russian*
Religion: Christianity, Islam
GDP per capita: $27,800
Life expectancy: 71 years

San Marino
Area: 24 sq mi
(61 sq km)
Population: 34,000
Percent urban: 97.2%
Capital: San Marino
Language: Italian
Religion: Christianity
GDP per capita: $58,600
Life expectancy: 83 years

Serbia
Area: 29,913 sq mi
(77,474 sq km)
Population: 7,078,000
Percent urban: 56.1%
Capital: Belgrade
Language: Serbian*
Religion: Christianity
GDP per capita: $15,000
Life expectancy: 76 years

Slovakia
Area: 18,933 sq mi
(49,035 sq km)
Population: 5,445,000
Percent urban: 53.7%
Capital: Bratislava
Language: Slovak*
Religion: Christianity
GDP per capita: $33,000
Life expectancy: 77 years

Slovenia
Area: 7,827 sq mi
(20,273 sq km)
Population: 2,102,000
Percent urban: 54.5%
Capital: Ljubljana
Language: Slovene*
Religion: Christianity
GDP per capita: $34,400
Life expectancy: 78 years

Spain
Area: 195,124 sq mi
(505,370 sq km)
Population: 49,331,000
Percent urban: 80.3%
Capital: Madrid
Language: Castilian Spanish*,
Catalan, Galician, Basque
Religion: Christianity
GDP per capita: $38,300
Life expectancy: 82 years

Sweden
Area: 173,860 sq mi
(450,295 sq km)
Population: 10,041,000
Percent urban: 87.4%
Capital: Stockholm
Language: Swedish*
Religion: Christianity
GDP per capita: $51,500
Life expectancy: 82 years

Switzerland
Area: 15,937 sq mi
(41,277 sq km)
Population: 8,293,000
Percent urban: 73.8%
Capital: Bern
Language: German*, French*,
Italian*, Romansch*
Religion: Christianity
GDP per capita: $61,400
Life expectancy: 83 years

FLAGS & FACTS

Ukraine
Area: 233,032 sq mi
(603,550 sq km)
Population: 43,952,000
Percent urban: 69.4%
Capital: Kyiv
Language: Ukrainian*, Russian
Religion: Christianity
GDP per capita: $8,700
Life expectancy: 72 years

United Kingdom
Area: 94,058 sq mi
(243,610 sq km)
Population: 65,105,000
Percent urban: 83.4%
Capital: London
Language: English, regional
languages
Religion: Christianity
GDP per capita: $44,100
Life expectancy: 81 years

Vatican City (Holy See)
Area: 0.17 sq mi
(0.44 sq km)
Population: 1,000
Percent urban: 100%
Capital: Vatican City
Language: Italian, Latin, French
Religion: Christianity
GDP per capita: NA
Life expectancy: NA

ASIA

Afghanistan
Area: 251,827 sq mi
(652,230 sq km)
Population: 34,941,000
Percent urban: 25.5%
Capital: Kabul
Language: Dari*, Pashto*, Uzbek
Religion: Islam
GDP per capita: $2,000
Life expectancy: 52 years

Armenia
Area: 11,484 sq mi
(29,743 sq km)
Population: 3,038,000
Percent urban: 63.1%
Capital: Yerevan
Language: Armenian*
Religion: Christianity
GDP per capita: $9,500
Life expectancy: 75 years

Azerbaijan
Area: 33,436 sq mi
(86,600 sq km)
Population: 10,047,000
Percent urban: 55.7%
Capital: Baku
Language: Azerbaijani (Azeri)*,
Russian
Religion: Islam
GDP per capita: $17,500
Life expectancy: 73 years

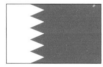

Bahrain
Area: 293 sq mi
(760 sq km)
Population: 1,443,000
Percent urban: 89.3%
Capital: Manama
Language: Arabic*, English, Farsi,
Urdu
Religion: Islam
GDP per capita: $48,500
Life expectancy: 79 years

Bangladesh
Area: 57,321 sq mi
(148,460 sq km)
Population: 159,453,000
Percent urban: 36.6%
Capital: Dhaka
Language: Bangla (Bengali)*
Religion: Islam, Hinduism
GDP per capita: $4,200
Life expectancy: 73 years

Bhutan
Area: 14,824 sq mi
(38,394 sq km)
Population: 766,000
Percent urban: 40.9%
Capital: Thimphu
Language: Dzongkha*, Sharchhopka,
Lhotshamkha
Religion: Buddhism, Hinduism
GDP per capita: $8,700
Life expectancy: 71 years

Brunei
Area: 2,226 sq mi
(5,765 sq km)
Population: 451,000
Percent urban: 77.6%
Capital: Bandar Seri Begawan
Language: Malay*, English, Chinese
Religion: Islam
GDP per capita: $78,200
Life expectancy: 77 years

Cambodia
Area: 69,898 sq mi
(181,035 sq km)
Population: 16,450,000
Percent urban: 23.4%
Capital: Phnom Penh
Language: Khmer*
Religion: Buddhism
GDP per capita: $4,000
Life expectancy: 65 years

China
Area: 3,705,405 sq mi
(9,596,960 sq km)
Population: 1,384,689,000
Percent urban: 59.2%
Capital: Beijing
Language: Standard Chinese or
Mandarin*, Yue or Cantonese, Wu,
Minbei, Minnan, Xiang, Gan, Hakka
dialects, numerous regionally
official languages
Religion: Folk religion, Buddhism,
Christianity
GDP per capita: $16,700
Life expectancy: 76 years

Georgia
Area: 26,911 sq mi
(69,700 sq km)
Population: 4,003,000
Percent urban: 58.6%
Capital: Tbilisi
Language: Georgian*
Religion: Christianity, Islam
GDP per capita: $10,700
Life expectancy: 76 years

India
Area: 1,269,219 sq mi
(3,287,263 sq km)
Population: 1,296,834,000
Percent urban: 34%
Capital: New Delhi
Language: Hindi*, English*, state
languages
Religion: Hinduism, Islam
GDP per capita: $7,200
Life expectancy: 69 years

Indonesia
Area: 735,358 sq mi
(1,904,569 sq km)
Population: 262,787,000
Percent urban: 55.3%
Capital: Jakarta
Language: Bahasa Indonesia*,
English, Dutch, Javanese, local
dialects
Religion: Islam, Christianity
GDP per capita: $12,400
Life expectancy: 73 years

Iran
Area: 636,371 sq mi
(1,648,195 sq km)
Population: 83,025,000
Percent urban: 74.9%
Capital: Tehran
Language: Persian (Farsi)*
Religion: Islam
GDP per capita: $20,200
Life expectancy: 74 years

Iraq
Area: 169,235 sq mi
(438,317 sq km)
Population: 40,194,000
Percent urban: 70.5%
Capital: Baghdad
Language: Arabic*, Kurdish*
Religion: Islam
GDP per capita: $17,000
Life expectancy: 75 years

Israel
Area: 8,019 sq mi
(20,770 sq km)
Population: 8,425,000
Percent urban: 92.4%
Capital: Jerusalem
Language: Hebrew*, Arabic, English
Religion: Judaism, Islam
GDP per capita: $36,300
Life expectancy: 83 years

Japan
Area: 145,914 sq mi
(377,915 sq km)
Population: 126,168,000
Percent urban: 91.6%
Capital: Tokyo
Language: Japanese*
Religion: Shintoism, Buddhism
GDP per capita: $42,800
Life expectancy: 85 years

Jordan
Area: 34,495 sq mi
(89,342 sq km)
Population: 10,458,000
Percent urban: 91%
Capital: Amman
Language: Arabic*, English
Religion: Islam
GDP per capita: $12,500
Life expectancy: 75 years

Kazakhstan
Area: 1,052,089 sq mi
(2,724,900 sq km)
Population: 18,949,000
Percent urban: 57.4%
Capital: Nur-Sultan (Astana)
Language: Kazakh*, Russian*
Religion: Islam, Christianity
GDP per capita: $26,300
Life expectancy: 71 years

Kuwait
Area: 6,880 sq mi
(17,818 sq km)
Population: 4,438,000
Percent urban: 100%
Capital: Kuwait City
Language: Arabic*, English
Religion: Islam, Christianity
GDP per capita: $66,200
Life expectancy: 78 years

Kyrgyzstan
Area: 77,201 sq mi
(199,951 sq km)
Population: 5,849,000
Percent urban: 36.4%
Capital: Bishkek
Language: Kyrgyz*, Uzbek, Russian*
Religion: Islam, Christianity
GDP per capita: $3,700
Life expectancy: 71 years

Laos
Area: 91,429 sq mi
(236,800 sq km)
Population: 7,234,000
Percent urban: 35%
Capital: Vientiane
Language: Lao*, French, English,
indigenous languages
Religion: Buddhism
GDP per capita: $7,400
Life expectancy: 65 years

Lebanon
Area: 4,015 sq mi
(10,400 sq km)
Population: 6,100,000
Percent urban: 88.6%
Capital: Beirut
Language: Arabic*, French, English,
Armenian
Religion: Islam, Christianity
GDP per capita: $19,400
Life expectancy: 78 years

Malaysia
Area: 127,355 sq mi
(329,847 sq km)
Population: 31,810,000
Percent urban: 76%
Capital: Kuala Lumpur
Language: Bahasa Malaysia (Malay)*
Religion: Islam, Buddhism
GDP per capita: $29,000
Life expectancy: 75 years

Maldives
Area: 115 sq mi
(298 sq km)
Population: 392,000
Percent urban: 39.8%
Capital: Male
Language: Dhivehi*, English
Religion: Islam
GDP per capita: $19,100
Life expectancy: 76 years

Mongolia
Area: 603,908 sq mi
(1,564,116 sq km)
Population: 3,103,000
Percent urban: 68.4%
Capital: Ulaanbaatar
Language: Mongolian*
Religion: Buddhism
GDP per capita: $13,000
Life expectancy: 70 years

Myanmar (Burma)
Area: 261,228 sq mi
(676,578 sq km)
Population: 55,623,000
Percent urban: 30.6%
Capital: Nay Pyi Taw
Language: Burmese*
Religion: Buddhism, Christianity,
Islam
GDP per capita: $6,200
Life expectancy: 68 years

Nepal
Area: 56,827 sq mi
(147,181 sq km)
Population: 29,718,000
Percent urban: 19.7%
Capital: Kathmandu
Language: Nepali*, Maithali
Religion: Hinduism
GDP per capita: $2,700
Life expectancy: 71 years

North Korea
Area: 46,540 sq mi
(120,538 sq km)
Population: 25,381,000
Percent urban: 61.9%
Capital: Pyongyang
Language: Korean
Religion: Buddhism, Confucianism,
indigenous beliefs
GDP per capita: $1,700
Life expectancy: 71 years

Oman
Area: 119,499 sq mi
(309,500 sq km)
Population: 4,613,000
Percent urban: 84.5%
Capital: Muscat
Language: Arabic*, English
Religion: Islam
GDP per capita: $45,200
Life expectancy: 76 years

Pakistan
Area: 307,374 sq mi
(796,095 sq km)
Population: 207,863,000
Percent urban: 36.7%
Capital: Islamabad
Language: Urdu*, English*, Punjabi,
Sindhi, Saraiki
Religion: Islam
GDP per capita: $5,400
Life expectancy: 68 years

Philippines
Area: 115,831 sq mi
(300,000 sq km)
Population: 105,893,000
Percent urban: 46.9%
Capital: Manila
Language: Filipino (Tagalog)*,
English*
Religion: Christianity
GDP per capita: $8,300
Life expectancy: 69 years

Qatar
Area: 4,473 sq mi
(11,586 sq km)
Population: 2,364,000
Percent urban: 99.1%
Capital: Doha
Language: Arabic*, English
Religion: Islam, Christianity,
Hinduism
GDP per capita: $124,500
Life expectancy: 79 years

Saudi Arabia
Area: 830,000 sq mi
(2,149,690 sq km)
Population: 33,091,000
Percent urban: 83.8%
Capital: Riyadh
Language: Arabic*
Religion: Islam
GDP per capita: $54,800
Life expectancy: 76 years

Singapore
Area: 269 sq mi
(697 sq km)
Population: 5,996,000
Percent urban: 100%
Capital: Singapore
Language: English*, Mandarin*,
Malay*, Tamil*
Religion: Buddhism, Christianity,
Islam, Taosim
GDP per capita: $93,900
Life expectancy: 85 years

South Korea
Area: 38,502 sq mi
(99,720 sq km)
Population: 51,418,000
Percent urban: 81.5%
Capital: Seoul
Language: Korean, English
Religion: Christianity, Buddhism
GDP per capita: $39,400
Life expectancy: 83 years

Sri Lanka
Area: 25,332 sq mi
(65,610 sq km)
Population: 22,577,000
Percent urban: 18.5%
Capital: Colombo (commercial),
Sri Jayewardenepura Kotta (official)
Language: Sinhala*, Tamil*, English
Religion: Buddhism, Hinduism,
Islam, Christianity
GDP per capita: $12,800
Life expectancy: 77 years

Syria
Area: 71,498 sq mi
(185,180 sq km)
Population: 19,454,000
Percent urban: 54.2%
Capital: Damascus
Language: Arabic*, Kurdish,
Armenian, Aramaic, Circassian,
French
Religion: Islam, Christianity
GDP per capita: $2,900
Life expectancy: 75 years

FLAGS & FACTS

Tajikistan
Area: 55,637 sq mi
(144,100 sq km)
Population: 8,605,000
Percent urban: 27.1%
Capital: Dushanbe
Language: Tajik*, Uzbek
Religion: Islam
GDP per capita: $3,200
Life expectancy: 68 years

Thailand
Area: 198,117 sq mi
(513,120 sq km)
Population: 68,616,000
Percent urban: 49.9%
Capital: Bangkok
Language: Thai*, English
Religion: Buddhism
GDP per capita: $17,900
Life expectancy: 75 years

Timor-Leste (East Timor)
Area: 5,743 sq mi
(14,874 sq km)
Population: 1,322,000
Percent urban: 30.6%
Capital: Dili
Language: Tetun*, Portuguese*,
Indonesian, English
Religion: Christianity
GDP per capita: $5,400
Life expectancy: 68 years

Turkey
Area: 302,535 sq mi
(783,562 sq km)
Population: 81,257,000
Percent urban: 75.1%
Capital: Ankara
Language: Turkish*, Kurdish
Religion: Islam
GDP per capita: $26,900
Life expectancy: 75 years

Turkmenistan
Area: 188,456 sq mi
(488,100 sq km)
Population: 5,411,000
Percent urban: 51.6%
Capital: Ashgabat
Language: Turkmen*, Russian
Religion: Islam, Christianity
GDP per capita: $18,100
Life expectancy: 70 years

United Arab Emirates
Area: 32,278 sq mi
(83,600 sq km)
Population: 9,701,000
Percent urban: 86.5%
Capital: Abu Dhabi
Language: Arabic*, Persian, English,
Hindi, Urdu
Religion: Islam
GDP per capita: $67,700
Life expectancy: 78 years

Uzbekistan
Area: 172,742 sq mi
(447,400 sq km)
Population: 30,024,000
Percent urban: 50.5%
Capital: Tashkent
Language: Uzbek*, Russian
Religion: Islam, Christianity
GDP per capita: $6,900
Life expectancy: 74 years

Vietnam
Area: 127,881 sq mi
(331,210 sq km)
Population: 97,040,000
Percent urban: 35.9%
Capital: Hanoi
Language: Vietnamese*, English
Religion: Buddhism, Christianity
GDP per capita: $6,900
Life expectancy: 74 years

Yemen
Area: 203,850 sq mi
(527,968 sq km)
Population: 28,667,000
Percent urban: 36.6%
Capital: Sanaa
Language: Arabic*
Religion: Islam
GDP per capita: $1,300
Life expectancy: 66 years

AFRICA

Algeria
Area: 919,595 sq mi
(2,381,741 sq km)
Population: 41,657,000
Percent urban: 72.6%
Capital: Algiers
Language: Arabic*, Berber*, French
Religion: Islam
GDP per capita: $15,200
Life expectancy: 77 years

Angola
Area: 481,353 sq mi
(1,246,700 sq km)
Population: 30,356,000
Percent urban: 65.5%
Capital: Luanda
Language: Portuguese*, Umbundu
Religion: Christianity
GDP per capita: $6,800
Life expectancy: 60 years

Benin
Area: 43,483 sq mi
(112,622 sq km)
Population: 11,341,000
Percent urban: 47.3%
Capital: Porto-Novo (official),
Cotonou (administrative)
Language: French*, Fon, Yoruba
Religion: Christianity, Islam,
indigenous beliefs
GDP per capita: $2,300
Life expectancy: 62 years

Botswana
Area: 224,607 sq mi
(581,730 sq km)
Population: 2,249,000
Percent urban: 69.4%
Capital: Gaborone
Language: English*, Setswana
Religion: Christianity
GDP per capita: $17,800
Life expectancy: 63 years

Burkina Faso
Area: 105,869 sq mi
(274,200 sq km)
Population: 19,743,000
Percent urban: 29.4%
Capital: Ouagadougou
Language: French*, indigenous
languages
Religion: Islam, Christianity
GDP per capita: $1,900
Life expectancy: 56 years

Burundi
Area: 10,745 sq mi
(27,830 sq km)
Population: 11,845,000
Percent urban: 13%
Capital: Bujumbura (commercial),
Gitega (official)
Language: Kirundi*, French*,
English*
Religion: Christianity
GDP per capita: $700
Life expectancy: 61 years

Cabo Verde
Area: 1,557 sq mi
(4,033 sq km)
Population: 568,000
Percent urban: 65.7%
Capital: Praia
Language: Portuguese*, Creole
Religion: Christianity
GDP per capita: $6,900
Life expectancy: 72 years

Cameroon
Area: 183,568 sq mi
(475,440 sq km)
Population: 25,641,000
Percent urban: 56.4%
Capital: Yaoundé
Language: English*, French*,
indigenous languages
Religion: Christianity, Islam
GDP per capita: $3,700
Life expectancy: 59 years

Central African Republic
Area: 240,535 sq mi
(622,984 sq km)
Population: 5,745,000
Percent urban: 41.4%
Capital: Bangui
Language: French*, Sangho,
indigenous languages
Religion: Christianity, indigenous
beliefs, Islam
GDP per capita: $700
Life expectancy: 53 years

Chad
Area: 495,755 sq mi
(1,284,000 sq km)
Population: 15,833,000
Percent urban: 23.1%
Capital: N'Djamena
Language: French*, Arabic*,
indigenous languages
Religion: Islam, Christianity
GDP per capita: $2,300
Life expectancy: 51 years

Comoros
Area: 863 sq mi
(2,235 sq km)
Population: 821,000
Percent urban: 29%
Capital: Moroni
Language: Arabic*, French*,
Shikomoro*
Religion: Islam
GDP per capita: $1,600
Life expectancy: 65 years

Congo
Area: 132,047 sq mi
(342,000 sq km)
Population: 5,062,000
Percent urban: 66.9%
Capital: Brazzaville
Language: French*, Lingala,
Monokutuba, other indigenous
languages
Religion: Christianity
GDP per capita: $6,600
Life expectancy: 60 years

**Congo, Democratic
Republic of the**
Area: 905,354 sq mi
(2,344,858 sq km)
Population: 85,281,000
Percent urban: 44.5%
Capital: Kinshasa
Language: French*, Lingala, other
indigenous languages
Religion: Christianity
GDP per capita: $800
Life expectancy: 58 years

Côte d'Ivoire (Ivory Coast)
Area: 124,504 sq mi
(322,463 sq km)
Population: 26,261,000
Percent urban: 50.8%
Capitals: Abidjan (administrative),
Yamoussoukro (legislative)
Language: French*, Dioula, other
indigenous languages
Religion: Islam, Christianity
GDP per capita: $3,900
Life expectancy: 59 years

Djibouti
Area: 8,958 sq mi
(23,200 sq km)
Population: 884,000
Percent urban: 77.8%
Capital: Djibouti
Language: French*, Arabic*, Somali,
Afar
Religion: Islam
GDP per capita: $3,600
Life expectancy: 64 years

Egypt
Area: 386,662 sq mi
(1,001,450 sq km)
Population: 99,413,000
Percent urban: 42.7%
Capital: Cairo
Language: Arabic*, English, French
Religion: Islam, Christianity
GDP per capita: $12,700
Life expectancy: 73 years

Equatorial Guinea
Area: 10,831 sq mi
(28,051 sq km)
Population: 797,000
Percent urban: 72.1%
Capital: Malabo
Language: Spanish*, French*,
Portuguese*, indigenous languages
Religion: Christianity, indigenous
beliefs
GDP per capita: $36,000
Life expectancy: 65 years

Eritrea
Area: 45,406 sq mi
(117,600 sq km)
Population: 5,971,000
Percent urban: 40.1%
Capital: Asmara
Language: Tigrinya*, Arabic*,
English*, indigenous languages
Religion: Islam, Christianity
GDP per capita: $1,600
Life expectancy: 65 years

Eswatini (Swaziland)
Area: 6,704 sq mi
(17,364 sq km)
Population: 1,087,000
Percent urban: 23.8%
Capital: Mbabane (administrative),
Lobamba (legislative and royal)
Language: English*, siSwati*
Religion: Christianity
GDP per capita: $9,900
Life expectancy: 52 years

Ethiopia
Area: 426,372 sq mi
(1,104,300 sq km)
Population: 108,386,000
Percent urban: 20.8%
Capital: Addis Ababa
Language: Amharic*, Oromo, Somali,
Tigrinya, Afar
Religion: Christianity, Islam
GDP per capita: $2,200
Life expectancy: 63 years

Gabon
Area: 103,347 sq mi
(267,667 sq km)
Population: 2,119,000
Percent urban: 89.4%
Capital: Libreville
Language: French*, indigenous
languages
Religion: Christianity
GDP per capita: $19,200
Life expectancy: 52 years

Gambia, The
Area: 4,363 sq mi
(11,300 sq km)
Population: 2,093,000
Percent urban: 61.3%
Capital: Banjul
Language: English*, indigenous
languages
Religion: Islam
GDP per capita: $1,700
Life expectancy: 65 years

Ghana
Area: 92,098 sq mi
(238,533 sq km)
Population: 28,102,000
Percent urban: 56.1%
Capital: Accra
Language: English*, Assanta, Ewe,
Fante
Religion: Christianity, Islam
GDP per capita: $4,700
Life expectancy: 67 years

Guinea
Area: 94,926 sq mi
(245,857 sq km)
Population: 11,855,000
Percent urban: 36.1%
Capital: Conakry
Language: French*, indigenous
languages
Religion: Islam
GDP per capita: $2,000
Life expectancy: 61 years

Guinea-Bissau
Area: 13,948 sq mi
(36,125 sq km)
Population: 1,833,000
Percent urban: 43.4%
Capital: Bissau
Language: Portuguese*, Creole,
Pular, Mandingo
Religion: Islam, Christianity,
indigenous beliefs
GDP per capita: $1,800
Life expectancy: 51 years

Kenya
Area: 224,081 sq mi
(580,367 sq km)
Population: 48,398,000
Percent urban: 27%
Capital: Nairobi
Language: English*, Kiswahili*,
indigenous languages
Religion: Christianity, Islam
GDP per capita: $3,500
Life expectancy: 64 years

Lesotho
Area: 11,720 sq mi
(30,355 sq km)
Population: 1,962,000
Percent urban: 28.2%
Capital: Maseru
Language: Sesotho*, English*, Zulu,
Xhosa
Religion: Christianity, indigenous
beliefs
GDP per capita: $3,600
Life expectancy: 53 years

Liberia
Area: 43,000 sq mi
(111,369 sq km)
Population: 4,810,000
Percent urban: 51.2%
Capital: Monrovia
Language: English*, indigenous
languages
Religion: Christianity, Islam
GDP per capita: $1,400
Life expectancy: 63 years

Libya
Area: 679,362 sq mi
(1,759,540 sq km)
Population: 6,755,000
Percent urban: 80.1%
Capital: Tripoli
Language: Arabic*, Italian, English,
Berber
Religion: Islam
GDP per capita: $10,000
Life expectancy: 77 years

Madagascar
Area: 226,658 sq mi
(587,041 sq km)
Population: 25,684,000
Percent urban: 37.2%
Capital: Antananarivo
Language: French*, Malagasy*,
English
Religion: Christianity, indigenous
beliefs, Islam
GDP per capita: $1,600
Life expectancy: 66 years

Malawi
Area: 45,747 sq mi
(118,484 sq km)
Population: 19,843,000
Percent urban: 16.9%
Capital: Lilongwe
Language: English*, Chichewa, other
indigenous languages
Religion: Christianity, Islam
GDP per capita: $1,200
Life expectancy: 62 years

FLAGS & FACTS

Mali
Area: 478,841 sq mi
(1,240,192 sq km)
Population: 18,430,000
Percent urban: 42.4%
Capital: Bamako
Language: French*, Bambara, other
indigenous languages
Religion: Islam
GDP per capita: $2,200
Life expectancy: 60 years

Mauritania
Area: 397,955 sq mi
(1,030,700 sq km)
Population: 3,840,000
Percent urban: 53.7%
Capital: Nouakchott
Language: Arabic*, indigenous
languages
Religion: Islam
GDP per capita: $4,400
Life expectancy: 63 years

Mauritius
Area: 788 sq mi
(2,040 sq km)
Population: 1,364,000
Percent urban: 40.8%
Capital: Port Louis
Language: Creole, English*
Religion: Hinduism, Christianity,
Islam
GDP per capita: $21,600
Life expectancy: 76 years

Morocco
Area: 172,414 sq mi
(446,550 sq km)
Population: 34,314,000
Percent urban: 62.5%
Capital: Rabat
Language: Arabic*, Tamazight*,
French
Religion: Islam
GDP per capita: $8,600
Life expectancy: 77 years

Mozambique
Area: 308,642 sq mi
(799,380 sq km)
Population: 27,234,000
Percent urban: 36%
Capital: Maputo
Language: Portuguese*, Emakhuwa,
Xichangana, other indigenous
languages
Religion: Christianity, Islam
GDP per capita: $1,200
Life expectancy: 54 years

Namibia
Area: 318,261 sq mi
(824,292 sq km)
Population: 2,533,000
Percent urban: 50%
Capital: Windhoek
Language: English*, indigenous
languages, Afrikaans
Religion: Christianity, indigenous
beliefs
GDP per capita: $11,300
Life expectancy: 64 years

Niger
Area: 489,191 sq mi
(1,267,000 sq km)
Population: 19,866,000
Percent urban: 16.4%
Capital: Niamey
Language: French*, indigenous
languages
Religion: Islam
GDP per capita: $1,200
Life expectancy: 56 years

Nigeria
Area: 356,669 sq mi
(923,768 sq km)
Population: 203,453,000
Percent urban: 50.3%
Capital: Abuja
Language: English*, indigenous
languages
Religion: Islam, Christianity,
indigenous beliefs
GDP per capita: $5,900
Life expectancy: 54 years

Rwanda
Area: 10,169 sq mi
(26,338 sq km)
Population: 12,187,000
Percent urban: 17.2%
Capital: Kigali
Language: Kinyarwanda*, French*,
English*, Kiswahili
Religion: Christianity
GDP per capita: $2,100
Life expectancy: 64 years

Sao Tome and Principe
Area: 372 sq mi
(964 sq km)
Population: 204,000
Percent urban: 72.8%
Capital: São Tomé
Language: Portuguese*, Forro
Religion: Christianity
GDP per capita: $3,200
Life expectancy: 65 years

Senegal
Area: 75,955 sq mi
(196,722 sq km)
Population: 15,021,000
Percent urban: 47.2%
Capital: Dakar
Language: French*, Wolof, other
indigenous languages
Religion: Islam
GDP per capita: $2,700
Life expectancy: 62 years

Seychelles
Area: 176 sq mi
(455 sq km)
Population: 95,000
Percent urban: 56.7%
Capital: Victoria
Language: Creole*, English*, French*
Religion: Christianity
GDP per capita: $28,900
Life expectancy: 75 years

Sierra Leone
Area: 27,699 sq mi
(71,740 sq km)
Population: 6,312,000
Percent urban: 42.1%
Capital: Freetown
Language: English*, Mende, Temne,
Krio
Religion: Islam, Christianity
GDP per capita: $1,600
Life expectancy: 59 years

Somalia
Area: 246,201 sq mi
(637,657 sq km)
Population: 11,259,000
Percent urban: 45%
Capital: Mogadishu
Language: Somali*, Arabic*, Italian,
English
Religion: Islam
GDP per capita: NA
Life expectancy: 53 years

South Africa
Area: 470,693 sq mi
(1,219,090 sq km)
Population: 55,380,000
Percent urban: 66.4%
Capital: Pretoria (Tshwane)
(administrative), Cape Town
(legislative), Bloemfontein (judicial)
Language: IsiZulu*, IsiXhosa*, other
indigenous languages*, Afrikaans*,
English*
Religion: Christianity
GDP per capita: $13,500
Life expectancy: 64 years

South Sudan
Area: 248,777 sq mi
(644,329 sq km)
Population: 10,205,000
Percent urban: 19.6%
Capital: Juba
Language: English*, Arabic,
indigenous languages
Religion: Animism, Christianity
GDP per capita: $1,500
Life expectancy: NA

Sudan
Area: 718,723 sq mi
(1,861,484 sq km)
Population: 43,121,000
Percent urban: 34.6%
Capital: Khartoum
Language: Arabic*, English*
Religion: Islam
GDP per capita: $4,600
Life expectancy: 64 years

Tanzania
Area: 365,754 sq mi
(947,300 sq km)
Population: 55,451,000
Percent urban: 33.8%
Capital: Dar es Salaam
(administrative), Dodoma (official)
Language: Kiswahili*, English*,
indigenous languages
Religion: Christianity, Islam
GDP per capita: $3,200
Life expectancy: 63 years

Togo
Area: 21,925 sq mi
(56,785 sq km)
Population: 8,176,000
Percent urban: 23.1%
Capital: Lomé
Language: French*, Ewe, Mina,
Kabye, Dagomba
Religion: Indigenous beliefs,
Christianity, Islam
GDP per capita: $5,600
Life expectancy: 76 years

Tunisia
Area: 63,170 sq mi
(163,610 sq km)
Population: 11,516,000
Percent urban: 68.9%
Capital: Tunis
Language: Arabic*, French, Berber
Religion: Islam
GDP per capita: $11,800
Life expectancy: 76 years

Uganda
Area: 93,065 sq mi
(241,038 sq km)
Population: 40,854,000
Percent urban: 23.8%
Capital: Kampala
Language: English*, Swahili*, Ganda
(Luganda)
Religion: Christianity, Islam
GDP per capita: $2,400
Life expectancy: 56 years

Zambia
Area: 290,587 sq mi
(752,618 sq km)
Population: 16,445,000
Percent urban: 43.5%
Capital: Lusaka
Language: English*, Bemba, Nyanja,
Tonga, other indigenous languages
Religion: Christianity
GDP per capita: $4,000
Life expectancy: 53 years

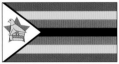

Zimbabwe
Area: 150,872 sq mi
(390,757 sq km)
Population: 14,030,000
Percent urban: 32.2%
Capital: Harare
Language: Shona*, Ndebele*, English*,
indigenous languages*
Religion: Christianity, indigenous
beliefs
GDP per capita: $2,300
Life expectancy: 60 years

AUSTRALIA,
NEW ZEALAND & OCEANIA

Australia
Area: 2,988,901 sq mi
(7,741,220 sq km)
Population: 23,470,000
Percent urban: 86%
Capital: Canberra, A.C.T.
Language: English
Religion: Christianity
GDP per capita: $50,300
Life expectancy: 82 years

Fiji
Area: 7,056 sq mi
(18,274 sq km)
Population: 927,000
Percent urban: 56.2%
Capital: Suva
Language: English*, Fijian*, Hindi
Religion: Christianity, Hinduism
GDP per capita: $9,800
Life expectancy: 73 years

Kiribati
Area: 313 sq mi
(811 sq km)
Population: 109,000
Percent urban: 54.1%
Capital: Tarawa
Language: English*, I-Kiribati
Religion: Christianity
GDP per capita: $2,000
Life expectancy: 67 years

Marshall Islands
Area: 70 sq mi
(181 sq km)
Population: 76,000
Percent urban: 77%
Capital: Majuro
Language: Marshallese*, English*
Religion: Christianity
GDP per capita: $3,400
Life expectancy: 73 years

Micronesia, Federated States of
Area: 271 sq mi
(702 sq km)
Population: 104,000
Percent urban: 22.7%
Capital: Palikir
Language: English*, indigenous
languages
Religion: Christianity
GDP per capita: $3,400
Life expectancy: 73 years

Nauru
Area: 8 sq mi
(21 sq km)
Population: 10,000
Percent urban: 100%
Capital: Yaren
Language: Nauruan*, English
Religion: Christianity
GDP per capita: $12,200
Life expectancy: 67 years

New Zealand
Area: 103,799 sq mi
(268,838 sq km)
Population: 4,546,000
Percent urban: 86.5%
Capital: Wellington
Language: English*, Maori*
Religion: Christianity
GDP per capita: $38,900
Life expectancy: 81 years

Palau
Area: 177 sq mi
(459 sq km)
Population: 22,000
Percent urban: 79.9%
Capital: Ngerulmud
Language: Palauan*, English*,
Filipino
Religion: Christianity
GDP per capita: $16,200
Life expectancy: 73 years

Papua New Guinea
Area: 178,703 sq mi
(462,840 sq km)
Population: 7,027,000
Percent urban: 13.2%
Capital: Port Moresby
Language: Tok Pisin*, English*, Hiri
Motu*, other indigenous languages
Religion: Christianity
GDP per capita: $3,700
Life expectancy: 67 years

Samoa
Area: 1,093 sq mi
(2,831 sq km)
Population: 201,000
Percent urban: 18.2%
Capital: Apia
Language: Samoan*, English*
Religion: Christianity
GDP per capita: $5,700
Life expectancy: 74 years

Solomon Islands
Area: 11,157 sq mi
(28,896 sq km)
Population: 660,000
Percent urban: 23.7%
Capital: Honiara
Language: English*, Melanesian
pidgin, indigenous languages
Religion: Christianity
GDP per capita: $2,200
Life expectancy: 76 years

Tonga
Area: 288 sq mi
(747 sq km)
Population: 106,000
Percent urban: 23.1%
Capital: Nuku'alofa
Language: Tongan*, English*
Religion: Christianity
GDP per capita: $5,600
Life expectancy: 76 years

Tuvalu
Area: 10 sq mi
(26 sq km)
Population: 11,000
Percent urban: 62.4%
Capital: Funafuti
Language: Tuvaluan*, English*,
Samoan, Kiribati
Religion: Christianity
GDP per capita: $3,800
Life expectancy: 67 years

Vanuatu
Area: 4,706 sq mi
(12,189 sq km)
Population: 283,000
Percent urban: 25.3%
Capital: Port Vila
Language: Bislama*, English*,
French*, indigenous languages
Religion: Christianity
GDP per capita: $2,700
Life expectancy: 74 years

Glossary

acid rain precipitation containing acid droplets resulting from the mixture of moisture in the air with carbon dioxide, nitrogen oxide, sulfur dioxide, and hydrocarbons released by factories and motor vehicles

archipelago group or chain of islands

atheist person or group that does not believe in any deity

basin area of land that is lower at the center than at the rim

bathymetry measurement of depth at various places in the ocean or other body of water

bay body of water, usually smaller than a gulf, that is partially surrounded by land

biomass total volume of organic material in a certain area or ecosystem that can be used as a renewable energy source (a biofuel)

border area along each side of the boundary that separates one country from another

boundary most commonly, a line that has been established by people to mark the limit of one political unit, such as a country or state, and the beginning of another. Geographical features such as mountains sometimes act as boundaries.

caloric supply measure of the amount of food available to a particular person, household, or community

canal human-made waterway that is used by ships or to carry water for irrigation

canyon deep, narrow valley that has steep sides

carat unit of weight for precious stones equal to 200 milligrams

cliff very steep rock face, usually along a coast or on the side of a mountain

climate change change in typical climate patterns, including temperature or precipitation; may result from natural cycles or from human activities such as use of fossil fuels

continent one of the seven main landmasses on Earth's surface

continental climate interior areas found only in the Northern Hemisphere north of mild climate regions; summer to winter temperature extremes

country territory with a government that is the highest legal authority over the land and people within its boundaries

Creole language formed from a mixture of different languages, such as French and an indigenous language

delta lowland formed by silt, sand, and gravel deposited by a river at its mouth

desert hot or cold region that receives 10 inches (25 cm) or less of rain or other forms of precipitation a year

desertification spread of desertlike conditions in semiarid regions that is the result of human pressures, such as overgrazing, removal of natural vegetation, and cultivation of land, as well as climatic changes

divide elevated boundary line separating river systems from which rivers flow in different directions

dry climate areas experiencing low annual precipitation and day to night temperature extremes

earthquake sudden movement or shaking of Earth's crust, often resulting in damage on the surface

elevation distance above sea level, usually measured in feet or meters

escarpment cliff that separates two nearly flat land areas that lie at different elevations

fault break in Earth's crust along which movement up, down, or sideways occurs

fjord/fiord long narrow coastal inlet associated with past glaciation, as in Norway and Chile

fork place where a river splits into two smaller streams

geographic pole 90° N or 90° S latitude; location of the ends of Earth's axis

glacier large, slow-moving mass of ice

greenhouse gases gases, such as carbon dioxide and methane, that contribute to atmospheric warming

gross domestic product (GDP) per capita total value of goods and services produced by a country's economy in a year divided by the country's total population. Figures in this atlas are in U.S. dollars and based on **purchasing power parity (PPP),** an economic calculation for comparing the value of different currencies that takes into account the cost of living in each country.

gulf portion of the ocean that cuts into the land; usually larger than a bay

harbor body of water, sheltered by natural or artificial barriers, that is deep enough for ships

hemisphere half a sphere. Earth can be divided into Northern and Southern Hemispheres, or Eastern and Western Hemispheres.

highland climate areas associated with mountains where elevation is the main factor in determining temperature and precipitation

highlands an elevated area or the more mountainous region of a country

hybrid car a car that is powered by gasoline and electricity

ice cap thick layer of ice and snow covering less than 19,300 square miles (50,000 sq km)

ice sheet thick layer of ice and snow covering more than 19,300 square miles (50,000 sq km)

indigenous naturally occurring in a particular area or region, as with people, languages, or religions

inlet narrow opening in the land that is filled with water flowing from an ocean, a lake, or a river

island landmass, smaller than a continent, that is completely surrounded by water

lagoon shallow body of water that is open to the sea but also protected from it by a reef or sandbar

lake body of water that is surrounded by land. Large lakes are sometimes called seas.

landform physical feature shaped by tectonic activity, weathering, and erosion. Earth's four major kinds are plains, mountains, plateaus, and hills.

landmass large area of Earth's crust that lies above sea level, such as a continent

large-scale map map, such as a street map, that shows a small area in great detail

Latin America cultural region generally considered to include Mexico, Central America, South America, and the West Indies. Spanish and Portuguese are the principal languages.

latitude measurement in degrees north or south of 0° (Equator) to 90°

leeward side away from or sheltered from the wind

life expectancy average number of years a person can expect to live

lingua franca language not native to the local population that is used as a common or commercial language

longitude measurement in degrees east or west from 0° (prime meridian) to 180°

magma molten rock in Earth's mantle

magnetic pole point at which the axis of Earth's magnetic field intersects Earth's surface. Compass needles align with Earth's magnetic field so that one end points to the north magnetic pole, the other to the south magnetic pole.

mesa eroded plateau, broader than it is high, found in arid or semiarid regions

metropolitan area a city and its surrounding suburbs or communities

Middle East term commonly used for the countries of southwestern Asia, but which can also include northern Africa from Morocco to Egypt

molten liquefied by heat; melted

mountain landform, higher than a hill, that rises at least 1,000 feet (300 m) above the surrounding land and is wider at its base than at its top, or peak. A series of mountains is called a range.

nation people who share a common culture or sense of history. It is often used as another word for "country," although people within a country may be of many cultures.

ocean the large body of salt water that surrounds the continents and covers more than two-thirds of Earth's surface

pack ice large blocks of ice that form on the surface of the sea, pushed together by wind and currents

peninsula extension of land that is surrounded by water on three sides

pidgin simplified form of speech that allows speakers of different languages to communicate

plain large area of relatively flat land that is often covered with grasses

plantation agriculture type of commercial agriculture specializing in one or two crops, such as coffee or bananas

plate tectonics theory that Earth's crust is broken into large sections, or plates, that slowly move over the mantle (diagram, p. 17)

plateau relatively flat area, larger than a mesa, that rises above the surrounding landscape

poaching illegal killing or taking of animals from their natural habitats

polar climate area north of the Arctic Circle and south of the Antarctic Circle where temperatures remain cold year-round and precipitation is low

population density in a country, the average number of people living on each square mile or square kilometer of land (calculated by dividing population by land area)

Prairie Provinces popular name for the Canadian provinces of Manitoba, Saskatchewan, and Alberta

prime meridian imaginary line that runs through Greenwich, England, and is accepted as the line of 0° longitude

projection process of representing the round Earth on a flat surface, such as a map

Glossary

rain shadow dry region on the leeward side of a mountain range

reef offshore ridge made of coral, rocks, or sand. A reef that lies parallel to a coastline and is separated from it by a lagoon is called a barrier reef.

renewable resources resources that are replenished naturally, but the supply of which can be endangered by overuse and pollution

revolution movement of Earth in its orbit around the sun (365 days/1 year)

rotation movement of Earth on its axis (24 hours/1 day)

rural relating to an area outside a city and its surrounding suburbs with low population density and an agricultural economy

Sahel semiarid grassland in Africa along the Sahara's southern border

savanna tropical grassland with scattered trees

scale on a map, a means of explaining the relationship between distances on the map and actual distances on Earth's surface

sea ocean or a partially enclosed body of salt water that is connected to the ocean. Completely enclosed bodies of salt water, such as the Dead Sea, are really lakes.

sea level average surface level of Earth's oceans from which the height of land areas can be measured

Silk Road ancient trade route stretching from China to the Mediterranean

slot canyon very narrow, deep canyon formed by water and wind erosion

small-scale map map, such as a country map, that shows a large area without much detail

sound long, broad inlet of the ocean that lies parallel to the coast and often separates an island and the mainland

Soviet Union shortened name for the Union of Soviet Socialist Republics (U.S.S.R.), a former Communist republic (1920–1991) in eastern Europe and northern and central Asia, made up of 15 republics, of which Russia was the largest

staple chief food of a people's diet

steppe Slavic word referring to relatively flat, mostly treeless temperate grasslands that stretch across much of the central parts of Europe and Asia

strait narrow passage of water that connects two larger bodies of water

Sunbelt U.S. region made up of southern and western states that are experiencing major population in-migration and economic growth

territory land that is under the jurisdiction of a country but is not a state or a province

topography features, such as mountains and valleys, that are evident on Earth's surface

tornado violently rotating column of air associated with thunderstorms

transshipment movement of goods or containers to one location before moving on, often by a different form of transportation, to a final destination

tributary stream that flows into a larger river

tropical cyclone large weather system that forms over warm tropical water. With sustained winds of at least 74 miles an hour (119 km/h), it is called a hurricane in the Atlantic Ocean and eastern Pacific; a cyclone in the Bay of Bengal, Indian Ocean, and South Pacific, and a typhoon in the western Pacific.

tropics region lying within $23\frac{1}{2}°$ north and south of the Equator that experiences warm temperatures year-round

tsunami very large ocean wave caused by an earthquake or other powerful underwater disturbance, such as a volcanic eruption

urban relating to a city and its densely populated surrounding area with a non-agricultural economy

valley long depression, usually created by a river, that is bordered by higher land

virgin forest forest made up of trees that have never been cut down by humans

volcano opening in Earth's crust through which molten rock erupts. A volcano that has not erupted in the past 10,000 years but is expected to erupt again is said to be dormant.

wat Buddhist monastery or temple in southeastern Asia

windward side or direction that faces the wind

Geo Facts & Figures

PLANET EARTH

Mass:
6,584,800,000,000,000,000,000 tons
(5,973,600,000,000,000,000,000 metric tons)
Distance around the Equator: 24,901 mi
(40,075 km)
Area: 196,940,000 sq mi
(510,072,000 sq km)
Land area: 57,506,000 sq mi
(148,940,000 sq km)
Water area: 139,434,000 sq mi
(361,132,000 sq km))

The Continents

Asia: 17,208,000 sq mi
(44,570,000 sq km)
Africa: 11,608,000 sq mi
(30,065,000 sq km)
North America: 9,449,000 sq mi
(24,474,000 sq km)
South America: 6,880,000 sq mi
(17,819,000 sq km)
Antarctica: 5,100,000 sq mi
(13,209,000 sq km)
Europe: 3,841,000 sq mi
(9,947,000 sq km)
Australia: 2,970,000 sq mi
(7,692,000 sq km)

Highest Mountain on Each Continent

Everest, Asia: 29,035 ft (8,850 m)
Cerro Aconcagua, South America:
22,831 ft (6,959 m)
Denali (Mt. McKinley), North America:
20,310 ft (6,190 m)
Kilimanjaro, Africa: 19,340 ft
(5,895 m)
El'brus, Europe: 18,510 ft (5,642 m)
Vinson Massif, Antarctica: 16,067 ft
(4,897 m)
Kosciuszko, Australia: 7,310 ft
(2,228 m)

Lowest Point on Each Continent

Byrd Glacier (depression), Antarctica:
−9,416 ft (−2,870 m)
Dead Sea, Asia: −1,424 ft (−434 m)
Lake Assal, Africa: −509 ft (−155 m)
Laguna del Carbón, South America:
−344 ft (−105 m)
Death Valley, North America:
−282 ft (−86 m)
Caspian Sea, Europe: −92 ft (−28 m)
Lake Eyre, Australia: −49 ft (−15 m)

Longest Rivers

Nile, Africa: 4,160 mi (6,695 km)
Amazon, South America: 4,150 mi
(6,679 km)
Yangtze (Chang), Asia: 3,880 mi
(6,244 km)
Mississippi-Missouri, North America:
3,710 mi (5,971 km)
Yenisey-Angara, Asia: 3,610 mi
(5,810 km)
Yellow (Huang), Asia: 3,590 mi (5,778 km)
Ob-Irtysh, Asia: 3,430 mi (5,520 km)
Amur, Asia: 3,420 mi (5,504 km)
Lena, Asia: 3,200 mi (5,150 km)
Congo, Africa: 3,180 mi (5,118 km)

Largest Islands

Greenland: 836,000 sq mi
(2,166,000 sq km)
New Guinea: 306,000 sq mi
(792,500 sq km)
Borneo: 280,100 sq mi (725,500 sq km)
Madagascar: 226,600 sq mi
(587,000 sq km)
Baffin: 196,000 sq mi (507,500 sq km)
Sumatra: 165,000 sq mi
(427,300 sq km)
Honshu: 87,800 sq mi (227,400 sq km)
Great Britain: 84,200 sq mi
(218,100 sq km)
Victoria: 83,900 sq mi (217,300 sq km)
Ellesmere: 75,800 sq mi
(196,200 sq km)

Oceans

Pacific: 69,000,000 sq mi
(178,800,000 sq km)
Atlantic: 35,400,000 sq mi
(91,700,000 sq km)
Indian: 29,400,000 sq mi
(76,200,000 sq km)
Arctic: 5,600,000 sq mi
(14,700,000 sq km)

Largest Seas (by area)

Coral: 1,615,500 sq mi
(4,184,000 sq km)
South China: 1,388,400 sq mi
(3,596,000 sq km)
Caribbean: 1,094,200 sq mi
(2,834,000 sq km)
Bering: 973,000 sq mi
(2,520,000 sq km)
Mediterranean: 953,300 sq mi
(2,469,000 sq km)
Okhotsk: 627,400 sq mi
(1,625,000 sq km)
Gulf of Mexico: 591,500 sq mi
(1,532,000 sq km)
Norwegian: 550,200 sq mi
(1,425,000 sq km)
Greenland: 447,100 sq mi
(1,158,000 sq km)
Japan (East Sea): 389,200 sq mi
(1,008,000 sq km)

Largest Lakes (by area)

Caspian Sea, Europe-Asia: 143,200 sq mi
(371,000 sq km)
Superior, North America: 31,700 sq mi
(82,100 sq km)
Victoria, Africa: 26,800 sq mi
(69,500 sq km)
Huron, North America: 23,000 sq mi
(59,600 sq km)
Michigan, North America: 22,300 sq mi
(57,800 sq km)
Tanganyika, Africa: 12,600 sq mi
(32,600 sq km)
Baikal, Asia: 12,200 sq mi
(31,500 sq km)

Geo Facts & Figures

Largest Lakes (cont'd)

Great Bear, North America: 12,100 sq mi
(31,300 sq km)

Malawi (Nyasa), Africa: 11,200 sq mi
(28,900 sq km)

Great Slave, North America: 11,000 sq mi
(28,600 sq km)

GEOGRAPHIC EXTREMES

Highest Mountain
Everest, China/Nepal:
29,035 ft (8,850 m)

Deepest Point in the Ocean
Challenger Deep, Mariana Trench, Pacific:
-36,037 ft (-10,984 m)

Hottest Place
Dalol, Danakil Depression, Ethiopia:
annual average temperature 93°F
(34°C)

Coldest Place
Ridge A, Antarctica:
annual average temperature -94°F
(-70°C)

Wettest Place
Mawsynram, Meghalaya, India: annual
average rainfall 467 in (1,187 cm)

Driest Place
Arica, Atacama Desert, Chile: barely
measurable rainfall

Largest Hot Desert
Sahara, Africa: 3,475,000 sq mi
(9,000,000 sq km)

Largest Cold Desert
Antarctica: 5,100,000 sq mi
(13,209,000 sq km)

PEOPLE

Most Populous Continent
Asia   4,641,055,000

Least Populous Continent
Antarctica   no permanent population
Australia   23,470,000

Population Density by Continent (highest to lowest)

Continent	Density
Asia	269.7 people/sq mi
	104.1 people/sq km
Europe	194.6 people/sq mi
	75.2 people/sq km
Africa	115.5 people/sq mi
	44.6 people/sq km
North America	62.7 people/sq mi
	24.2 people/sq km
South America	62.6 people/sq mi
	24.2 people/sq km
Australia	7.9 people/sq mi
	3.0 people/sq km

Most Populous Country
China   1,384,689,000

Least Populous Country
Vatican City   1,000

Most Densely Populated Countries

Monaco	39,000.0 people/sq mi
	(19,500.0 people/sq km)
Singapore	22,280.6 people/sq mi
	(8,602.6 people/sq km)
Vatican City	5,886.3 people/sq mi
	(2,272.7 people/sq km)
Bahrain	4,917.6 people/sq mi
	(1,898.7 people/sq km)
Malta	3,680.1 people/sq mi
	(1,420.9 people/sq km)
Maldives	3,407.0 people/sq mi
	(1,315.4 people/sq km)
Bangladesh	2,781.8 people/sq mi
	(1,074.0 people/sq km)
Barbados	1,764.8 people/sq mi
	(681.4 people/sq km)
Mauritius	1,731.7 people/sq mi
	(668.6 people/sq km)
Lebanon	1,519.1 people/sq mi
	(586.5 people/sq km)

Least Densely Populated Countries

Mongolia	5.1 people/sq mi
	(2.0 people/sq km)
Australia	7.9 people/sq mi
	(3.0 people/sq km)
Namibia	8.0 people/sq mi
	(3.1 people/sq km)
Iceland	8.7 people/sq mi
	(3.3 people/sq km)
Guyana	8.9 people/sq mi
	(3.4 people/sq km)
Canada	9.3 people/sq mi
	(3.6 people/sq km)
Suriname	9.5 people/sq mi
	(3.7 people/sq km)
Mauritania	9.6 people/sq mi
	(3.7 people/sq km)
Libya	9.9 people/sq mi
	(3.8 people/sq km)

Most Populous Metropolitan Areas

Tokyo, Japan	37,468,000
Delhi, India	30,291,000
Shanghai, China	27,058,000
São Paulo, Brazil	22,043,000
Mexico City, Mexico	21,782,000
Dhaka, Bangladesh	21,006,000
Cairo, Egypt	20,901,000
Beijing, China	20,463,000
Mumbai (Bombay), India	20,411,000
Osaka, Japan	19,165,000

Countries With the Highest Population Growth Rate

Syria	4.25%
Niger	3.66%
Angola	3.43%
Benin	3.40%
Uganda	3.34%
Malawi	3.30%
Chad	3.18%
Democratic Republic of the Congo	3.18%
Mali	2.95%
Zambia	2.89%

Countries With the Lowest Population Growth Rate

Lebanon	-6.68%
Lithuania	-1.13%
Latvia	-1.12%
Moldova	-1.08%
Bulgaria	-0.65%
Estonia	-0.65%
Federated States of Micronesia	-0.6%
Croatia	-0.5%
Serbia	-0.47%
Romania	-0.37%

Countries With the Highest Life Expectancy

Monaco	89 years
Japan	85 years
Singapore	85 years
Andorra	83 years
Iceland	83 years
Israel	83 years
San Marino	83 years
South Korea	83 years
Switzerland	83 years
Australia	82 years
Austria	82 years
Canada	82 years
France	82 years
Italy	82 years
Liechtenstein	82 years
Luxembourg	82 years
Norway	82 years
Spain	82 years

Countries With the Lowest Life Expectancy

Chad	51 years
Guinea-Bissau	51 years
Afghanistan	52 years
Eswatini (Swaziland)	52 years
Gabon	52 years
Central African Republic	53 years
Lesotho	53 years
Somalia	53 years
Zambia	53 years
Mozambique	54 years
Nigeria	54 years

Countries With the Highest Percent Urban Population

Kuwait	100%
Monaco	100%
Nauru	100%
Singapore	100%
Vatican City	100%
Qatar	99.1%
Belgium	98%
San Marino	97.2%
Uruguay	95.3%
Malta	94.6%

Countries With the Lowest Percent Urban Population

Burundi	13%
Papua New Guinea	13.2%
Liechtenstein	14.3%
Niger	16.4%
Malawi	16.9%
Rwanda	17.2%
Samoa	18.2%
Sri Lanka	18.5%
St. Lucia	18.7%
South Sudan	19.6%

Countries With the Highest Gross Domestic Product per Person (PPP)

Liechtenstein	$139,100
Qatar	$124,500
Monaco	$115,700
Luxembourg	$104,000
Singapore	$93,900
Brunei	$78,200
Ireland	$75,500
Norway	$71,800
United Arab Emirates	$67,700
Kuwait	$66,200

Countries With the Lowest Gross Domestic Product per Person (PPP)

Burundi	$700
Central African Republic	$700
Democratic Republic of the Congo	$800
Malawi	$1,200
Mozambique	$1,200
Niger	$1,200
Yemen	$1,300
Liberia	$1,400
South Sudan	$1,500
Comoros	$1,600
Eritrea	$1,600
Madagascar	$1,600
Sierra Leone	$1,600

Geo Facts & Figures

With an adult's help, check out these websites for more information about various topics discussed in this atlas.

Antarctica
www.coolantarctica.com

Biomes
www.blueplanetbiomes.org

Climate change
climate.nasa.gov

Climates
www.worldclimate.com

Countries of the world (statistics)
www.cia.gov/library/publications
/resources/the-world-factbook

Endangered species
www.iucnredlist.org

Extreme facts about the world
www.extremescience.com

Flags of the world
www.crwflags.com/fotw/flags

Languages: "Say Hello"
www.ipl.org/div/hello

Mapping the world
www.google.com/earth

National anthems
www.nationalanthems.info

Natural disasters
Earthquakes:
earthquake.usgs.gov/earthquakes
Hurricanes: www.nhc.noaa.gov
Tsunamis: www.tsunami.noaa.gov
Volcanoes:
volcanoes.usgs.gov/index.html

Population
Population clock:
www.census.gov/popclock
World population: www.prb.org/
2020-world-population-data-sheet

Religions of the world
www.adherents.com

Solar system
solarsystem.nasa.gov/planets

Time
Time around the world:
www.worldtimeserver.com
Time zones: worldtimezone.com

Weather around the world
weather.com

World Heritage sites
whc.unesco.org/en/list

ABBREVIATIONS

°E	degrees East	L.	Lake	N.Z.	New Zealand
°N	degrees North	LA.	Louisiana	OKLA.	Oklahoma
°S	degrees South	LIECH.	Liechtenstein	OREG.	Oregon
°W	degrees West	LUX.	Luxembourg	P.E.I.	Prince Edward Island
°C	degrees Celsius	m	meters	p.	page
°F	degrees Fahrenheit	MASS.	Massachusetts	pp.	pages
AFGHAN.	Afghanistan	MD.	Maryland	PA.	Pennsylvania
ALA.	Alabama	ME.	Maine	Pen.	Peninsula
ARK.	Arkansas	mi	miles	R.I.	Rhode Island
B.&H.	Bosnia and Herzegovina	MICH.	Michigan	Rep.	Republic
BELG.	Belgium	MINN.	Minnesota	S	South
COLO.	Colorado	MISS.	Mississippi	S. DAK.	South Dakota
CONN.	Connecticut	MO.	Missouri	S.C.	South Carolina
D.C.	District of Columbia	MONT.	Montana	sq km	square kilometers
DEL.	Delaware	MONT.	Montenegro	sq mi	square miles
DEM.	Democratic	Mt.	Mount, Mountain	St., Ste.	Saint, Sainte
E	East	Mts.	Mountains	Str.	Strait
FLA.	Florida	N	North	SWITZ.	Switzerland
ft	feet	N. DAK.	North Dakota	TENN.	Tennessee
GA.	Georgia	N. MEX.	New Mexico	U.A.E.	United Arab Emirates
GDP	Gross Domestic Product	N.B.	New Brunswick	U.K.	United Kingdom
I.	Island	N.C.	North Carolina	U.S./U.S.A.	United States
ILL.	Illinois	N.H.	New Hampshire	VA.	Virginia
IND.	Indiana	N.J.	New Jersey	VT.	Vermont
Is.	Islands	N.P.	National Park	W	West
KANS.	Kansas	N.Y.	New York	W. VA.	West Virginia
km	kilometers	NEBR.	Nebraska	WASH.	Washington
KY.	Kentucky	NETH.	Netherlands	WIS.	Wisconsin
KYRG.	Kyrgyzstan	NEV.	Nevada	WYO.	Wyoming

Metric Conversions

CONVERSION TO METRIC MEASURES

SYMBOL	WHEN YOU KNOW	MULTIPLY BY	TO FIND	SYMBOL
		LENGTH		
in	inches	2.54	centimeters	cm
ft	feet	0.30	meters	m
yd	yards	0.91	meters	m
mi	miles	1.61	kilometers	km
		AREA		
in²	square inches	6.45	square centimeters	cm²
ft²	square feet	0.09	square meters	m²
yd²	square yards	0.84	square meters	m²
mi²	square miles	2.59	square kilometers	km²
--	acres	0.40	hectares	ha
		MASS		
oz	ounces	28.35	grams	g
lb	pounds	0.45	kilograms	kg
--	short tons	0.91	metric tons	t
		VOLUME		
in³	cubic inches	16.39	milliliters	mL
liq oz	liquid ounces	29.57	milliliters	mL
pt	pints	0.47	liters	L
qt	quarts	0.95	liters	L
gal	gallons	3.79	liters	L
ft³	cubic feet	0.03	cubic meters	m³
yd³	cubic yards	0.76	cubic meters	m³
		TEMPERATURE		
°F	degrees Fahrenheit	5/9 after subtracting 32	degrees Celsius (centigrade)	°C

CONVERSION FROM METRIC MEASURES

SYMBOL	WHEN YOU KNOW	MULTIPLY BY	TO FIND	SYMBOL
		LENGTH		
cm	centimeters	0.39	inches	in
m	meters	3.28	feet	ft
m	meters	1.09	yards	yd
km	kilometers	0.62	miles	mi
		AREA		
cm²	square centimeters	0.16	square inches	in²
m²	square meters	10.76	square feet	ft²
m²	square meters	1.20	square yards	yd²
km²	square kilometers	0.39	square miles	mi²
ha	hectares	2.47	acres	--
		MASS		
g	grams	0.04	ounces	oz
kg	kilograms	2.20	pounds	lb
t	metric tons	1.10	short tons	--
		VOLUME		
mL	milliliters	0.06	cubic inches	in³
mL	milliliters	0.03	liquid ounces	liq oz
L	liters	2.11	pints	pt
L	liters	1.06	quarts	qt
L	liters	0.26	gallons	gal
m³	cubic meters	35.31	cubic feet	ft³
m³	cubic meters	1.31	cubic yards	yd³
		TEMPERATURE		
°C	degrees Celsius (centigrade)	9/5 then add 32	degrees Fahrenheit	°F

Index

Map references are in boldface (**58**) type. Letters and numbers following in lightface (D12) locate the place-names using the map grid. (Refer to page 7 for more details.)

1st Cataract — Arkansas

Happy Valley — Juiz de Fora

Lake Region – Marcus Island

Namsos — Oodaaq Island

Prince Patrick Island — St. Lucia

Solimões — Tibet, Plateau of

Vladikavkaz – Arabian Sea

Arafura Sea — Galápagos Fracture Zone

Galápagos Rift – North Australian Basin

Map Data Sources

8 (Find Your House, Computer Enhanced Views of...), Esri, Maxar, Earthstar Geographics, CNES/Airbus DS, USDA FSA, USGS, Aerogrid, IGN, IGP, and the GIS User Community; 16 (A Look Within), Tibor G. Tóth; (Continents on the Move) C. R. Scotese PALEOMAP Project; 17, 32, 69 (Tectonic Features, Natural Disasters, Dangerous Foundation), USGS Earthquake Hazards Program and USGS National Earthquake Information Center (NEIC). earthquake.usgs.gov; 17, 20 (Earth Shapers, Exploring the Landscape), Chuck Carter, Eagre Games Inc.; 22 (Climatic Zones), © H.J. de Blij, P.O. Muller, and John Wiley & Sons, Inc.; 25 (Land and Ocean Temperature Averages), NOAA National Centers for Environmental Information, *State of the Climate: Global Climate Report for July 2019*, published online August 2019, https://www.ncdc.noaa.gov/sotc/global/201907; 26 (Vegetation Zones), *Biodiversity*. NG Maps for *National Geographic* magazine. February 1999; 28 (Human Footprint), Venter, O., E.W. Sanderson, A. Magrach, J.R. Allan, J. Beher, K.R. Jones, H.P. Possingham, W.F. Laurance, P. Wood, B.M. Fekete, M.A. Levy, and J.E.M. Watson. "Sixteen years of change in the global terrestrial human footprint and implications for biodiversity conservation." *Nature Communications*, doi:10.1038/ncomms12558, 2016; Watson, J.E.M., D.F. Shanahan, M. Di Marco, J. Allan, W.F. Laurance, E.W. Sanderson, B. Mackey, and O. Venter. "Catastrophic Declines in Wilderness Areas Undermine Global Environment Targets." *Current Biology*, doi:10.1016/j.cub.2016.08.049, 26, 2016; 28 (Environmental Stresses), Halpern, B. S. et al. "Spatial and temporal changes in cumulative human impacts on the world's ocean. " *Nat. Commun.* 6:7615 doi:10.1038/ncomms8615 (2015); *Millennium Ecosystem Assessment*. Ecosystems and Human Well-Being, Synthesis; World Health Organization (WHO); (Human Footprint) Wildlife Conservation Society-WCS, and Center for

International Earth Science Information Network-CIESIN-Columbia University. 2005; Last of the Wild Project, Version 2, 2005 (LWP-2): Global Human Footprint Dataset (Geographic). Palisades, NY: NASA Socioeconomic Data and Applications Center (SEDAC). https://doi.org/10.7927/H4M61H5F; United Nations Department of Economic and Social Affairs (DESA), Population Division; 30 (Number of Threatened Species, 2020), IUCN 2020. The IUCN Red List of Threatened Species. Version 2020-1. http://www.iucnredlist.org; 32 (Natural Disasters), National Geophysical Data Center/World Data Service: NCEI/WDS Global Historical Tsunami Database. NOAA National Centers for Environmental Information. doi:10.7289/V5PN93H7; 32, 69 (Natural Disasters, Dangerous Foundation) Smithsonian Institution, Global Volcanism Program. volcano.si.edu; USGS and the International Association of Volcanology and Chemistry of the Earth's Interior. vulcan.wr.usgs.gov; National Geophysical Data Center/World Data Service (NGDC/WDS): NCEI/WDS Global Significant Volcanic Eruptions Database. NOAA National Centers for Environmental Information. doi:10.7289/V5JW8BSH; 36 (Population Density), Landscan 2018 Population Dataset created by UT-Battelle, LLC, the management and operating contractor of the Oak Ridge National Laboratory acting on behalf of the U.S. Department of Energy under Contract No. DE-AC05-00OR22725. Distributed by East View Geospatial: geospatial.com and East View Information Services: eastview.com/online/landscan; (Urban Area Population), United Nations Department of Economic and Social Affairs (DESA), Population Division; 38 (Projected Population Change (%), 2015–2050), CIA. *The World Factbook*. cia.gov; Population Reference Bureau. prb.org/DataFinder; (Population Pyramids) United Nations, Department of Economic and Social Affairs,

Population Division. *World Population Prospects: The 2019 Revision*. (Medium variant); 40 (Migration) United Nations Department of Economic and Social Affairs (DESA), Population Division; 42 (Major Language Families Today), Harald Hammarström, Thom Castermans, Robert Forkel, Kevin Verbeek, Michel A. Westenberg, and Bettina Speckmann. 2018. "Simultaneous Visualization of Language Endangerment and Language Description." *Language Documentation & Conservation*, 12, 359–392; 44 (Predominant Religion), CIA. *The World Factbook*. cia.gov; 46 (Dominant Economic Sector), CIA. *The World Factbook*. cia.gov; 48 (World Economies), World Bank. data.worldbank.org; 48 (Commodity-Dependent Economies), United Nations Conference on Trade and Development (UNCTAD), *State of Commodity Dependence 2019*, https://unctad.org/en/pages/PublicationWebflyer.aspx?publicationid=2439; 49 (Major Regional Trade Agreements), APEC (apec.org); ASEAN (asean.org); COMESA (facebook.com/ComesaSecretariat/); ECOWAS (ecowas.int); EU (europa.eu); MERCOSUR (mercosur.int); USMCA (ustr.gov/usmca); SAFTA (saarc-sec.org); 50 (Renewable Freshwater Resources per Capita), Food and Agriculture Organization. AQUASTAT data; 52 (Crop Allocation), Global Landscapes Initiative, Institute on the Environment, University of Minnesota. Hooke, Roger LeB., and José F. Martín-Duque. "Land Transformation by Humans: A Review." *GSA Today (2012)*, Volume 22 (12): 4–10; 54 (Total Energy Consumption, Major Energy Deposit), EIA (U.S. Energy Information Administration); 99 (Old-Growth Forest), Sabatini, F.M. et al. "Where are Europe's last primary forests? " *Diversity and Distributions*. DOI: 10.1111/ddi.12778 (2018); 139 (Changing the Land), UN Food and Agricultural Organization. www.fao.org/docrep/008/y5744e/y5744e04.htm.

Photo Credits

AS: Adobe Stock; ASP: Alamy Stock Photo; GI: Getty Images; NGIC: National Geographic Image Collection; SS: Shutterstock

Cover
(Arches National Park), Lunamarina/Dreamstime; (Earth), Anton Balazh/SS; (Saint Petersburg), Potapov Alexander/SS; (elephant), BonnieBC/SS; (surfer), Belinda Howell/GI; back cover (tarsier), R.M. Nunes/AS; (Uxmal ruins) Martin Gray/NGIC; (Sydney Opera House) Sam Abell/NGIC; (soccer player) Pollyana Ventura/GI

Front of Book
1, Anton Balazh/SS; 2 (UP), Anton Balazh/SS; 2 (LO LE), R.M. Nunes/AS; 2 (LO CTR LE), Tom Murphy/NGIC; 2 (LO CTR RT), Pollyana Ventura/GI; 2 (LO RT), Richard Nowitz/NGIC; 3 (LO LE), Peter Betts/SS; 3 (LO CTR LE), Bogdan Lazar/AS; 3 (LO CTR RT), Barbara Schneider/scxh; 3 (LO

RT), Brand X; 4 (LE), Tomasz Tomaszewski/NGIC; 4 (CTR), Todd Gipstein/NGIC; 4 (RT), Richard Nowitz/NGIC; 5 (LE), Taylor S. Kennedy/NGIC; 5 (CTR LE), Cary Wolinsky; 5 (CTR RT), Frans Lanting/NGIC; 5 (RT), Nick Garbutt/Steve Bloom Images/ASP; 10, Mark Theissen & Becky Hale; 11, NASA/JPL-Caltech; 14-15 (UP), David Aguilar; 20 (LO LE), GVS/AS; 20 (LO CTR LE), Bill Hatcher/NGIC; 20 (LO CTR RT), Durktalsma/Dreamstime; 20 (LO RT), Carsten Peter/NGIC; 21 (LO LE), Kryssia Campos/GI; 21 (LO CTR LE), davidrh/AS; 21 (LO CTR RT), Carsten Krueger/AS; 21 (LO RT), Stepo/AS; 25 (UP), Kevin Rivoli/AP Photo; 25 (LO), Weiss and Overpeck, The University of Arizona; 26 (LO LE), Andrei Stepanov/AS; 26 (LO CTR LE), Raymond Gehman/NGIC; 26 (LO CTR RT), damedias/AS; 26 (LO RT), vgabusi/AS; 27 (LO LE), PhotoItaliaStudio/SS; 27 (LO CTR LE), Szymon/AS; 27 (LO CTR RT), Chris/AS; 27 (LO RT), Maria Stenzel/NGIC; 28 (LO RT), James P.

Blair/NGIC; 29 (LO LE), William Thompson; 29 (LO CTR), Steve McCurry/NGIC; 29 (LO RT), SEYLLOU/AFP via GI; 31 (UP LE), Nick Garbutt/Nature Picture Library; 31 (UP CTR LE), Martin Harvey/GI; 31 (UP CTR RT), Suzi Eszterhas/Minden Pictures; 31 (UP RT), Martin Willis/Minden Pictures; 31 (LO LE), Mike Bowie, Lincoln University, NZ; 31 (LO CTR LE), Christophe Courteau/Nature Picture Library; 31 (LO CTR RT), samantoniophoto/AS; 31 (LO RT), Peter Himmelhuber/Zoonar/ASP; 32 (UP), Ron Gravelle/NGIC; 32 (LO), Paul Dempsey/SS; 33 (UP), Fotos593/SS; 33 (LO LE), Adhitya Hendra/Pacific Press/Alamy Live News; 33 (LO RT), JIJI PRESS/AFP via GI; 37, Justin Guariglia/NGIC; 40, ajansen/GI; 41 (UP), Khalil Mazraawi/AFP via GI; 41 (LO LE), Liu Jin/AFP via GI; 41 (LO RT), Joe Raedle/GI; 42, Maria Stenzel/NGIC; 43 (LE), Justin Guariglia/NGIC; 43 (RT), Yasser Chalid/GI; 44 (LE), Martin Gray/NGIC; 44 (CTR), Randy

Olson/NGIC; 44 (RT), Amit Dave/Reuters; 45 (LE), REZA/NGIC; 45 (RT), Richard Nowitz/NGIC; 46 (LE), Jon Parker Lee/ASP; 46 (RT), Justin Guariglia/NGIC; 47 (LE), Mike Goldwater/ASP; 47 (RT), Phil Schermeister/NGIC; 48, hxdyl/SS; 50, Jodi Cobb/NGIC; 52, Owen Franken/GI; 53 (UP LE), Wavebreak Media/AS; 53 (UP RT), Stephen St. John/NGIC; 53 (CTR RT), Joel Sartore/NGIC; 53 (LO LE), James P. Blair/NGIC; 53 (LO RT), Michael Nichols/NGIC; 55 (LE), Walter Rawlings/ASP; 55 (CTR LE), Richard Nowitz/NGIC; 55 (CTR RT), Sarah Leen/NGIC; 55 (RT), Marc Moritsch/NGIC

North America
60 (UP), José A. Castellanos/ASP; 60 (LO), Tomasz Tomaszewski/NGIC; 61 (UP), Michael Melford/NGIC; 61 (LO LE), Rex Stucky/NGIC; 61 (LO RT), Warren Metcalf/SS; 62 (UP LE), Ira Block/NGIC; 62 (UP RT & LO LE), George F. Mobley/NGIC; 62 (LO RT), Martin Gray/NGIC; 63 (UP), Damocean/iStockphoto; 63 (LO LE), espiegle/AS; 63 (LO RT), Brad Mitchell/ASP; 64 (CTR), Alaska Stock LLC/NGIC; 64 (LO), Richard Nowitz/NGIC; 65 (UP), Tim Laman/NGIC; 65 (LO), Michael S. Yamashita/NGIC; 66 (UP), Zeljko Radojko/SS; 66 (LO), Todd Gipstein/NGIC; 66-67 (LO), Norbert Rosing/NGIC; 67 (UP), Brooks Walker/NGIC; 68 (UP), Chris Jenner/SS; 68 (LO), UlrikeStein/GI; 69 (UP LE), Macduff Everton/NGIC; 69 (UP RT), worldswildlifewonders/SS; 70 (UP), Sean Drakes/LatinContent via GI; 70 (CTR), Steve Raymer/NGIC; 70-71, lavizzara/AS; 71 (UP), Michael Melford/NGIC; 71 (LO), Kamira/SS

South America
76 (UP), Jason Edwards/NGIC; 76 (LO), Pablo Corral Vega/NGIC; 77 (UP), Stephanie Maze/NGIC; 77 (LO LE), vadim_ozz/AS; 77 (LO RT), Todd Gipstein/NGIC; 78 (UP LE), Jimmy Chin/NGIC; 78 (UP RT), giedriius/AS; 78 (LO LE), Ed George/NGIC; 78 (LO RT), Curioso.Photography/AS; 79 (UP), Richard Nowitz/NGIC; 79 (LO LE), Joel Sartore/NGIC; 79 (LO RT), Melissa Farlow/NGIC; 80 (UP), tirc83/GI; 80 (LO), Pablo Corral Vega/NGIC; 80-81, ecuadorquerido/AS; 81, O. Louis Mazzatenta/NGIC; 82 (UP), Elsa/GI; 82 (LO), Priit Vesilind/NGIC; 83 (UP), Joel Sartore/NGIC; 83 (LO), James L. Amos/NGIC; 84 (CTR), O. Louis Mazzatenta/NGIC; 84 (LO), sunsinger/SS; 85 (UP), Maria Stenzel/NGIC; 85 (CTR), Joel Sartore/NGIC

Europe
90 (UP), Richard Nowitz/NGIC; 90 (LO LE), Priit Vesilind/NGIC; 90-91, Pavel Svoboda Photography/SS; 91 (UP LE), Melissa Farlow/NGIC; 91 (UP RT), ZimmermannPhotogr..Y/AS; 92 (UP LE), Taylor S. Kennedy/NGIC; 92 (LO LE), F8studio/AS; 92 (LO RT), Sisse Brimberg/NGIC; 92-93, Richard Nowitz/NGIC; 93 (CTR), Nicole Duplaix/NGIC; 93 (LO LE), Richard Nowitz/NGIC; 93 (LO RT), James P. Blair/NGIC; 94 (UP), Karen Kasmauski/NGIC; 94 (LO LE), Priit Vesilind/NGIC; 94 (LO RT), mantaphoto/GI; 95, INTERFOTO/ASP; 96 (UP), Richard Nowitz/NGIC; 96 (CTR), Cees Van Leeuwen; Cordaiy Photo

Library Ltd./Corbis; 96 (LO), Jim Richardson/NGIC; 97, Richard Nowitz/NGIC; 98 (UP & LO), Catherine Karnow/NGIC; 99 (LE & RT), Sisse Brimberg/NGIC; 100 (UP), James P. Blair/NGIC; 100 (LO LE), Freesurf69/Dreamstime; 100 (LO RT), Richard I'Anson/GI; 101, James L. Stanfield/NGIC; 102 (UP & LO), Steve Raymer/NGIC; 103, Richard Nowitz/NGIC

Asia
108 (UP), Taylor S. Kennedy/NGIC; 108 (LO), Steve McCurry/NGIC; 109 (UP), Steve Raymer/NGIC; 109 (LO LE), natalia_maroz/AS; 109 (LO RT), David Edwards/NGIC; 110 (UP LE), Fred de Noyelle/Godong/Corbis; 110 (LO LE), moofushi/AS; 110 (LO RT), Justin Guariglia/NGIC; 110-111, Todd Gipstein/NGIC; 111 (LO LE), Michael Nichols/NGIC; 111 (LO RT), Justin Guariglia/NGIC; 112 (UP), Maria Stenzel/NGIC; 112 (LO), Steve Winter/NGIC; 113 (UP), Steve Raymer/NGIC; 113 (LO), Alexander Zemlianichenko Jr./Bloomberg via GI; 114 (UP), Medford Taylor/NGIC; 114 (LO), Shamil Zhumatov/Reuters; 115 (UP), Wild Wonders of Europe/Shpilenok/Nature Picture Library; 115 (LO), Dean Conger/NGIC; 116 (UP), H. Edward Kim/NGIC; 116 (LO), Justin Guariglia/NGIC; 117 (UP), David Edwards/NGIC; 117 (LO), O. Louis Mazzatenta/NGIC; 118 (UP), James L. Stanfield/NGIC; 118 (LO), Alex Webb/NGIC; 119 (UP), Martin Gray/NGIC; 119 (LO), Ulrich Baumgarten via GI; 120 (UP LE), Morteza Nikoubazl/Reuters; 120 (UP RT), ZambeziShark/GI; 120 (LO), Robb Kendrick/NGIC; 121 (UP), Bill Lyons; 122 (UP), Ed George/NGIC; 122 (LO), James P. Blair/NGIC; 123 (UP), Gleb Semenov/iStockphoto; 123 (LO), Bobby Model/NGIC; 124 (UP LE), Paul Chesley/NGIC; 124 (UP RT), R.M. Nunes/AS; 124 (LO), UV70/SS; 125 (UP), John Lander/500px/GI; 125 (LO), Steve Raymer/NGIC; 126 (UP), Darren Whiteside/Reuters; 126 (LO), Alexandra Boulat/NGIC; 127 (UP LE), Paul Chesley/NGIC; 127 (UP RT & LO), Tim Laman/NGIC

Africa
132 (UP), Joel Carillet/GI; 132 (LO LE), Michael Nichols/NGIC; 132 (LO RT), Vividrange/SS; 133 (UP), Skip Brown/NGIC; 133 (LO LE), Bill Curtsinger/NGIC; 133 (LO RT), Cary Wolinsky; 134 (UP), Georg Gerster/NGIC; 134 (LO LE), Digital Vision/GI; 134 (LO RT), Kenneth Garrett/NGIC; 135 (UP), Jaakko/AS; 135 (LO LE), Bill Curtsinger/NGIC; 135 (LO RT), Michael Nichols/NGIC; 136 (CTR), Thomas J. Abercrombie/NGIC; 136 (LO), mtcurado/GI; 137 (UP), Dan Breckwoldt/Dreamstime; 137 (CTR), Typhoonski/Dreamstime; 137 (LO), Christian Wilkinson/ASP; 138 (UP), Eric Lafforgue/ASP; 138 (LO LE), Linda Hughes Photography/SS; 138 (LO RT), Robert W. Moore/NGIC; 139, James L. Stanfield/NGIC; 140 (UP), WLDavies/GI; 140 (LO LE), Michael Lewis/NGIC; 140 (LO RT), Steve De Neef/NGIC; 141 (UP), Suzi Eszterhas/Minden Pictures; 141 (LO), Bobby Haas/NGIC; 142 (UP), Last Refuge/robertharding/ASP; 142 (LO), Hermes Images/AGF Srl/ASP; 143 (UP), Werner Forman/Universal Images Group/GI; 143 (LO), Florent Vergnes/AFP via GI; 144 (UP), George F. Mobley/NGIC; 144

(LO), Tim Laman/NGIC; 145 (UP), Kenneth Garrett/NGIC; 145 (LO), HandmadePictures/AS

Australia, New Zealand & Oceania
150 (UP), Nicole Duplaix/NGIC; 150 (LO), Frans Lanting/NGIC; 151 (UP), beau/AS; 151 (LO LE), Tim Laman/NGIC; 151 (LO RT), Nicole Duplaix/NGIC; 152 (UP), Medford Taylor/NGIC; 152 (CTR), N.Minton/SS; 152 (LO), John Seaton Callahan/GI; 152-153 (UP), Tim Laman/NGIC; 152-153 (LO), travellight/SS; 153 (CTR), Paul Chesley/NGIC; 153 (LO), Mark Cosslett/NGIC; 154 (LE), Jim Agronick/SS; 154 (RT), Sam Abell/NGIC; 155 (LE), Jason Edwards/NGIC; 155 (RT), Paul Chesley/NGIC; 156 (UP), bumihills/SS; 156 (LO), Carsten Peter/NGIC; 157 (UP LE), Martin Gray/NGIC; 157 (UP RT), Richard Carey/AS; 157 (LO), Jodi Cobb/NGIC

Antarctica
160, Nick Garbutt/Steve Bloom Images/ASP; 161 (UP), Vicki Beaver/ASP; 161 (LO), Alex Huizinga/Minden Pictures; 162 (UP), Philip Spindler/National Science Foundation/Science Source; 162 (LO), Robert Harding Picture Library/NGIC; 163 (UP), Paul Nicklen/NGIC; 163 (LO), Norbert Wu/Minden Pictures

The Oceans
167 (UP), NOAA; 167 (LO LE), Scripps Institute of Oceanography; 167 (LO RT), NASA; 168 (UP), Wolcott Henry/NGIC; 168 (LO), Karen Kasmauski/NGIC; 170 (UP), Tom Murphy/NGIC; 170 (LO LE), John Eastcott And Yva Momatiuk/NGIC; 170 (LO RT), Emory Kristof/NGIC; 172, Hans Fricke/NGIC; 174 (LE), Paul Nicklen/NGIC; 174 (RT), Norbert Rosing/NGIC

NATIONAL GEOGRAPHIC and Yellow Border Design are trademarks of the
National Geographic Society, used under license.

Since 1888, the National Geographic Society has funded more than 12,000
research, exploration, and preservation projects around the world.
The Society receives funds from National Geographic Partners, LLC,
funded in part by your purchase. A portion of the proceeds from this book
supports this vital work. To learn more, visit natgeo.com/info.

For more information, visit nationalgeographic.com, call 1-877-873-6846,
or write to the following address:

National Geographic Partners, LLC
1145 17th Street N.W.
Washington, DC 20036-4688 U.S.A.

For librarians and teachers: nationalgeographic.com/books/
librarians-and-educators

More for kids from National Geographic: natgeokids.com

National Geographic Kids magazine inspires children to explore their world
with fun yet educational articles on animals, science, nature, and more.
Using fresh storytelling and amazing photography, *Nat Geo Kids* shows kids
ages 6 to 14 the fascinating truth about the world—and why they should care.
kids.nationalgeographic.com/subscribe

For rights or permissions inquiries, please contact National Geographic Books
Subsidiary Rights: bookrights@natgeo.com

Designed by Kathryn Robbins and Ruthie Thompson

**National Geographic supports K–12 educators with ELA Common Core
Resources. Visit natgeoed.org/commoncore for more information.**

Trade paperback ISBN: 978-1-4263-7227-8
Hardcover ISBN: 978-1-4263-7228-5
Reinforced library binding ISBN: 978-1-4263-7229-2

The publisher would like to thank everyone who worked to make this book come
together: Judith Painter, writer and reviewer; Grace Hill, project manager;
Michelle Harris, fact-checker; Nicole Overton, reviewer; Angela Modany,
associate editor; Hilary Andrews, associate photo editor; Mike McNey, map
production; Maureen J. Flynn, map research and edit; Chris Philpotts, illustrator;
Joan Gossett, production editor; and Gus Tello and Anne LeongSon, design
production assistants.

Printed in Hong Kong
21/PPHK/1

There's always more ...
TO EXPLORE!

National Geographic Kids has the perfect atlas for kids of every age, from preschool through high school—all with the latest age-appropriate facts, maps, images, and more.

The atlas series is designed to grow as kids grow, adding more depth and relevant material at every level to help them stay curious about the world and to succeed at school and in life!

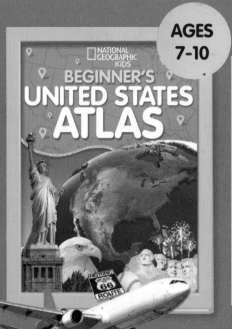

AGES 7-10

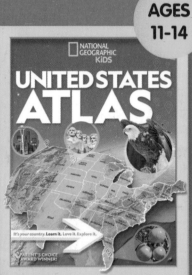

AGES 11-14